# HEAVENLY EARTH

## A VISION FOR RURAL PROSPERITY

"Empowering Remote Communities: A Vision for Joyful Li...

### A GLANCE OF RURAL LIVING

## RAVINDRAN KOLAPARAMBIL

ISBN
Hardcase 979-8-89544-259-3
Paperback 979-8-89475-378-2

# CONTENTS

# ❧ Contents ❦

# AUTHOR'S PLEA TO RURAL COMMUNITIES

In this thought-provoking piece, the author appeals to the rural public, sharing insights on how everyday individuals can transform their financial circumstances. The path to prosperity lies not in grand schemes or elusive secrets but in practical actions accessible to all. Let us explore this alternative perspective together.

This book is on how to overcome the countryside / rural people who ultimately suffer from criminal activities and have the utter lowest lifestyles, with many kinds of illnesses/sicknesses and the poorest conditions. Without even basic facilities, suffering without daily bread, is explaining about the change of mindset for unity is a different thought can attain and solve their entire problems.

May the novel concept within this book illuminate and rejuvenate your minds, encouraging you to embrace every aspect that enhances your lives—the warmth of love, the solace of home, the delight of your children and friends, and the unwavering support of your entire family. Their compassionate hearts stand ready to accept and treat all fellow human beings with equality, fostering an environment enriched by knowledge and the vibrant tapestry of diversity.

In the vast expanse of remote areas, where challenges abound and suffering often prevails, a beacon of hope emerges—an advanced thought that transcends mere survival. This thought envisions not just existence but a **joyful life** for the teeming population dwelling in these far-flung corners.

At its core lies a powerful lesson: **unity among people**. It is the thread that stitches together the fabric of progress. This lesson, imparted through the pages of a remarkable book, holds the key to transforming adversity into opportunity. But this book is no ordinary reading material; it is a call to action.

**Readers**, take heed! Beyond absorbing words, you must contemplate the practical implementation of these insights within your own communities. Imagine a ripple effect—a collective effort that ensures everyone finds their **daily sustenance**. As we prioritize development and prosperity, we elevate ourselves. No longer will we remain unnoticed; no longer will our potential go untapped.

Let this book be more than ink on paper; let it be the catalyst for change. For unity in purposeful action lies the promise of a brighter future. — A future where suffering gives way to joy and where every individual thrives.

In our vast world, hopes and dreams permeate every corner. Each of us harbors desires waiting to be fulfilled. Let us become beacons of happiness, guiding one another along the path. As we extend our helping hands, unity, serenity, and lasting peace will flourish within us. Amidst the present challenges and rural hardships, I contemplate practical, enduring solutions.

With an unwavering commitment to technical excellence and a shared passion for innovation, I am confident that collaboration within remote areas can foster integration. By focusing on land development tailored for agriculture and other long-term opportunities, we can provide meaningful employment to the rural population. This endeavor not only benefits individuals but also contributes lasting value to our world.

*May the fresh concepts within this book illuminate your thoughts and encourage you to embrace each aspect that enriches your life— whether it's the warmth of love, the solace of home, the joy of childhood friendships, or the unwavering support of your family.*

**Metamorphosis** occurs when one transitions from an actor to the President of the U.S.A. This transformation serves as a prime example of metamorphosis. Similarly, when a caterpillar undergoes the remarkable change into a butterfly, it too exemplifies metamorphosis. Your journey from being an ordinary individual to achieving wealth through this unit system can also be seen as a form of transformation.

Let us harbor hope that our dreams come true across the entire world and that the aspirations of each individual find fulfillment. May your inner light guide others, serving as helping hands to strengthen unity, serenity, and inner peace, ultimately dispelling sadness.

**Remember:** perseverance is the hallmark of success.

"The upcoming unit members and all associated functionaries can wholeheartedly embrace participation if the rural population is willing. Throughout this book, I present ideas in a fresh, innovative, and straightforward manner using simple English. Instead of merely reading, let's actively apply these concepts and work together toward a better future."

"When faced with an insurmountable problem, seeking assistance from others can often lead to a swift resolution. By collaborating with others, you not only enhance your own personality but also create a unique family dynamic."

"Furthermore, team members within the unit are strategically positioning themselves based on their individual skills and abilities. This approach extends to the unit's operations at a corporate level, where all members collaboratively leverage their previously untapped influence.

This concerted effort is fostering genuine diversity, a departure from the existing subpar lifestyle."

**Inclusive Collaboration for Success**: The members should adopt an inclusive and collaborative approach, transforming the unit into a platform for performance and seamless integration. By doing so, we can maximize our chances of success.

**Empowering All Members**: Let go of the notion that only selected individuals can elevate the union. In reality, each one of you possesses the capability to safeguard our collective interests, so there's no need to create hierarchical positions like director or executive director. Instead, recognize that this unit belongs to all of us, and we are collectively responsible for its success.

**Uniting as a Family Business**: Treat this unit as your family business. "As the boss and paymaster," you have the authority to make decisions. Unite your strengths and experiences to ensure the unit thrives.

**Remember:**, you are more than capable of handling all affairs and growing in strength through practical experience.

The members can collaborate inclusively, turning the unit into a dynamic platform for performance and seamless integration. The unit's success hinges on collective effort. There exists a tradition that assumes only select members can elevate the union, but this notion is purely imaginative.

Each of you possesses equal competence in safeguarding your properties. There's no need to establish directorial roles or sign agreements entrusting the unit to others. \

**Remember**, this unit belongs to all of you—you are the bosses and paymasters. Treat it like a family business, uniting your strengths.

You have more than enough capability to manage affairs effectively and gain strength through experience."

**Unit Accountability and Protection**: All members of the unit are **accountable** and subject to scrutiny for any negative actions, even ordinary members. However, there exists an additional clause aimed at safeguarding the unit against internal deception or cheating by its own members.

**A New Mindset for a Bright Future**: To overcome your current challenges, you must cultivate a different mindset. As you step into the unit, confront your present obstacles with determination. Your fresh perspectives and innovative thoughts will pave the way toward a brighter future.

**Stalin and the Live Chicken**: While the tale of Josef Stalin plucking feathers from a live chicken in front of his followers may be a fable, it vividly portrays the brutality associated with the Soviet dictator. According to the narrative, Stalin forcefully held the squawking bird and stripped it of its feathers, leaving a lasting impression on those who witnessed the act.

Stalin placed the grain on the floor and watched as the bird eagerly pecked it up. "Observe," he said to those around him. "See how that chicken follows me for food?" He drew a parallel: "People can be just like that. Even if you cause them immense suffering, they may still cling to you, driven by their basic needs."

The question lingers: Are we becoming Stalin's chickens, blindly following those who provide sustenance, regardless of the cost?

In my work with rural communities, I've employed proverbs, quotes, and relatable examples to ensure that even the most economically disadvantaged can grasp the essence of the message. Empowering them with wisdom and understanding is essential for their progress.

**RAVINDRAN KOLAPARAMBIL**
597, 2ND FLOOR, 2A, SHREE KRISHNA BLOSSOM, 7TH MAIN, 11TH CROSS, 3RD PHASE, J.P.NAGAR, BANGALORE 560 078 – KARNATAKA –INDIA
**E-mail:** heavenly.earth1987@gmail.com

# CHAPTER I

# THE CURRENT STATE OF RURAL AREAS

In many rural communities, the pervasive influence of drugs casts a shadow over daily life. When faced with unpleasant situations, individuals often choose to escape from reality, abandoning their true responsibilities. They seek refuge in the company of friends and neighbors who are already ensnared by addiction to alcohol or drugs.

These individuals embark on a life of substance consumption, believing it will bring them happiness. They even extol the virtues of this lifestyle to others. Their argument holds some truth: without a conscience, they can evade the burdens of responsibility while perpetually under the influence of substances.

Unfortunately, this habit leads to addiction—to alcohol, drugs, and a downward spiral. Once stable homes are now teetering on the brink of destitution, parents find themselves powerless to help their children due to financial constraints. Living in households plagued by alcoholism, these individuals receive no aid from their neighbors.

It is time to rethink our approach—to break free from this cycle and envision a different path for rural communities. Let us explore innovative solutions that can uplift lives and restore hope where it has been lost.

Most of the drunkards have ruined their lives, affecting not only themselves but also those close to them. They rarely consider the impact on their families and loved ones. Their laziness and destructive habits have turned their homes into hellish environments. But what now? You've been slow to contemplate positive change, the change your family has been hoping for.

You're running out of time. Prepare to break free from this harmful habit—whether through treatment or sheer self-confidence. Choose a path that aligns with the expectations others have for you. Your future is bright, and the power to transform lies in your hands. You can make a triumphant comeback.

Your current pitiful state was influenced by others' decisions. Perhaps someone cunning in your society sought a life of pleasure at your expense. Illiteracy, inefficiency, and blind obedience contributed to their privileged existence.

The snares set by others have ensnared you into a lifetime of servitude, causing perpetual suffering. Elevating the lives of those in rural areas is no simple task; it involves numerous complex factors. Rescuing you from this wretched existence is a tension-filled process. Why should I or anyone else bear the responsibility of protecting you? Additionally, there exists a class of people who actively work against your well-being.

## GUIDANCE BEYOND BOUNDARIES

This unit serves as your guide, leading you toward a new life that has remained elusive until now. Instead of merely following the footsteps of your ancestors, who never envisioned a positive path for their future, you find yourself trapped in a cycle devoid of optimism. The days pass, yet there is no proactive consideration of what lies ahead.

Within this web of circumstances, there is no benevolent force stepping forward to make your existence pleasant. You remain ensnared by external influences, waiting for assistance that may never materialize. But realization dawns: the power to change your life lies within you. Positive thinking becomes the key—a prerequisite for making decisions aligned with your deepest desires.

Your calculations, once hopeful, now echo futility. Years slip away, and yet you fail to explore remedies that could alter your trajectory. Even as your family grows, their needs expand beyond your grasp, intertwining with the neighboring community. The weight of responsibilities presses upon you, and you contemplate escape.

In moments of despair, you consider self-sabotage, disregarding the well-being of your loved ones. Precious years vanish, casualties of misguided thoughts about your own future. But perhaps, just perhaps, a shift in mindset can unlock the door to transformation.

**Remember**, *the power to shape your destiny lies not in external circumstances but within your own perception and choices.*

**Persisting Through Challenges** – This unwavering force will labor tirelessly on your behalf until circumstances shift in your favor. Rather than dwelling on your past, consider it a period of adversity that you successfully navigated. Now, you find yourself on the right path, leading a genuinely pragmatic life alongside family, neighbors, and friends.

**Facing the Shadows** – You recognize that drugs may offer temporary respite from life's sorrows, but they are not a lasting solution. To overcome these challenges, you need a resolute mindset. While substances can cloud your consciousness, they also wreak havoc on your health. Your family can only weep for you, their dreams buried under the weight of your choices.

**A New Resolve** – Yet, your decision to reclaim your life is astute. Many stand ready to welcome you back. This unit comprises numerous members—near and dear—who will accompany you on the remaining journey. Your life isn't wasted; it serves your family, neighbors, and nation in myriad ways. Strive, achieve, and make a difference—for yourself and others.

1. **Embracing Life's Challenges**: We all encounter hardships throughout our lives. No one is exempt from problems. These daily struggles are an integral part of existence. When we confront life's threats head-on, we truly live. But have you ever considered that if everyone followed your approach to facing life, humanity would cease to exist—it would turn to dust?

2. **Beyond Self-Centeredness**: Focusing solely on oneself is a selfish mindset. Instead, connecting with others and sharing both joys and sorrows leads to a more fulfilling life—one that resonates with everyone. Genuine friendships and shared experiences create a sense of normalcy and acceptance.

3. **Escaping Sorrows and Finding Joy**: Some seek a sorrow-free existence, chasing joy through dependence on alcohol and drugs. For them, this becomes their definition of life. However, true fulfillment lies in making others happy. By doing so, we discover the essence of life—a journey that teaches us how to live joyfully and appreciate every moment.

4. **Innate Wisdom and Common Sense**: We are all equipped with the innate ability to navigate life's consequences and pleasures.

No specialized skills are necessary—common sense suffices. Many lead fulfilling lives by cherishing their loved ones and embracing the ordinary. After all, every common person holds the potential for a heavenly existence.

**Observe Your Surroundings and Discover Answers** – Take a moment to listen to your surroundings and observe them closely. Often, the answers we seek are right there, waiting to be noticed. Perhaps you've encountered someone whom you initially dismissed as 'good for nothing.' However, consider that their life, like yours, is a unique blend of inborn talents and clever attitudes. Recognize this truth.

**Life's Short, Make the Most of It** – Your life is a canvas waiting to be painted. It's not just about fulfilling obligations to others or yourself; it's about savoring every moment. Amidst your busy schedule, find time to love and listen to others. These seemingly small acts can enrich your life and create ripples of positive impact. Helping others becomes an integral part of your existence.

**Dream of a Joyful Life** – Imagine a life that transcends the ordinary—a luxurious, Hi-Fi existence devoid of sadness. Each one of us has the power to create such a reality. By living harmoniously with others, we infuse our lives with vibrant colors. This new way of living, though not novel, awaits those who dare to take the first step."

**Remember**, *life is a canvas, and you hold the brush.* –

1. **Transformation and Progress**: Through this system, we must initiate a profound transformation, dismantling the obstacles that hinder our progress. Slowing down is a luxury we cannot afford. This approach holds the promise of fulfilling our tireless efforts, yielding results we eagerly await.
2. **Opportunities and Individuality**: Once, there existed a belief that these opportunities were reserved for others—perhaps too

distant for us to grasp. But such thoughts are mere shackles of negativity. Instead, recognize that you are a unique individual destined to lead and possess something extraordinary.

3. **A Fresh Mindset**: Embracing a fresh mindset—one that dares to think differently—ushers in a new systematic existence. For many, this shift can create ripples through various systems, effecting positive change.

4. **Wealth and True Peace**: Consider this: ill-gotten wealth never brings true peace. Every possession, every property unwittingly minted by someone else, reflects the immaturity of their mind. It's a folly beyond measure.

1. **Exploring This System:"** Within The Confines Of This Intricate System, You'll Unearth Not Just Practical Wisdom But Also Novel Concepts That Enhance And Elevate The Experience Of Life.

2. **"Urban Realities:"** Amidst the hustle and bustle of cities, where competition flourishes, and tensions ebb and flow, keep in mind that the affairs of others are not our burden to bear.

1. **The Current System and Unintended Criminals**: The existing system inadvertently pushes many individuals into criminal activities simply because they are struggling to make ends meet. These people find themselves compelled to enter the world of crime out of sheer necessity.

2. **Balancing Sacrifice and Comfort**: No one is demanding that you sacrifice your well-being or endure extreme hardships. Life is fleeting, and it's perfectly acceptable to enjoy the fruits of your hard-earned money. Remember that the suffering experienced by others isn't your fault; it often results from deliberate actions taken by someone else.

3. **The Purpose of Employment**: The primary goal of any employment opportunity, whether large or small, should be to provide individuals with enough to sustain themselves. When you achieve self-sufficiency and financial stability, consider extending

a helping hand to others. Offering short-term loans with reasonable interest rates can assist fellow community members without compromising the unit's hard-earned resources.

4. **Responsibility and Compassion**: Let's reconsider our perspective on beggars. Rather than assuming they lack strong individuals to protect them, let's recognize that the system sometimes fails them. Instead of burdening children with begging pots, we should hold parents accountable from the outset. By doing so, we can create a more compassionate and responsible society.

**Accountability for Our Elders** – It is essential to recognize that elderly individuals also have families—relatives, sons, and daughters—who should be held accountable for their well-being. Unfortunately, some responsible people are quietly abandoning their parents and children on the streets, evading authorities due to systemic flaws. This situation constitutes a grave offense—one that demands immediate change for our nation's progress.

**Sustainable Living and Responsible Inheritance** – Each of us can strive to earn what is necessary for ourselves and our families. Moderation is key; accumulating excessive wealth to pass on to future generations can lead to lifelong sorrow. Instead, focus on a reasonable standard of living.

**The Pitfalls of Inefficient Donations** – Donating through intermediaries or organizations without proper scrutiny is unwise. Some entities exploit the vulnerable, masquerading as charitable causes. These include those who beg for funds under the guise of aiding handicapped, children, and elderly inmates. The government must take decisive action to ban such deceptive organizations and protect those who fall victim to their schemes.

**A Life in Confinement** – Consider the lives of these categorized inmates, who are confined to small buildings with numerous restrictions. Their existence is akin to that of animals. If we neglect their care, they may resort to desperate measures, becoming unwitting criminals seeking their rights through force.

**Remember:** *our collective actions shape society's future. Let us prioritize compassion and responsibility, ensuring the well-being of all, regardless of age or circumstance.*

**Why Does This System Encourage Disregard for Systematic Regulation?** The existing system seems to inadvertently promote non-compliance with systematic regulations. It raises questions about why certain rules apply selectively and not universally. Particularly concerning are the exemptions for vulnerable groups who lack advocates to protect their interests.

**Neglecting the Most Vulnerable** The system's failure to extend its protective umbrella to impoverished individuals is concerning. These marginalized categories often lack support networks or influential voices to champion their cause. It's as if there's an unspoken assumption that they can fend for themselves, even when the reality is far from it.

**Reconsidering the Old Adage,** There's an old saying that if a child has a mouth, someone will feed them. However, perhaps it's time for the government to reevaluate this notion. Abolishing such a system could pave the way for a more compassionate approach—one that recognizes that as people grow, their needs multiply. By doing so, we can build a society that truly considers the well-being of all its members.

## "EMBRACE LIFE'S OPPORTUNITIES"

Life presents opportunities to many, so don't shy away from them. Your chances are not exclusive; they are shared by clever individuals across various walks of life. Unfortunately, a lack of unity often hinders progress. Facing challenges alone is no easy feat, and sometimes, it leads to lives unraveling rather than resilience.

People often limit themselves to their immediate family circle. Despite being aware of their accomplishments, they cannot fully possess what they've earned. Illegally accumulated wealth only exacerbates the misery of others.

If you find yourself in such a position, recognize that consuming everything won't bring peace of mind to your family. The root of societal problems lies in the unequal distribution of resources. When resources are plundered, disappointment and violence ensue. The solution lies in inequitable resource allocation, fostering a peaceful coexistence devoid of jealousy and enmity.

Acknowledging these truths, let's strive for a brighter future by sharing our talents, valuables, and skills. Together, we can cultivate positive thinking and boldness within our collective team.

"A sound mind often leads us to dream about our future, envisioning a life filled with possibilities. However, upon reflection, we encounter memories that sting—the choices we made and the pain we endured. Despite this, personal growth shapes us, altering our perspectives and embedding us in a web of beliefs.

One prevailing belief is that our existence is perpetual, unaffected by external events. We convince ourselves that what transpires around us merely impacts others, leaving us unscathed. Yet, this mindset proves insufficient. We must navigate life's twists and turns, ruling our minds as we journey through countless years.

Even as science and technology advance, our resolute minds remain impervious. Self-interest prevails, and change requires deliberate intention. In this intricate dance of beliefs and self-perception, we remain the architects of our own transformation."

## SEEKING PEACE BEYOND WEALTH

Many believe that a peaceful life can only be attained through riches or affluence. From our earliest days, we've been surrounded by the notion that money governs everything. But what if there exists an alternative path—a permanent solution—that remains hidden from most? Perhaps it lies in simplicity, in embracing circumstances that others dismiss as poverty.

The allure of wealth can cloud our minds, preventing us from connecting with those who lack financial parity. We hesitate to extend a compassionate embrace to those who don't share our economic status. Yet, there are individuals who genuinely value the lives of rural communities who work tirelessly for their well-being. Sadly, their efforts often go unnoticed, overshadowed by the prevailing belief that their philosophy yields no tangible results.

Consider this: it's not your fault that you haven't found a remedy for your struggles. Others, too, fail to provide trustworthy advice. But here's the crux—if you're unwilling to change, no external force can rescue you. These rare souls, who genuinely care from the depths of their hearts, remain a beacon of hope in our society.

The ultimate outcome of life lies in either **ignoring the struggles of others** or **remaining indifferent to them.** Consider this: why would you choose to live a life akin to that of a comedian—devoid of peace and joy, not just for yourself but also for those around you? The time you've spent is precious; reflecting on past situations can illuminate your mistakes.

Have you ever found yourself ensnared by someone else's cunning ideas, unwittingly allowing them to disrupt your life? Even after years have passed, you may remain oblivious to the trap you're in—a trap from which they benefit while you continue along that same path.

Whether you're rich or poor, the shared experience is one of lacking love and affection. The immensely wealthy suffer just as much as those without life's basic necessities. Perhaps it's time to consider an alternative: ponder the intersection of science and technology, seeking understanding and balance.

## "EMPOWER YOUR FUTURE: YOUR LIFE, YOUR CHOICE"

It's crucial to recognize that someone's vested interests may be influencing your decisions, potentially leading you astray. Remember, nobody can deceive you without your consent or awareness. Your willingness becomes their advantage. Some individuals exploit the freedom they have in your life, ultimately affecting not only you but your entire family.

Over time, their interference might render you incapable of leading a normal life. They may pretend to be helpful, subtly ingraining themselves as essential figures. However, breaking free from your current obstacles—whether through mental strength or professional treatment—can transform your situation. You'll rise above others and no longer be hindered by addiction or bad habits.

Embrace this newfound freedom. With a clear mind, you'll contribute fresh ideas, collaborate with others, and shape a brighter future for yourself and your loved ones.

"Collectively, each of you should contemplate how to propel the unit forward. The trajectory of progress hinges on your mindset and unwavering effort. Strive to elevate it to new heights swiftly.

The concerted efforts of families, coupled with resolute determination, dictate how effectively you steer the unit. Avoid shortcuts; instead, focus on sustainable growth.

Building self-confidence among members and securing necessary funds is paramount. Further insights on these aspects are elaborated in other sections. A thorough exploration will clarify any lingering doubts.

Remember, no task is insignificant, and no challenge is insurmountable. You're not alone; you're part of a vast family. Embrace this collective strength.

Resolve to overcome adversity without hesitation. Pledge to minimize reliance on external factors—whether government, relatives, or friends. Your self-sufficiency is your greatest asset.

All the suffering you endure now is only for a few more months. With a little hard work, we can overcome our sorrows permanently and easily. You are shaping your destiny as you move along the path of your next life chapter, surrounded by family and neighbors. Instead of waiting aimlessly, work with purpose. Many are part of this joint venture, eagerly anticipating the fortune that lies ahead. Life is a journey through highs and lows, fueled by positive thinking and dreams of a heavenly existence just a few steps away.

This isn't mere imagination; it's a tangible destination you're striving to reach—a spot carved out by your earlier efforts. Your collective endeavors give rise to new hopes for life, ensuring success for all. Recognize that this joint venture, fueled by strength and determination, will etch each of you into the annals of history. Before embarking on this journey, prepare an estimate with your plans. Whether the members create it themselves or seek expert assistance, this estimate will guide you forward, minimizing obstacles along the way."

1. **Recognizing Financial Constraints**: It's essential to acknowledge that envisioning a sustainable income source without adequate funds is akin to dreaming with empty pockets. Unfortunately, this predicament is more prevalent in marginalized and underprivileged communities. In such circumstances, seeking financial assistance from the government becomes a viable option.

2. **Self-Sufficient Units and Government Support**: Many self-sustaining units have emerged, effectively reducing the government's reliance on rural funds. If your unit is among those seeking assistance, presenting a well-prepared estimate and project report can open doors. The government may extend support in the form of funding or long-term loans.

3. **Empowering Local Development**: A unit comprising committed members and sufficient resources can catalyze transformative developments in the area. As a result, dreams can materialize, and positive outcomes can be realized within a few months. Conversely, insufficient funds—whether in business ventures or unit investments—often lead to setbacks and increased debt.

4. **Charting the Path Ahead**: While the unit will undoubtedly support your endeavors, the project report remains pivotal. It's up to you to chart the course for the future based on this crucial document.

**Remember**, *thoughtful planning and collaboration can turn aspirations into reality.*

## SUFFICIENT INVESTMENT: A PATH TO SUCCESS

In the realm of business and start-ups, **adequate financial investment** plays a pivotal role. Without sufficient funds, operational efficiency becomes elusive, impacting not only the business itself but also causing personal distress. Imagine facing a financial crisis that compels you to deplete the working capital you've diligently invested in your venture. Such moments can cast a shadow over your entire project.

Why do adversities often weigh us down? The answer lies not in external circumstances but rather within ourselves. When we grapple with sorrows from all directions, our ability to think positively wanes, leaving us devoid of effective solutions. It's as if we're impoverished in our outlook.

Yet, there exists a remedy—a beacon of hope. When life's challenges seem insurmountable, seek assistance from others. Collaboratively, problems become solvable. Curiously, while we discuss this theory, few have truly applied it to their own lives. Perhaps your latent abilities, skills, and intelligence remain untapped, waiting for the right moment to shine.

## A NOVEL APPROACH TO ALLEVIATING RURAL POVERTY

In the vast countryside, where poverty casts a long shadow over countless lives, we found ourselves pondering an urgent and large-scale solution. The answer emerged from the collective efforts of neighbors banding together for a brighter future—the birth of the **unit system**.

This innovative idea has captured the imagination of many. As social creatures, humans rely on each other; life without mutual support is an arduous journey. While some of us are well aware of this truth, there remain a few who need to broaden their perspective and recognize the potential of our invitation.

1. **The Joint Venture**: Our unconventional approach—a joint venture—addresses the multifaceted needs of a suffering population. These individuals have spent their entire lives with little purpose, yearning for a different path—one that leads to prosperity, fueled by innate courage and skill.
2. **Surprising Possibilities**: When we discussed this concept with others, their surprise was palpable. Not only does it offer a lifeline to countless illiterate and impoverished rural residents, but it also empowers the government to implement policies on a scale far beyond what cities alone can achieve.

This unit system represents hope—a collaborative effort to uplift lives and create a more equitable future.

3. **Unlocking New Perspectives**: By opening their inner eye, individuals find life becoming easier. They embrace discipline, seeking a unique existence where they need not rely on anyone else. Filled with hope, they believe that through concerted effort, they can achieve anything within a few months.

4. **Dreaming Beyond Survival**: Previously, many merely anticipated daily work to earn their bread. However, forming a cohesive unit compels them to dream bigger. They recognize the abundance of resources around them—money, manpower, and other valuable assets. It's time to harness these resources effectively.

5. **Collective Impact**: The difference between the efforts of a single person and a united group is immense. Our motto is "Employment for All." We'll tap into previously idle resources and utilize them fully. Regular work and consistent income transform mindsets, empowering everyone involved.

**Why Group/Unit Systems Manage Properties, Wealth, and Expenses Jointly** In the group or unit system, the collective management of properties, wealth, and expenses offers several advantages. Let's explore why this approach is beneficial:

1. **Pooling of Minds and Skills**: When all members collaborate, a diverse range of minds and skills come together. Each individual contributes unique perspectives and expertise. This collective intelligence ensures thorough decision-making, especially when handling complex financial matters

2. **Specialization in Money Matters**: Within the group, there is often a designated focus on financial management. Some individuals specialize in handling money-related affairs. Their expertise ensures efficient allocation, investment, and tracking of resources.

3. **Emotional Neutrality**: Unlike individual decision-making, where emotions can sway choices, group decisions remain relatively

neutral. Emotions need not be immediately disclosed to others. This emotional detachment allows for rational and strategic financial planning.

4. **Preserving Funds**: Group management ensures that funds remain in the collective account until a significant investment opportunity arises. Rather than impulsive spending, the group patiently waits for the right moment to invest wisely.

5. **Merits and Demerits**: Of course, there are pros and cons to both approaches. While group decisions benefit from shared knowledge and accountability, individual decisions allow for personal autonomy. It's essential to weigh these factors based on the specific context.

6. **Countryside Considerations**: In rural areas, where literacy levels may be lower, group decisions become even more valuable. Illiterate individuals can collectively navigate large quantities of wealth effectively, leveraging the combined wisdom of the group.

In summary, joint management fosters collaboration, expertise, emotional balance, and prudent financial stewardship. Whether in urban or rural settings, thoughtful decision-making remains key.

## INDIVIDUAL EMOTIONS AND COLLECTIVE VENTURES

The emotions and inner thoughts of an individual tend to be resistant to change. However, when operating within a group, that individual becomes just one among many. Consider this: have you ever contemplated a joint venture with an erstwhile enemy neighbor? Such collaboration could address gaps, alleviate suffering, and enhance the quality of your peaceful days and youthful experiences.

Successfully effecting change through joint ventures relies on a result-oriented, universally agreed-upon system—one that is straightforward to follow. Now, imagine achieving greatness from a starting point of "zero" in life, surpassing even your wildest expectations. Yet, upon realizing this possibility, you might wonder why it wasn't accomplished long ago by your ancestors.

The answer lies in the systems that existed—systems that both the powerful and the powerless could not tolerate, ultimately leading to adverse consequences. These persistent thoughts continue to hinder progress in rural areas and impact the lives of a substantial population. Your forward-thinking mindset and adaptability are commendable. By overcoming defeatist attitudes, you can positively impact the world, allowing more people to savor life's abundance.

**In Pursuit of Self-Interest –** *The collective well-being of society often hinges on individuals sacrificing their own comfort and overcoming challenges. However, this system can be transformed through wise decision-making.*

**Remember**, *your life belongs to you—none of you exist solely for others. This realization marks a profound shift in mindset.*

**Unity and Resolution –** Within this community, many of you can come together to abandon trivial disputes, especially when genuine enmity is absent. Consider resolving conflicts permanently—for the sake of your family, children, and their future. Why cling to ego when you can save time, youth, and the remaining years of your life? What do you truly gain?

**A New Path Ahead –** Both you and your neighbors have endured years of hardship. Now, let go of the past and work diligently for the unit's growth. Embrace abundance rather than sorrow.

**Remember**: *the struggles faced by your ancestors were simply their fate. Let us empathize and move forward.*

## CHALLENGES IN RURAL WELFARE PROGRAMS

The government has implemented various schemes aimed at improving the lives of rural populations. These initiatives involve coordination across multiple departments and banks. However, the outcomes have been less than satisfactory.

While some individuals have received benefits, it is difficult to determine whether they are the true beneficiaries. Eligibility assessments are often made by outsiders who lack a deep understanding of the local context. Consequently, many rural residents remain excluded from these benefits.

The process of enumerating beneficiaries without direct interaction poses challenges. Collecting information from third parties is common, especially in remote areas where reaching out to outsiders can be cumbersome.

In summary, despite efforts, the impact of rural welfare programs remains limited due to these inherent challenges.

1. The concerned official sat in a public place, gathering random details about the rural population. However, the approach to collecting data about rural family's needs a transformation. Most officials hesitate to visit the humble thatched homes and understand their lifestyle.

2. If this situation persists in assessing the lives of rural individuals and their families, a drastic change is necessary. To improve the well-being of the poor, significant adjustments must occur. Although it's a challenging task, the solution lies in establishing a permanent unit that sincerely serves all populations in remote areas.

3. The primary goal of these units is to uplift rural communities, treating them as equals and integrating them into the mainstream population. Unfortunately, the government often implements rural development schemes through outsiders who lack interest in working within such remote areas. As a result, the intended benefits often elude the real beneficiaries, leaving them unaware of how to access the funds meant for their betterment.

**Community Units and Rural Development** – This community unit shoulders the burdens and responsibilities of its members. Comprising rural residents selected from a specific area, the unit is dedicated to promoting development and well-being. Their sincere efforts contribute to the successful implementation of government schemes within their region. By efficiently managing development projects and executing beneficial programs, these units play a crucial role. Additionally, their meticulous record-keeping ensures transparency and accountability.

**Identifying Real Beneficiaries** – Beyond the administrative level, it is essential for officials to identify the true beneficiaries. Regular visits to local communities—ideally 4-5 times a year—allow for firsthand assessments. Collecting progress reports, conducting inspections, and maintaining accurate records are vital steps in ensuring effective governance and equitable distribution of resources.

## EMPOWERING RURAL UNITS FOR POSITIVE CHANGE

In the context of rural development, certain processes often prove more costly than the funds allocated for their implementation and oversight. However, the landscape is changing. Numerous similar units exist in rural areas, and now, these units can take charge of local development initiatives.

Consider the following facts: The average rural individual eagerly anticipates a transformative shift in their life—a dream that remains close to their heart. Neither beneficiaries nor government officials have found a definitive solution. Enter the voluntary units—collectives formed for the well-being of their members. These units now step forward to act on behalf of the government.

Their commitment is unwavering. These units, driven by a sense of responsibility, actively engage in addressing the needs of their family members. Their goal? To bring about lasting change and alleviate the sorrows faced by their community. For them, the unit is more than an organization; it is their very essence. They aspire to live lives akin to those of the average person.

As we enter a new era, we must harness technological advancements, scientific progress, and innovative ideas. Together, we can work toward a brighter future—one that benefits all members of our community. Our confidence in achieving this collective vision remains steadfast.

**Our Collective Agenda: Living Lavishly and Trusting One Another** – "Repeat it many times in your mind: I aspire to live a life of abundance alongside my family and neighbors. Our shared agenda is simple: honesty, trust, and mutual support."

**Rejecting Passivity: A Call to Combat Deceit and Power Abuse** – "Let us not be mere supplicants. Instead, let's stand against cheating and the misuse of power."

**The Collective Shield: Thousands Unite for Your Well-Being** – "Previously, you relied on a small family of five for support. Now, envision more than a thousand individuals bolstering you. Their watchful eyes safeguard you, just as a family would. No one will deceive or threaten you. You belong to a protective collective—a unit and its members."

**Unlocking Hidden Resources: Unity and Diligence as Our Path** – "Within our unit's boundaries lie scattered resources. Join forces, explore, and uncover them. Your effort, skills, hard work, and positive mindset will ensure our collective well-being. Walk alongside your fellow travelers, for together, we thrive."

"The prevailing circumstances beckon all of you to come together, uniting your efforts to fortify the scattered rural communities and promote their development and well-being. By supporting and relying on one another, you can forge a distinct path in life.

This path leads toward the prosperity of the rural population. Though it was once shrouded in darkness, now it unfolds before you. Together with others, you can stride toward the goal of abundant living. Focus solely on progress within the community; let other concerns fade away.

Discover the fundamental solution to the poverty and hardship that has plagued your life for years. Recognize that a harmonious social existence requires a profound shift in mindset. Your groundbreaking approach to uplifting the poor and most vulnerable will garner global recognition.

Embrace this significant ethical responsibility and collaborate with others to implement it unanimously. Feel the transformative power within you—a turning point that can elevate your life. Be kind and supportive, and share positive thoughts to yield beneficial outcomes for all."

## COMMUNITY COOPERATIVE: EMPOWERING RURAL LIVELIHOODS

Our community cooperative encompasses **200 households** nestled in the serene countryside. Within this diverse group, we find both **privileged and unprivileged families**, all united as a cohesive unit. Our shared purpose? To forge a path toward sustainable livelihoods through collective effort and unwavering determination

**Abundant Resources Wait:**

**Land**: Our fertile soil stretches out, promising prosperity.

**Skilled Workforce**: A blend of artisans, laborers, and experts—each contributing their unique talents.

**Water Sources**: Lifelines that sustain our endeavors

**Geography**: The lay of the land, its contours, and hidden treasures— our compass to success.

**Catalysts for Dreams –** Luck favors those who toil. Our fertile lands, like seeds awaiting cultivation, await your efforts. As you sow, so shall you reap? Let your sweat be the catalyst that transforms potential into reality.

**Investment Wisdom –** Your investment—whether in sweat, skills, or resources—holds the key to a fulfilling life. Categorize our skilled workers, honor the casual laborers, and never underestimate anyone. Beneath each facade lies wisdom and untapped potential.

**Registering Potential: Names, ages, education, and special skills are** meticulously recorded within our unit. These details form the bedrock of collaboration. The unit, like a skilled artisan, can mold and refine its services, elevating each member to new heights.

*Together, we weave a tapestry of prosperity, where unity fuels progress and dreams take flight.*

## EMPOWERING RURAL COMMUNITIES: OVERCOMING CHALLENGES

In rural areas, many individuals have endured challenging circumstances for years. Despite overall development, the lives of the countryside population remain largely unaffected. However, if someone steps forward, they could rally support from others.

Guidance is crucial to navigate these circumstances. A helping hand could transform them into a self-sufficient team, enabling them to carve out their own destinies. Although hardworking, they often face poor outcomes due to insufficient support, leading them to resign themselves to fate.

The absence of education, proper guidance, and sound advice fosters negative thinking among rural residents. Changing their mindset is no small feat. They remain divided, influenced by ancestral beliefs, and sometimes even harbor discontent toward their neighbors.

While uniting and uplifting them seems daunting, it's not impossible. If someone in your area is willing to shoulder the risk and responsibility, positive change can ripple through their lives and those of their neighbors.

## EMPOWERING RURAL DEVELOPMENT THROUGH COMMUNITY UNITS

In a remarkably short span of time, these community units have the potential to elevate remote areas to an above-average status. Unlike the government's rural development schemes, which often struggle to gain traction in distant regions, these units can effectively bridge the gap.

Outsiders, understandably, show limited interest in the progress of remote areas due to the challenging living conditions. Moreover, the government staff assigned to supervise these projects are often from the other locality, making it difficult to ensure corruption-free services. Overcoming these hurdles is crucial to unlocking the true benefits of government initiatives.

Unlike individual contractors or companies working in the area, the unit operates differently. Its members collectively transform the countryside environment, offering a platform for population growth and holistic family solutions. Born out of necessity, these units empower communities that have long endured tragic and challenging lives.

Now, having formed these units, residents feel safer and more secure. Their unity fuels their confidence that, with collective support, the unit can achieve financial stability and lasting impact.

1. The countryside population is living without basic facilities, and infrastructure is continuing even after hundreds of years. This unit brought you the chance in the countryside to make a permanent remedy to your sorrowful lives.
2. Many had lived and died, serving the influential and clever among them as slaves. Still, many of their followers are continuing the same path with much suffering, the after-effects of that everlasting pain, sickness, and pandemics.
3. The political revolution is expecting mass developments in the countryside and the people. They have many limitations and have to satisfy their party and alliance parties. If you fail to demand your portion with a big majority, then your portion will be considerably tiny in size.
4. The political support and benefits depend as it is not in the hands of individuals, but the masses are deciding. Besides, they are not bothered about the individual's suffering from an area, whereas

they consider many based on the support evaluated by way of vote.

## REVISED VERSION

In rural areas, the population endures a life devoid of even basic facilities and infrastructure, persisting for centuries. However, this unit presents an opportunity—a chance to permanently alleviate the hardships faced by those living in the countryside.

Generations have served the influential and cunning as slaves, their lives marked by suffering. Even today, many followers continue down the same path, bearing the enduring consequences of pain, illness, and pandemics.

The impending political revolution anticipates substantial progress in rural communities. Yet, limitations persist, and satisfying party and alliance demands remains crucial. Failing to assert your rights with a strong majority could leave you with a disproportionately small share.

Political support and benefits lie not in the hands of individuals but in the collective will. While they may overlook individual suffering in specific areas, their decisions hinge on the support gauged through votes.

"The unit operates with a distinct purpose, driven by its members. Their intentions and decisions are solely focused on the unit's growth. This has been evident from the outset. The primary aim is for unit members to collectively work toward overcoming poverty permanently. Any additional progress the unit achieves is a testament to their diligent efforts."

## YOU ARE NOT SCAPEGOATS

In the quiet corners of the countryside, many exploit the local populace for their own gain. Amidst your boundless sorrows, they offer what seems like assistance, yet their intentions remain far from altruistic.

These opportunists ensnare you in fresh traps, capitalizing on your vulnerable state. You find yourself with no recourse but to acquiesce to their terms.

Education, once a beacon of hope, now stands impotent for these rural souls. Even securing daily sustenance becomes an insurmountable challenge. The systems that should protect them lie dormant, and no one extends a hand to uplift them. It's a lamentable state of affairs.

Two-thirds of the world's countryside dwellers languish in idleness, year after year. They grapple with purposelessness while solutions elude them. Employment opportunities remain elusive, and the remedy remains unexplored. But there is a glimmer of transformation—the unit system—a catalyst for profound change beyond mere economic growth.

This unit, like a magic elixir, has the power to quell their unemployment woes, elevating them on a global scale. Yet, in remote corners, educated minds forsake their roots, seeking refuge in towns and cities. Even the smallest of reasons—jobs, modest shops—draw them away. Meanwhile, their brethren in the countryside sacrifice silently, their untapped potential hidden beneath layers of ignorance.

The resources lay scattered, waiting for discovery. Knowledge, like a dormant seed, yearns for fertile minds to cultivate it. Perhaps, one day, the countryside will awaken to its own brilliance, transcending the shackles of ignorance and reclaiming its rightful place in the sun.

## LIVING FOR SOMEONE CLEVER

You hold the power to change your life; no one else can do it for you. Decisions lie within your grasp. If you allow others to exploit you, no external assistance can truly help until you shift your mindset. Consider an alternative perspective, and you'll find yourself leading a more opulent existence. Your followers will be your cheerleaders, urging you forward.

**Returning to Tranquility: The Rural Affluent** Once, the rural rich and prosperous departed their remote homelands in pursuit of business or career opportunities. Now, they return, seeking solace in the serene countryside after amassing wealth. City life, once vibrant, has left them weary. However, their priorities extend beyond personal comfort—they seldom contemplate improving the lives of their fellow countrymen. Instead, they exploit your vulnerability, seeking cheap services throughout their lifetime.

**Challenges in Rural Adoption Schemes** While many banks and organizations have attempted rural adoption schemes, success remains elusive due to inadequate follow-up. The benefits fail to reach the intended recipients. The absence of local staff to oversee fund utilization and other activities hinders progress. A concerted effort, backed by sufficient manpower, is essential for these initiatives to thrive.

"The government faces significant expenses when implementing plans and projects involving numerous staff members, subordinates, and control officials. Additionally, the willingness of staff to work in remote areas plays a crucial role. These endeavors result in substantial costs, which may not align with the government's primary agenda focused on rural development.

However, there's a solution: the establishment of a local unit. By situating the unit's office and members within the countryside, the area's status gradually shifts from remote to developing. This unit becomes instrumental in successfully executing government interests and schemes for the benefit of the community.

Under the unit's purview, every development initiative within the area receives attention. Beneficiaries receive shared benefits within specified time limits, and the government maintains proper records throughout the unit.

Interestingly, while many banks attempted to implement government schemes for rural and remote area development, their efforts fell short of expectations. <u>Instead, they primarily provided loans to those capable of repayment."</u>

# CHAPTER II

# THE SIGNIFICANCE OF THIS UNIT SYSTEM

Within this small group, members have the ability to independently manage and address various aspects promptly. The immediate assessment of each action represents a significant achievement. Conversely, prolonged issue resolution can hinder the unit's growth.

Time holds immense value here. The rural community has invested substantial time, which directly impacts their progress. Our unit aims to achieve substantial goals. Despite government efforts to develop rural areas, they have yet to yield significant returns.

Enforcing government regulations among unit members is straightforward. Adherence to these rules ensures a high-quality culture within the group. This commitment fosters peace and eliminates criminal and illegal activities from our midst.

Once, a minister engaged in rampant corruption, amassing great wealth through illicit means. Despite his ill-gotten riches, he led a modest life, refraining from donning extravagant attire. His son, privy to his father's secrets and vulnerabilities, seized this knowledge as leverage. Blackmail ensued, and a substantial portion of the minister's ill-gotten gains was extorted from him.

Persisting on his corrupt path, the minister clung to his insatiable desire for wealth, displaying a lunatic determination. He forsook the pursuit of a dignified existence, instead fixated on accumulating more money—his fate or perhaps the state of his mind driving him relentlessly.

Unfortunately, when public figures harbor such weaknesses, it detrimentally impacts the nation's progress and the well-being of its citizens.

## DECEPTION – THROUGH FALSE PROMISES: A GROWING CONCERN

At the inception of any endeavor, one anticipates reaping the fruits of labor throughout their lifetime, alongside their family. However, despite the existence of comprehensive rules governing various aspects of life, corruption remains pervasive, eroding ethical standards among citizens.

The legal frameworks in many countries inadvertently harbor loopholes that allow wrongdoers to perpetrate their offenses repeatedly. These provisions, ostensibly part of the law, inadvertently shield criminals from the full weight of justice. Sometimes, even the innocent find themselves ensnared by circumstance, yet the system often dismisses or closes such cases prematurely.

Regrettably, once a case concludes, it fades into oblivion with little consideration for its impact. Perhaps it is time we collectively address these issues and strive for a more just and accountable society.

Most rules, especially those related to cheating, have legal provisions. For instance, if you lend someone money through a handshake agreement without registering it, that agreement is not considered valid. However, you can rectify this by paying additional stamp duty and penalties to make the document legally binding.

Your friend, aware of how to deceive, advises against registering the agreement. They try to convince you that they will repay you promptly.

You trust their words and accept a check along with the agreement and an undertaking letter. Unfortunately, these documents alone are insufficient for recovering your money. This is a separate issue you might not be aware of.

If you believe you know your friend well, you may think spending thousands on registration is unnecessary. However, this decision could put your hard-earned money at risk, especially if your friend turns out to be untrustworthy.

**Navigating Sticky Loans and Legal Matters**: When faced with burdensome loans, it's essential to consider legal implications. An unregistered agreement is essentially worthless—a mere scrap of paper. Unfortunately, this oversight can result in losing not only the money paid but also strain relationships. To avoid such pitfalls, seek legal advice and adhere to applicable laws. Going forward, a dedicated unit will handle your financial transactions lawfully and address any related issues.

**Upholding Rules and Ethics: A Call to Awareness** – In every country, a multitude of rules and regulations exists, often bewildering ordinary citizens. These guidelines touch every aspect of life, from civic duties to personal conduct. As members of society, we must strive to comprehend these norms and ensure their dissemination.

Within any organization or community unit, fostering awareness is paramount. Whether through contact classes, meetings, or circulars, we can empower our members and extend this knowledge to the public. By doing so, we contribute to a well-informed citizenry.

Our collective aspiration is simple: to lead decent lives through honest toil. Despite facing poverty and scarcity, many of us remain steadfast in upholding our nation's ethics. This commitment reflects a desire for a tranquil existence—a life guided by principles.

The broader public, too, plays a crucial role. They willingly adhere to the rules and regulations set forth by their nation. However, a small minority grapples with financial hardship, leading them to rebel against these norms. To overcome such challenges and realize our dreams, we must explore alternative paths—one that our ancestors could not fathom in their time.

Let us continue to uphold integrity, foster awareness, and collectively shape a better future for all.

**Community Unit and Responsible Living**: The bond among neighbors can transform lives. Many prefer a peaceful environment over violence. Often, people heed their ancestors' advice without questioning, relying solely on their experience. Unfortunately, this approach can leave them feeling unfulfilled. Moving forward, let's prioritize cooperation over excessive rules within our community. By supporting one another and understanding our nation's regulations, we can foster smooth growth together.

**Empowering Choices and Realizing Responsibilities**: Each of us shares responsibilities. One crucial aspect is recognizing how birth rates impact individual development. While some laws have loopholes allowing criminals to escape, we must also acknowledge personal limitations. Raising a child involves more than just providing food, clothing, and education. Even with limited income, societal expectations may pressure us to marry and reproduce. Let's think twice about our choices and consider the bigger picture.

**Financial Stability and Earning Potential**: The rising birth rate places greater demands on financial stability for child-rearing, including necessities like food, clothing, and education. Many find themselves contemplating alternative ways to earn money to meet these daily requirements. However, if you are a bonded laborer lacking specific skills, your income potential remains limited.

**Being a Responsible Citizen** – As a proud citizen of any nation, there are numerous responsibilities you must uphold. Simple actions like walking on the road, driving, and treating others respectfully can help you avoid penalties in your daily life.

**Addressing Agitation and Government Interaction** – The collective protests over seemingly trivial issues against the government—

such as inadequate ration and water supply—need to cease. These demonstrations often attract the attention of vulnerable, illiterate individuals who are easily swayed by media advertisements. It is crucial to take such matters seriously and curb any fraudulent practices that exploit the weaker sections of society.

**Collaboration between the Government and Organizations –** Effective collaboration between government bodies and private entities is essential. By fostering mutual understanding and cooperation, both parties can support each other. It is vital not to evade payments owed to the government, as doing so may lead to unforeseen consequences. Even small service charges serve to protect citizens' rights. Skipping these payments for minor gains can result in significant losses.

Operating within legal boundaries is crucial for any organization. The government provides support, and it is our responsibility to ensure that sufficient funds are available. Levies and taxes contribute to the nation's development and aid various groups, including ours.

**Avoiding Legal Pitfalls in Financial Transactions –** When you assist others by evading the lawful amount they owe to the government, you commit a serious offense. Skipping out on proper registration of agreements disproportionately benefits those who seek to exploit you. By supporting such individuals, you inadvertently violate the very rules designed to safeguard your rights

in these transactions – The consequence? You risk losing your hard-earned money due to the absence of proper legal documentation.

Consider this: When the law is circumvented, it aids the looter in evading both rightful payments to the government and the amounts owed to you. Those who pilfer from you gain an advantage, effectively closing the door on your ability to make claims against them indefinitely.

Meanwhile, those who engage in illegal assistance during times of hardship will ultimately suffer the consequences.

To avoid these pitfalls, exercise caution in all transactions—whether familiar or unknown. Entrust transactions within your unit to a vigilant manager who ensures compliance with legal requirements. Going forward, all dealings on behalf of members or the unit must adhere strictly to the law.

Remember, lawful transactions not only safeguard your finances and time but also provide peace of mind. Upholding the rules ensures that no loopholes are exploited. Reject any advice to the contrary; after all, the unit's funds are public, and you remain accountable for their proper handling.

**The Significance of Legal Transactions** – We recognize that amending laws is no simple task, but the legal framework exists precisely to prevent deceit and fraud. It is not solely the government's responsibility to enforce these laws; it is our duty as citizens to adhere to existing regulations and avoid falling into traps.

Within our community, a dedicated unit remains vigilant about financial and other matters affecting individuals and families. By channeling all financial transactions through this unit, we safeguard our rights.

Despite the multitude of laws governing various aspects of life, lack of awareness often leads people into legal disputes—whether at police stations or in courtrooms. However, with the establishment of these units, many neighborhood conflicts can be resolved proactively, preventing unnecessary legal battles.

Furthermore, these units educate their members on essential legal knowledge that every common person should possess. Through contact classes with police authorities and online learning, unit members can elevate their understanding of legal matters.

**Educated Members: A Valuable Asset** Well-educated members serve as the unit's treasure. Their presence not only helps avoid unnecessary legal complications but also fosters unity among like-minded individuals, ultimately contributing to the unit's growth.

**Government Welfare and Village Development** While the government extends welfare measures to its citizens, it often remains unaware of their effective utilization and lacks direct involvement in village development. Units can bridge this gap by identifying suitable machinery and resources for the betterment of humanity.

**Harmonious Living and Proactive Initiatives** – By maintaining integrity and avoiding conflicts with neighbors, unit members can collectively brainstorm and implement positive changes in their lives. Additionally, the unit should actively engage in members' affairs, making decisions based on genuine considerations.

**Financial Transparency: No Unaccounted Money** – Once a unit is formed, borrowing money among members becomes unnecessary.

The unit takes charge of all financial matters, ensuring transparency and accountability for every penny. Unaccounted money has no place within the unit's framework.

## "ENSURING TRANSPARENCY: UNACCOUNTED MONEY – UNIT MEMBERS"

When a unit is formed, strict guidelines prevent members from borrowing money from each other. All financial matters are directly managed by the unit itself. Consequently, any illicit money-making activities cannot be carried out by individual members. The sources of funds are meticulously tracked and documented within the unit.

The unit operates like a close-knit family, with all assets benefiting each member equally. Whether based on official records or mutual understanding, every member has a rightful claim to these assets. Upholding the best interests of its members, the unit strictly prohibits any malpractice.

Furthermore, the funds held by the unit must maintain a pristine record. This ensures transparency and prevents any individual member from bending the rules in favor of themselves or their family.

## FUND CANVASSING FOR UNIT MEMBERS

Unit members should be informed that they have the option to bring deposits from their friends and relatives outside the unit. These deposits can significantly contribute to urgent development projects within the unit. If the interest rates on such deposits exceed those offered by banks, it will attract more depositors.

To ensure transparency and compliance, the unit must prominently display a notice. This notice should clarify that any deposited amount related to black money or any other illegal activity is the sole responsibility of the depositor. Along with the deposit application form, the unit can obtain a declaration from the depositor confirming the legitimacy of the funds.

By adhering to this process, the unit can protect itself from legal repercussions and unnecessary formalities. Refusing to accept deposits without a proper declaration ensures that the depositor explicitly states that the money deposited is their own. Additionally, they express no objection if the information is disclosed to the government. This approach will be particularly beneficial if attractive interest rates attract deposits from various sources.

**Efficient Deposit Handling**: To prevent any misunderstandings, consider receiving deposits directly into the unit's account. However, it's crucial to adhere to money transaction rules, especially when dealing with amounts exceeding the authorized limit set by the authorities.

**Legal Compliance and Accountability**: Your unit must remain free from legal repercussions. If you receive an amount that is potentially involved in illegal activities, follow the relevant rules and handle it according to the directives provided by court or government personnel.

**Deposit Practices**: Units should refrain from interfering in matters related to illicit money possession by depositing funds into their accounts. <u>While accepting deposits from outsiders introduced by members, exercise good faith and offer competitive interest rates, but avoid exceeding what a bank charges for a loan or overdraft</u>.

# CHAPTER III

# ADVANTAGE OF THE UNIT SYSTEM

## ADVANTAGES OF THE UNIT SYSTEM FOR GOVERNMENT

The unit system operates independently, focusing on the welfare of rural and countryside residents. While it has its limitations, it also provides valuable support to the government. Notably:

1. **Identification and Regularization of Illegal Stays**: The unit plays a crucial role in identifying and regularizing illegal settlements. By ensuring that every family is recognized, it facilitates the issuance of statutorily approved documents for each individual. This process grants legal identities, allowing people to claim their nationality through the unit. **Remember**, *the unit system bridges the gap between remote areas and legal recognition, benefiting both individuals and the government*.

**Identification and Fate**: In our country, there exist individuals without proper identification. This unit plays a crucial role in tracing such families or individuals. Once identified, the government can then determine their fate.

**Countryside Traces**: Families residing in rural areas for many years can also be traced through this unit. They have the option to continue with their existing identified documents, or their fate will be decided by the government. Additionally, this unit helps identify waste that has been dumped in remote regions over the years.

**Uniting the Scattered Population** The unit serves as a hub, organizing the scattered population under one roof. Remarkably, people from backward rural backgrounds are transforming into more developed individuals. They now enjoy life within the unit, adapting to new infrastructure, habits, and a distinct culture.

"The residents of this self-sufficient community possess remarkable mental wealth, and their unity catalyzes gradual transformations in their habits. Consequently, the local economy has surged to unprecedented heights. Remarkably, this growth occurs effortlessly, without any direct intervention from the government.

Living a distinct life of health and prosperity, these individuals have acquired substantial knowledge across various domains. Their population remains limited, granting them effective control over all aspects within their community. The unit's members diligently safeguard the area, ensuring it remains entirely free from anti-social elements. Despite facing threats from external sources, including gangsters, their unwavering unity and considerable strength allow them to fend off crises.

Moreover, the economic landscape of this region has flourished, satisfying the needs and aspirations of all its inhabitants. Remarkably, this community takes on the responsibility of assessing government properties within its boundaries. Without any government intervention, they meticulously track trespassers and categorize properties as wet, dry, or barren."

**Efficient Land Management**: If any trespass occurs on government lands within the unit's boundaries, it can be promptly traced. The identified property can then be allocated to the unit or its members through the unit management. Necessary formalities and documentation can facilitate property registration at the Sub-registrar office.

**Streamlined Revenue Collection**: This unit serves as an effective conduit for collecting revenue owed to the government or its undertakings. By remitting funds directly to the relevant bank accounts, the government can save considerable effort. Even in rural areas, outstanding dues can be collected without the need for additional expenses like staff salaries.

**Transparent Eligibility and Accountability**: Individual eligibility becomes crystal clear due to well-documented transactions and accounts. The continuous efforts of dedicated members — approximately 1,000 individuals from 200 families —contribute to the improvement of the specific area.

**Black-and-White Transactions:** All financial dealings are transparent, leaving no room for speculation or criticism. This collaborative effort is not a one-person show; shortcuts are eschewed in favor of genuine development. As an open book, the government can always request records for further assistance.

"All unit records are meticulously based on real counts and precise measurements, ensuring that anyone can find satisfaction and accurately relay their records and accounts." These units serve as a foundation for cultivating high-quality citizens —individuals with exemplary habits, discipline, cultural awareness, and a comprehensive understanding of their surroundings.

Within these units, members remain up-to-date in fulfilling their government dues, demonstrating unwavering sincerity and loyalty to one another. They view each other as part of a single-family, devoid of enmity, as was previously the case.

Moreover, these units have the potential to permanently eradicate the criminal backgrounds of rural residents. By doing so, the previously wasted manpower spent on court proceedings can be redirected toward productive endeavors. Besides all these achievements not only benefit the unit but also contributes to the nation's progress Certainly! Let me rephrase that for you:

"<u>By implementing a unit system in rural areas, which cover the largest portion of the world (about 2/3), and enhancing production, inflation can be effectively controlled.</u>"

As all homes within the unit are members, tax payments and other charges levied by government authorities — such as rural, water, and electricity authorities — are consolidated into a single lump-sum payment, ensuring timely compliance."

**Streamlined Transactions and Rural Development**: – The government and other authorities need not send notices or bill collectors to the unit. Under the present system, no dues will accumulate.

The unit's adoption of online payments for every transaction is a progressive step, especially in rural areas. Most payments occur in lump sums through banks, making future verification easier.

By ensuring thorough bank transactions, the government's desired implementation becomes feasible. A significant portion of the rural population relies solely on accounted pure money banking.

**Empowering Youth and Family Businesses** – Youngsters gain exposure at all levels by actively participating in various unit tasks. Allocating them to different sections allows them to develop their careers within the unit, akin to a family business.

**Parental Responsibility for Birth Control**: – To manage the birth rate, parents must provide 100% protection to their children within the unit.

## THE UNIT ASSERTS THE FOLLOWING PRINCIPLES

**Shared Responsibility**: Parents bear equal responsibility for their children's well-being.

**Birth Rate Control**: This unit actively manages birth rates.

**Exemplary Model**: It aims to serve as a model for both the nation and the world. Parents must not evade their duties, including providing **food, shelter, and education** to their children.

Support should continue until the children achieve self-sufficiency or reach a certain age. Children should not suffer due to parental conflicts; both parents share liability and accountability.

While government regulations alone cannot effectively control birth rates, this unit adheres strictly to its own rules. Generalizing policies that benefit society is essential. Having lived without proper guidance, many residents here face extreme poverty.

**Unit Awareness and Birth Control**: The members constitute the unit, and the unit belongs to them. It is crucial for the unit to recognize the importance of birth control. As part of your support, you should present this matter during your meeting as an agenda item.

**Challenges with Charitable Efforts**: – Unfortunately, most charitable endeavors fall short due to insincerity among the beneficiaries. Additionally, the system should reconsider accepting donations for charity, as some individuals misuse these funds while living extravagant lives. Tolerating such behavior perpetuates a natural cycle of deception.

**Rethinking Collective Knowledge** – *The unit's formation involves its members, leading to a shared pool of knowledge about life. However, we need to shift our approach. Instead of mindlessly adopting the outcomes of others' experiences, we should hold parents responsible for ensuring that their children learn valuable lessons.*

## THE CHARADE OF CHARITY:

Interestingly, some clever individuals exploit the concept of charity. By labeling their endeavors as such, they attract easy money, akin to different types of liquor packaged in various bottles of diverse colors.

The beneficiaries are tearing up every day in the practice – None of them are spring and age or gender are not differentiating their sorrows. Our inquiry must be for finding out the real cause and its route and the child must get the life than the effect of the father's / mother's prestige.

In the olden days, there were facilities to safeguard them instead of entrusting them to the charitable to provide them sufficient wealth, which was very rare only done – the remaining grown under criminal-minds were turn anti-social elements.

The present system of charity is a source to lavishly live for somebody cleverly presenting it in front of others is a different kind of begging and the government is allowing rebates besides encouraging them to such donations. It is not an easy task to pull out of this system because many are living with this permanent source of income.

The pity mind behind all these is they are very politely cheating others, even influencing the government for tax exemptions, which is very well-known to all. The unit can control this so that in the coming years onwards, they can work on this and abolish this system, which will come under the crime of cheating.

Moreover, the relatives of each home admitted in old-age or children's homes can find out through these units and can rescue them even if very few only remain – for them also, the unit can find a remedy. Now, there are many people in the countryside who do not have an address to express their identity.

**Empathy and Equality**: Every day, beneficiaries face challenges in their daily lives. Regardless of age or gender, their sorrows remain undifferentiated. Our inquiry aims to uncover the true causes and pathways to address these issues. Above all, we prioritize the well-being of the child over the prestige of their parents.

**Historical Safeguards**: In the past, protective facilities existed to shield vulnerable individuals. Rather than entrusting them solely to charitable organizations, efforts were made to provide them with sufficient resources. Unfortunately, some grew up in environments influenced by criminal tendencies, leading to anti-social behavior.

**Charity's Complex Landscape**: Today's charitable system often blurs the line between genuine assistance and strategic presentation.

While some genuinely help those in need, others cleverly manipulate the system. Government incentives and rebates further complicate matters.

Escaping this cycle is challenging, especially when many rely on it as a permanent income source.

**Polite Deception**: Beneath the surface, some individuals subtly deceive others. They influence the government for tax exemptions, perpetuating a flawed system. Addressing this issue requires vigilance; failure to do so risks perpetuating a crime of deception.

**Uniting Families**: Even amidst these complexities, there's hope. Units can identify and rescue relatives admitted to old-age or children's homes. Their efforts matter, especially when so many people lack a fixed address to express their identity.

**Addressing the Homeless Population**: *In the coming years, it will be possible for local units to identify and integrate the homeless population into regular society. These individuals will likely have some connection to existing community members. By doing so, we can permanently address this issue and ensure their inclusion.*

**Government's Advantage in Addressing Homelessness**: From each local unit, there may be a few homeless individuals. Identifying and integrating them would be advantageous for the government. These newly recognized citizens can contribute by participating in elections, supporting political parties, and becoming part of the nation. The government can proudly showcase this initiative.

**Empowering Children with Stability**: Children deserve stability. A simple white paper petition to the relevant authorities should grant them the right to a permanent address and meaning in life. Their gratitude will extend to the government or any other supporters who facilitate this change.

**Assisting the Unaffiliated Population**: Despite our efforts, there remain around 1000 individuals who are not associated with any local unit. The government must take steps to provide them with land and facilities, especially in rural areas. While 100% assistance may not be feasible, the government's intervention is crucial.

**Eliminating Child Beggars and Laborers**: No child should be forced into begging or child labor on the streets. Our nation should be free from such hardships. Instead of merely enforcing rules or removing them, we must reinstate these children with basic facilities to improve their lives.

**Unit Cooperation in Identifying Citizens**: By identifying individuals related to existing unit members, the government can swiftly recognize their subjects and regularize their status. The unit's assistance in shedding light on these unidentified citizens is invaluable.

**Member Identification and Accountability**: – Members of this specific area play a crucial role in identifying any doubtful individuals. They should recognize that this responsibility is on their shoulders. If any doubts arise, the manager has the authority to reject membership applications.

**Enhancing Unit Identity and Government Recognition**: – The unit's primary objective is to foster self-sufficiency among its members. By organizing small clusters of 200 households, the unit can directly manage all internal affairs. This proactive approach not only strengthens the unit's identity but also garners government attention toward creating a crime-free community.

**Leaderless Harmony and Comfort**: – Unlike traditional structures, this unit operates without a designated leader or unwanted interference. Consequently, it cultivates a comfortable and pleasant environment within its boundaries.

**Optimizing Manpower and Streamlined Operations**: Inmates who remain unaffected by adverse circumstances happily contribute to the unit and their families. The unit's intention is to achieve 100% manpower utilization. Workflows will flow seamlessly, unencumbered by hierarchical constraints. Regular classes and meetings further shape the unit's collective mindset.

**Safeguarding Vulnerable Individuals**: – The unit extends its protective umbrella to include the elderly, children, mentally challenged individuals, and those suffering from various ailments. Whether they come from orphanages or join the unit directly, their well-being remains a priority.

**Nurturing Mental Well-Being**: – To maintain mental vitality, active engagement is essential. Patience during the transition period ensures that everyone adapts smoothly. Showering them with love and unwavering support is the key to their successful integration into the unit's fabric.

**Encouraging Growth and Respect**: Allow individuals to work or collaborate with other teams but set clear limits. This approach fosters mental improvement and helps them reach a more normal level of functioning.

Discourage disruptive behavior or insults stemming from personal shortcomings. Instead, encourage understanding and empathy among team members. If they have parents, they should prioritize caring for them.

**Protecting Vulnerable Children: Put an end to using children for hard labor**, child exploitation, or anti-social activities within the unit. Irresponsible parenting may contribute to their mental health issues.

Avoid making them feel like orphans. Parents should not exploit their children for begging or criminal purposes.

**Unit Integrity and Transparency**: The unit operates for the collective benefit of its members. Individual gains are not prioritized, ensuring fairness.

All financial transactions are meticulously recorded, preventing any unaccounted money or corruption.

## SOCIAL IMPACT AND SAFETY:

**Eradicate begging, theft, and other anti-social activities within the unit's boundaries**. Vigilance by unit members can eliminate child kidnappings and threats against women. Regular training and information sharing enhance safety awareness.Together, these measures create a supportive and secure environment for all unit members.

**Access Control and Safety Measures**: The unit must implement strict access controls to regulate the entry of visitors and vendors into the residential area. If necessary, visitors should be directed through the unit office. This approach offers several advantages, including limiting unwanted entries and ensuring security.

**Managing Frequent Visitors**: Frequent visitors, such as product vendors and promoters, can be managed effectively by the unit office itself. If there is no valid reason, they should not be allowed inside the residential premises. By fencing the unit boundaries, we can restrict entry to the main gate adjacent to the unit office, enhancing control and safeguarding our members from potential threats.

**Separating Business and Residential Areas** – A gated community designating specific zones for business purposes while keeping the rest for residential use is essential. In the future, we may consider an apartment system for all members. This approach ensures that unwanted third parties do not enter residential areas and allows unit members to immediately recognize them.

**Enhancing Security and Community Well-Being**: As unit members interact with each other, they can promptly identify outsiders. This ability helps restrict external interference and prevents any disruption to the pleasant environment within the unit.

**Turning Dormant Individuals Productive**: Individuals struggling with addiction or alcoholism can transform their lives and become valuable contributors to the unit. Supporting their recovery and overall health enables active participation in unit activities.

**Zero Tolerance for Theft and Cheating**: Among members, theft and cheating cases are strictly prohibited. Any such behavior should be swiftly addressed and eliminated to maintain the integrity of our unit community.

**Addressing Harmful Individuals:** "He poses a greater threat than the average criminal, consuming smaller entities like a predator. It's crucial to be cautious from the outset and avoid associating with such individuals, as they can contaminate the environment with their toxic influence."

**Combating Prostitution and Anti-Social Activities:** "Prostitution can be eradicated from our area if we take proactive steps. Once rescued, those involved in prostitution should never return to it. By addressing prostitution and related anti-social behaviors within our community, we can create a safer environment."

**Eliminating Poverty and Starvation:** "With collective effort and a few days of hard work, we can immediately eliminate 100% of poverty and starvation within our community. This will directly benefit our families."

**Education System and Poverty Eradication:** "We should establish an education system managed by our units. While education is essential, our primary commitment remains poverty eradication. Let's focus on achieving that goal first."

"Once we achieve our objective, we can provide educational facilities for those in need. Understanding the basics required to run our unit, including production and sales, is essential."

**Empowering Members and Overcoming Employment Challenges:** Consider starting a small production unit that doubles as a training center for our members. Our children can receive training and become self-sufficient in their work."

"Every member should recognize our limitations in educating everyone. Rather than emphasizing formal education, our units aim to lift members out of poverty. Many parents educate their children despite the lack of nationwide employment opportunities."

**Empowering the Unit and Addressing Poverty:** The unit aims to distribute employment opportunities among all its members, harnessing 100% of its manpower to address the current poverty situation; consequently, unemployment does not adversely affect the unit.

**Education and Future Plans:** While we work toward accumulating sufficient funds and resources, our immediate focus remains on meeting the day-to-day needs of our members. In the future, through collaborative efforts involving five units, we aspire to establish a school for our children.

**Selecting Land and Property Management:** When choosing a location for the school, consider barren land with access to water and road facilities. As five units collectively manage and share equal rights, decisions regarding property registration fall under the purview of the management. We have decided to proceed with the purchase.

**Running the School:** By pooling the available resources, jointly all five units can efficiently operate the school. We can appoint teachers and staff from within our ranks or even seek skilled educators from nearby units.

Kindergartens and primary classes should be established within each unit's boundaries to ensure convenience for the children. Additionally, provisions for food and other amenities must be made available for both teachers and students.

**Employment and Qualifications:** Members interested in continued employment within the unit should undergo training and gain experience. While we value inborn skills, we also emphasize a minimum level of qualification. Positions requiring education cannot be filled by members lacking the necessary qualifications.

**Effective Work Allocation:** Regularly distributing work across different sections of the unit ensures that everyone possesses the requisite skills and contributes effectively.

**Enhancing Education in Remote Areas:** Education in remote regions has seen significant improvements compared to earlier times. Residents now acquire essential skills to interact with each other and outsiders. However, due to financial constraints, achieving a highly qualified workforce by bringing everyone together remains challenging.

**Empowering Rural Living:** Our primary goal is to elevate the standard of living in remote areas. We aim to provide essential amenities and facilities, enabling residents to lead self-sufficient lives without relying on external assistance. The mindset of struggling for daily sustenance must shift, ensuring people are no longer plagued by poverty and water scarcity.

**Addressing Laziness in Education:** Laziness often begins during school-level studies. In many cases, students should actively seek solutions rather than passively accepting difficulties. Encouraging proactive problem-solving can prevent a persistent pattern of laziness.

**Healthcare Infrastructure and Indigenous Medicine:** Establishing hospitals is crucial, and this can be achieved through joint ventures with other units, as previously proposed. Additionally, we need to identify suitable locations for primary health centers and Ayurveda dispensaries. These units should also promote indigenous medicinal practices, benefiting both patients and the nation.

**Indigenous and Ayurvedic Medicine Promotion**: Given that these units are often situated in remote areas, they heavily rely on indigenous treatment methods. The advantage lies in their ability to address common ailments without adverse effects. By emphasizing indigenous and Ayurveda medicines, along with mandatory cultivation of medicinal plants, units can contribute to overall well-being.

**Fostering Unity and Eradicating Enmity**: Villagers can overcome enmity and poverty by working together. Their shared goal is simple: to lead content lives with their families. Building brotherly relationships among unit members and fostering unity will lead to significant improvements.

**Data-Driven Progress and Skill Enhancement**: Census operations are costly for the government. However, units can provide essential data about their members, allowing for real-time assessment of progress. This data can inform development plans and programs. Furthermore, progress reports on individual efforts within the unit contribute to skill enhancement.

**Enhancing Rural Development through Community Units:** In our pursuit of rural development, we face the critical challenge of effective birth control is possible.. Despite existing laws and regulations, their implementation remains inadequate, hindering growth in rural areas and perpetuating poverty. Our primary agenda is to address this issue..

Within the framework of community units, the government can channel its efforts more efficiently. These units are responsible for delivering high-quality services tailored to their specific needs. As global dynamics shift, we must explore new opportunities. Many countries seek industrial products, and our units can play a pivotal role in meeting these demands.

To achieve this, we propose enhancing industrial capacity by upgrading machinery and ensuring skilled workers operate them. Dormant villagers can be empowered to contribute actively. Moreover, we must eradicate years of accumulated dirt in rural areas through these small units.

Unit-based governance allows seamless implementation of policies and regulations. From combating smoking, drug abuse, and prostitution to preventing theft and attacks, our units can foster a safer environment. If each member commits to improving their lifestyle and unit, we can uplift families and neighbors, creating a world-class rural life.

## ADDRESSING BIRTH CONTROL AND RURAL DEVELOPMENT

Making informed decisions about birth control is essential. Despite existing laws and regulations, proper implementation remains a challenge, particularly in rural areas. This deficiency hinders growth and perpetuates poverty. Our primary agenda is to address this issue.

Within our unit, the government can efficiently channel high-quality work. As global dynamics shift, we explore new opportunities. Many countries seek industrial products, and we can tap into this demand. By enhancing machinery capacity and selecting skilled workers, we meet rising requirements. Dormant villagers can transform into productive contributors.

In rural regions, accumulated dirt and waste pose long-standing problems. Our small units aim to eliminate these issues permanently. Through innovative approaches, we enforce policies and regulations, including bans on smoking, drugs, prostitution, theft, and attacks.

If each unit member commits to improving their lifestyle and environment, they can positively impact their families and neighbors. Together, we strive for a world-class standard of living.

## UNLOCK OUR POTENTIALS

**Unlocking Water Resources:** There are many resources to be tapped, wastage of dam water and river flow can be transformed into a solution for a global challenge: access to clean drinking water. Within our unit, this need is well-addressed. By collaborating across units, we can identify water sources and ensure adequate supply.

**Government-Approved Water Supply Scheme**: With special permission from the government, this scheme becomes feasible due to the existing pipeline infrastructure that often traverses government properties. Even if the units are located in remote areas, water supply from the dam and river can be extended to these units.

Erecting water treatment plants within these units enables water filtration and bottling, potentially for commercial purposes. Any surplus water can significantly benefit communities by providing safe drinking water. Moreover, these units can supply water at a nominal cost, leveraging government subsidies even in distant regions.

**Leveraging Leaking Dam Water**: While the burden on individual units can be substantial, collaborative efforts among neighboring units can alleviate this challenge. Instead of relying solely on dam water, consider utilizing the leaking water from the dam. Despite being overlooked, this water volume amounts to many gallons daily.

By channeling it through pipes, we can transform this wastewater into a valuable resource. This innovative approach not only addresses local water crises but also contributes to global sustainability.

**Turning Waste Water into Solution**: The strategic use of dam-side leaking water, previously considered useless, has now become a significant solution. By converting it into drinking water and supporting agricultural needs, we tackle a long-standing global issue.

Through these units, seemingly insurmountable problems can find a resolution. Additionally, this approach has the potential to resolve political disputes and agitations related to water scarcity.

Water, being essential for life, warrants government support — even if the initial investment is slightly higher.

**Water Solutions and Unit Collaboration:** Consider this as a lasting solution for water scarcity: units working together. Whether it's a community or an organization, collective efforts can address the critical issue of access to clean drinking water. By pooling resources and expertise, we can find innovative ways to ensure water availability for all.

**Combating Laziness in Education**: The seeds of laziness often sprout during school-level studies. It's crucial to identify and address this early on. Instead of allowing students to perpetuate lazy habits, let's actively seek solutions. Timely intervention can prevent long-term consequences and foster a proactive learning environment.

**Healthcare Collaboration and Holistic Approaches**: Hospitals play a vital role in our well-being. To enhance healthcare accessibility, consider joint ventures among different units. Imagine a primary health center and an Ayurveda dispensary working hand in hand. Let's also encourage indigenous medicinal practices alongside conventional treatments. Together, we can promote holistic health.

**Indigenous Medicine and Plant-Based Healing:** Many units operate in remote areas, relying on traditional healing methods. The advantage? These methods often have minimal side effects. Let's actively promote indigenous and Ayurveda medicines. Additionally, mandatory cultivation of medicinal plants in specific regions can benefit both unit members and the nation at large.

**Unity and Eradicating Enmity**: Within villages, unnecessary conflicts can breed poverty. But imagine a united front – a team committed to happiness and family well-being. When unit members treat each other like family, enmity dissipates. Their collective strength becomes a catalyst for improvement.

**Data-Driven Progress and Development**: :Census-taking is resource-intensive for governments. However, units can provide valuable data. Each unit's records, meticulously maintained, can offer insights into progress. Armed with this information, we can strategize and lead units toward development. Progress reports from unit members further contribute to growth.

## COLLABORATION AND DATA-DRIVEN DECISIONS ARE KEY TO POSITIVE CHANGE!

"Each unit can participate in this facility by sharing the expenses incurred for the project equally. Although the supply through pipes can be costly, the large pipe size and sometimes kilometer-long lengths must be taken into account, along with periodic maintenance.

With special government permission, this scheme becomes feasible, especially since the pipes often traverse government properties. Even if the units are located in remote areas, water can be supplied from the dam and river to the unit members.

By establishing a water treatment plant within the unit, water filtering and bottling become viable for selling purposes. Any surplus can contribute to providing drinking water to many. These units can offer water at a nominal price, with government subsidies extending even to faraway places.

Given the burden on individual units, collaborative efforts with other units can be beneficial when laying the pipes. Although the water originates from the leaking dam, its daily volume — often in gallons — can significantly benefit numerous households for agricultural and drinking purposes.

The global water crisis affects many, leaving them desperate for drinking water. Utilizing this flowing wastewater through pipes for productive purposes is a wise approach.

The plan to repurpose the leaking water from the dam's sides—once wasted—now serves as both drinking water and irrigation. This solution addresses a long-standing global challenge.

Through these units, we can tackle seemingly insurmountable issues, including persistent political problems like poverty and criminal activities."

**Addressing the Core Agendas** – Our primary focus revolved around three key objectives. Let's delve into how we tackled them:

**Water Source: Bore Wells.** – Rather than having hundreds of individual wells, we propose limiting the number of bore wells to 5–10 within our unit. These bore wells should have a larger diameter, such as 8" or 10," ensuring sufficient water supply for 50–100 members per well.

Securing permission from local government officials is crucial before digging these bore wells, especially if they are located in public spaces.

Always obtain written permission to avoid legal complications down the line. While infrastructure development is essential, our primary concern remains the welfare of our members.

**Exploring Alternative Water Sources** – Consider utilizing paddy fields within our unit. These naturally wet areas can serve as excellent locations for digging large wells.

Despite their distance from residential areas, these wells offer a cost-effective solution compared to additional bore wells. Water can be conveniently supplied through pipelines.

**Remember** *to seek written consent from relevant authorities when laying pipelines, even on government land.*

**Exploiting Water Sources** – To harness the water source effectively, construct a bund across the river at its narrowest point. This will create a wet area with abundant water. Next, dig wells on both sides of the river, ensuring they remain consistently filled. To supply this water to our unit, pipes must be used, and proper filtration must be implemented before consumption.

These two water-sourcing methods are preferable over processing directly at the riverside. Be cautious of rainwater accumulation near the well during the rainy season. Being too close to the river can disrupt plant operations and impact water supply.

For wells located by the riverside or near dams, it's essential to build compound walls on the sides facing away from external water sources. This prevents direct contamination and maintains the wall height in line with the probable watershed near the well.

Additionally, consider constructing a protective wall around the well and motor shed, allowing convenient access while safeguarding the motor and other equipment. Keep the motor shed above the anticipated water level to prevent contamination from river overflow.

**Harnessing Dam Water for Electricity Generation:** Every day, significant amounts of dam water are lost due to leaks and electricity generation. Instead of waste, we can utilize this water for our unit's needs, including drinking.

To achieve this, create a small bund to intercept the water's flow. While not blocking it entirely, allow controlled overflow either near the dam or at a suitable point along its path. By doing so, we can prevent unnecessary loss and make better use of this valuable resource.

**Water Sources and Rural Progress**: Adequate water sources and availability are crucial for progress in the entire surrounding region, particularly in agriculture and allied activities.

**Eradicating Starvation and Poverty**: The three major, urgent agendas that have long impacted the lives of rural populations are now being addressed. We've discovered ways to purify contaminated water from dams and rivers, converting it into a valuable resource.

While this investment may be somewhat costly, it's essential for our unit's growth. By selling bottled water widely, we can recover these expenses and generate substantial income.

**Ensuring Accessible, Pure Water**: Despite the prevalence of substandard water due to cheating and adulteration, we aim to overcome this challenge. Our goal is to provide 100% pure and affordable water to all.

While not every unit has surplus water sources, we can manage this effectively and avoid direct competition.

## GOODWILL OF A UNIT

The **organic standard for oils** used in food preparations mandates that they be sourced directly through sealed packs. This ensures the highest quality and purity, and anything negative can be easily accountable.

"The water bottles provided by the manufacturing units must bear responsibility; they attract accountability. A unit cannot prioritize selling contaminated products to make quick profits."

Additionally, our unit benefits from **ample water supply**, allowing us to cultivate all the land under our purview for a variety of crops. From essential food crops to fruits, vegetables, flowers, and even medicinal plants, we have the potential to directly market and supply these products to end-users.

This approach not only fosters goodwill but also positions us favorably in the market, making product sales effortless.

Beyond oils, our unit handles other products as well, often fulfilling **bulk orders** based on our strategic marketing approach. However, let's delve into an intriguing possibility —

## THE SEAWATER TREATMENT

While it can be expensive compared to alternative methods, we should consider it seriously once our financial position improves. Units located near the seashore could benefit significantly from this source.

For a sustainable solution to drinking water, consider **collaborating with neighboring units**. By joining forces, we can address any shortages in water supply. Desalination, although costly and energy-intensive, remains a viable option. Perhaps, as our financial stability grows, we can explore incorporating solar energy into the process.

Our mission is clear: **provide 100% pure and affordable sweet water** to all. While not every unit enjoys surplus water sources, we can avoid direct competition by strategically pricing our hygienic bottled water. Your unit's production capacity and market demand will guide the pricing strategy. Remember, we're not just competing with other brands; we're creating a sustainable water solution for everyone.

**Seawater Treatment: A Costly but Vital Source: W**hen no other water source is available within a unit, seawater treatment becomes a consideration. However, it is undeniably expensive compared to alternative methods. We should only contemplate this option once our financial position improves. In such cases, units located near the seashore are the most viable choice.

**A Permanent Solution for Drinking Water:** When the existing water source proves insufficient, joining forces with at least ten or more units becomes essential. However, desalination, while effective, is costly and energy-intensive. During our initial stages, affordability is a challenge. Perhaps solar-powered solutions can be explored later once our financial stability is assured.

**Benefits for Politics:** Political parties that support and assist these units can secure a lasting vote bank. This alternative yet permanent solution significantly benefits rural populations. Villagers express immense gratitude to those who aid them during critical times.

**For Unit Members:** Unit members' awareness will improve as they experience a new lease on life. Interaction with others allows them to grasp novel concepts. By abandoning their past routines, they can transition from disinterest to productivity.

Strict adherence to banking practices ensures awareness of regular transactions and safeguards against cheating. The unit should actively promote financial literacy among its members, with younger individuals playing a crucial role in providing assistance.

## INFRASTRUCTURE

Improving road access and other facilities within the unit is crucial. Rather than treating this as a temporary measure, we should invest in creating a permanent asset. Our financial constraints currently prevent us from doing so, but our primary focus remains the welfare of our members rather than solely environmental and infrastructural concerns.

The properties involved in road development and infrastructure are government-owned. Consequently, we can only request that their authorities review our project reports. We hope for their support, recognizing that government resources can significantly benefit our projects beyond what the unit alone can achieve.

Our members harbor a unique perspective: transforming a remote area into a tourist destination with comprehensive amenities managed by the unit. Their determination, coupled with the challenges faced by rural communities, fuels their dreams.

## THE GOVERNMENT WILL ASSIST IN YOUR ENDEAVOR.

When communicating with the government, provide detailed information about your unit, including new projects and essential road and infrastructure requirements. While we shouldn't engage in recurring work due to our rural investment and developmental stage, local government authorities can handle such tasks more effectively.

By taking on government-assigned work, your members will contribute to the community while benefiting from the high-quality results you deliver.

**Remember**, *the unit's success need not come at the cost of financial strain.*

## UNIT-BASED COMMUNITY DEVELOPMENT

When individuals express a strong desire for change, their only recourse is to leave the community unit. These units are specifically designed to address poverty and other hardships faced by their members. The arrangement within these units is permanent and tailored to meet the needs of the community.

Partitioning among households is virtually non-existent within these units. Members receive comprehensive facilities and support, rendering the idea of separation unappealing. Instead, they remain within the unit, benefiting from assured income and permanent employment. The nuclear family setup becomes unnecessary in this context.

In cases where deserving individuals find themselves living frugally, they must carefully consider their options. Privately earning income is not an option within the unit; all financial transactions are part of the collective system. Any remaining balance is credited to individual home accounts, reinforcing the strong bond among house members.

The unit's educated team explores innovative ideas approved by fellow members, creating additional employment opportunities and income-generating projects. Multinational companies also recognize the skills of trained unit members and offer career openings. The unit actively supports individual growth and adaptation.

**Political Implications –** These community units, backed by political parties if offer a lasting solution for rural populations. *By supporting* *these units, politicians can secure a perpetual vote bank. The villagers stand to benefit significantly from this alternative approach.*

**Facilities and Hospitality**:-When arranging facilities for sightseeing or other purposes, it's advisable to utilize our own vehicles rather than involving external parties. This not only ensures safety but also enhances the overall experience for visitors. Additionally, we should prioritize providing acceptable food options and other facilities..

Rather than offering a five-star hotel experience in remote areas, we aim to create an affordable and delightful treat for our guests. This approach encourages repeat visits and word-of-mouth recommendations.

**The Power of Word-of-Mouth Advertising**: Remember that word-of-mouth advertising is incredibly potent. Impressions made through genuine hospitality leave a lasting impact. Guests often extend help voluntarily, without any persuasion or formal requests.

**Creating a Positive Impression**: – Our hosts play a crucial role in influencing tourists' perceptions. While we may not provide five-star facilities in remote areas, we should focus on creating an appealing setup with proper safety measures.

**Infrastructure Considerations**: Improving road access and other infrastructure within our unit is essential. Although our financial constraints limit permanent solutions, we can request government authorities to review our project reports. Their support will significantly benefit our endeavors.

**Bank Financing** – Banks are often eager to invest because they typically have substantial funds at their disposal. When you present your projects to them, they become even more interested. The requirements of each business unit often involve significant capital, and banks are pleased to see these funds being put to good use.

Moreover, since bank branches are often located within the premises of these units, they can closely monitor day-to-day progress and fund utilization.

The financing arrangement benefits both the banks and their clients. The substantial amount involved is fully secured, minimizing the risk of loans turning into non-performing assets (NPAs). Banks can observe how the funds are being utilized by the business unit, especially since they operate right on-site. As a result, banks are more than willing to assist these units.

To determine the appropriate loan amount, banks consider the unit's requirements and project reports. In some cases, opening a branch or an extension counter of the nearest bank within the unit's vicinity allows for even closer monitoring. This proximity enables timely advice to the unit's management and direct reporting to higher-ups within the bank.

Should a project face insufficient funding, banks promptly assess the situation and report to their higher authorities. Being fully secured, banks disburse funds incrementally based on the project reports submitted earlier. Transparency in transactions ensures that banks are satisfied and payments are disbursed accordingly.

This approach empowers the unit to manage payment risks effectively while the bank closely monitors progress.

Additionally, the well-trained unit members, guided by their peers and managers, are less susceptible to fraudulent practices. Effective communication further strengthens the relationship between the bank and the unit.

## THE PROCESS OF TURNING RAW MATERIAL INTO PURE GOLD

"Similar to gold, many individuals undergo suffering and challenges within this unit. Their experiences serve to refine them, much like the process of turning raw material into pure gold. Now, they possess a valuable skill set — their working capital — and each member has a stage upon which to perform.

Their success is a combination of luck and their willingness to seize every opportunity provided by this unit. These dedicated individuals demonstrate that none of them are useless or dormant. Instead, they work diligently for the betterment of the unit.

Over time, a once-dormant population has become active, shedding bad habits and contributing to the unit's growth. They stand ready to achieve victory alongside their peers, proudly identifying themselves as unit members who hold significant positions.

Their achievements are not the result of magic; rather, they stem from hard work and a willingness to embrace challenges. Living without unnecessary burdens, they thrive on positive energy. The system's progress is not due to someone else's exploitation; rather, it is driven by the collective responsibility of unit members who take ownership.

Unity has fortified them against life's threats. No longer alone, they stand strong, supported by thousands who share their resolve. A change in mindset can transform an entire life. Now, this unit functions as a cohesive team, proving that anything is possible when all aspects align.

Furthermore, the unit serves as a business organization, granting equal rights to all members and safeguarding their homes."

**Eye Donation: A Lifesaving Gift** Eye donation is a powerful and accessible way to spread awareness and encourage people to contribute to a noble cause. By donating their eyes and other body parts, individuals can make a significant impact on the lives of those in need.

The process becomes more straightforward when organized through donation centers. These centers, comprising 5 to 10 units, pool resources and equally distribute funds. This collaborative effort ensures that the donation lab functions optimally while any surplus resources can benefit other organizations.

Thanks to this coordinated approach, the combined efforts of these units can meet the eye transplantation requirements of the same unit, nearby facilities, and even city-side labs. But once our internal teams and units have finished their tasks, it's essential to consider other areas."

While supplying the donated eyes, the units may charge according to their operational costs, considering factors like staff salaries and facility maintenance.

Additionally, it's essential for one of the participating units to provide facilities to the donation lab free of charge. This selfless act ensures that the lab can operate efficiently, benefiting recipients and honoring the spirit of eye donation. In case of any disputes, the involved units should resolve them equitably, emphasizing the collective advantage of their collaboration.

"Consolidating the lab into one or two units would enhance the independent movement within its space. This consolidation is akin to a charitable act, ensuring that resources are efficiently distributed to those in need and deserve. By removing the constraints of unit boundaries, we can eliminate any limitations and operate the lab in a more sophisticated manner, benefiting both donors and recipients."

# CHAPTER IV

# THINKING DIFFERENTLY: EMPOWERING DORMANT RURAL POPULATIONS

**Aim of the unit** This chapter is dedicated to the rural population, aiming to eliminate the negative impacts that have plagued their lives. By embracing hard work and sacrifice, rural communities can infuse elements of urban living into their existence. Let's set aside animosity and forge new connections among ourselves.

Across the globe, countless rural areas harbor unprivileged individuals who have endured hardship for years. If you're willing to step forward and confront your current tragic circumstances, this guide offers a path to transform your life. The approach may seem unconventional, but it holds the promise of making rural life captivating and appealing.

Remember, no single person can alter the fate of others. However, when a collective effort emerges, lives can be reshaped. Consider it a joint venture for your well-being—one that will undoubtedly illuminate a brighter future, wiping away tears and sorrows.

1. **Building Resilience through Unity**: When faced with the challenges of poverty and despair, cultivating a defensive mindset is crucial. Recognize that you are not alone in your struggles; the collective strength of unity can fortify you against the hardships you encounter daily. By standing together, you gain the courage to confront life's obstacles head-on.

2. **Unyielding Determination for Unity**: An insatiable drive to persistently work toward unity, both within your family and beyond, can significantly impact your well-being. Rather than relying solely on external assistance, take ownership of your destiny. Even when faced with adversity, maintain your resolve to collaborate with others and effect positive change.

3. **Rural Perspectives on Government Support**: In rural areas, there exists a deep-seated belief that the government should be responsible for their welfare. However, only a minority actively take the initiative to improve their own lives. Lack of personal guidance and self-motivation hinders progress, leaving many untouched by positive transformation.

1. **Challenges of Self-Motivation**: Many individuals struggle with self-motivation. Despite being insensate due to addiction or other factors, they grapple with decision-making and yearn for change in their lives. Unfortunately, this often leads to persistent poverty and a sense of utter despair.

2. **A Mathematician's Wisdom**: *Imagine your love for family and friends as a perfect circle—no sides to break, no ends to terminate, and no angles to measure*. Similarly, your life should be a reflection of this unbounded love. As a single person, you face limitations, but these challenges can be overcome through collective effort.

3. **Politics within the Unit**: While many households harbor multiple political beliefs, active politics should not infiltrate our unit. Let our policy be clear: members can hold any political views, but engaging in active politics within the unit is prohibited by our bylaws.

"We stand united to transform the current situation, especially among the rural population. These individuals endure hardships merely to survive and protect their families indefinitely. Our collective ambition is to rise above these challenges by joining forces.

Every member has the freedom to cast their votes according to their preferences. Our organization operates as both a family welfare association and a family business. Our primary goal is to foster economic growth for each member. However, we recognize that politics isn't accessible to the underprivileged like us.

While it may benefit a few, it cannot address the entire societal spectrum. Our involvement is limited to supporting through voting. Given your limited time, set aside your sorrows and sufferings. There are others who will actively engage, and our silent moral support will empower deserving leaders to make decisions based on the collective voice of the masses."

## "EMBRACE YOUR HUMANITY"

To operate as a cohesive unit, the collective skills of its members suffice. By harnessing this synergy, you can propel the unit to great heights. Such elevation not only transforms your own life but also brings about significant change in your surroundings.

In rural areas, regardless of education, some individuals exhibit behavior akin to aggressive mongrel dogs. Unfortunately, much of the relevant news—both good and bad—fails to reach them. It is imperative for the entire rural population to shift their mindset and embrace a more human existence.

A select few lead slightly better lives due to their distinct mindset. However, there are those who still cling to superstitious beliefs, waiting for a miraculous day. Yet, your personal experiences should have taught you that no one but yourself truly cares for your well-being.

If you spend years hoping for external assistance, you squander your life, mirroring the faith-based passivity of your ancestors. Break free from this cycle. Neither they nor you should live solely for others; each of you must shatter the shell of laziness that envelops you.

**Remember:** *your actions shape your humanity*.

**Rethinking Solutions: A Different Path:** You find yourself treading the same path, adhering to familiar beliefs, and yet, the solution eludes you. It's time to recognize that your experiences and the stories passed down by your ancestors hold valuable insights. Consider them from a fresh perspective—one that diverges from the beaten track. The remedy lies in this shift of mindset.

**Seeking Assistance from Others:** Family—a miniature universe woven with threads of love and sacrifice—holds immense power. When you prioritize your kin, acknowledging their significance, love and sacrifice become the essence of life. This unit, akin to a single-family, thrives on these bonds.

Think beyond your immediate circle. Extend your love and willingness to sacrifice to encompass not only family but also neighbors. By doing so, you'll weave magic into your existence. This transformative effort will propel you toward success, ensuring you never look back.

**Embrace Change and Empowerment:** In this transformative era, it is essential to break free from the shackles of helplessness. Rather than accepting defeat, take an oath to think differently. Draw upon the skills, knowledge, and experiences passed down by your ancestors. These invaluable tools can serve as your weapons in the battle against poverty and life's hardships.

Consider the application of technology in your rural community. Seek ways to uplift the impoverished conditions faced by you, your family, and fellow citizens. It is your responsibility to drive positive change that benefits not only you but also the collective whole.

Regrettably, many rural youth have squandered their potential over the years. Instead of contributing to their own growth or that of others, they remain dormant. Break this cycle. Ponder solutions to your challenges and actively work toward overcoming them. Your transformation can be a beacon of hope for the entire community.

**Collaborating with Neighbors for Solutions –** When faced with challenges, consider joining forces with your neighbors to find solutions.

In the following pages, we'll explore how collective decision-making can be the most effective path forward. When an individual confronts a difficult situation, seeking assistance from others becomes the most viable remedy.

**Prioritizing Your Well-Being** – It's essential to recognize that everyone experiences their share of struggles—whether it's hunger, poverty, or other hardships. Often, these difficulties persist because we fail to think beyond our immediate limitations. *For years, rural communities have witnessed sympathetic gestures from outsiders— kind words and small monetary contributions for a meal. Yet, these fleeting acts rarely lead to lasting change.*

To break this cycle, consider a more permanent solution: harness the power of collaboration. By pooling resources and efforts, you can create opportunities for mutual prosperity. Your challenge lies in transforming helplessness into collective growth.

1. **Stuck in a Cycle**: You find yourself unable to discover a solution to your problems. Despite your relentless search, you remain stagnant, unable to reach your desired destination. *Unfortunately, this lack of direction makes you vulnerable to exploitation by others who offer enticing promises but lead you into criminal activities.*

2. **Grateful for Basic Necessities**: *At times, you feel grateful for the assistance you receive, even if it's just a meal.* However, your perspective is limited. Those who provide for you are well aware of this, <u>and they capitalize on your poverty</u>. Your potential for a better life remains untapped while you reap the benefits.

3. **Exploitation and Substance Abuse**: Instead of genuinely supporting you, some exploit your vulnerability. Rather than nourishing your body, they introduce drugs and alcohol, preventing any positive transformation. You've never contemplated your

own or your family's future because your circumstances keep you from thinking beyond survival—a situation they exploit to their advantage.

**Unlocking Productivity: A Shift in Perspective** – Often, seeking assistance can be misconstrued as laziness. We fail to recognize that accepting help is not a sign of weakness but rather a way to navigate life. Health and wealth surround us, yet they remain scattered and untapped. Despite this abundance, we sometimes feel utterly helpless, trapped by circumstances or superstitions.

However, there lies a solution—a joint effort. Rather than facing challenges alone, we can create a collective unit. Imagine a community formed for the welfare of all, encompassing both urban and rural populations. This joint venture holds the key to unlocking our true potential and transforming our lives.

## NOTHING IS FREE – IT COSTS YOUR LIFE

Your ancestors were accustomed to waiting for government assistance, and even today, the mindset of rural populations remains heavily influenced by this dependency. Many political leaders provide aid, treating you like mere animals, with an eye on their own future gains. You continue to exist, merely surviving on the resources at hand.

However, as a human being, you must aspire to more. To lead a better life, you need to shift your mindset. Be prepared to work diligently and invest your time for the collective benefit. Don't delay any longer; consider what lies ahead and how you can attain it.

Are you content following the same path as your ancestors? If your answer is "No," consider this: you have the power to lead a different lifestyle. Rural communities come together and explore joint ventures for the welfare of all villagers. Divide the village into smaller sections, each contributing to the greater good.

## EMPOWERING CHANGE THROUGH COMMUNITY ACTION

In our quest for progress, numerous projects await consideration. Rather than relying solely on government rural funds, why not explore the potential of joint ventures? Waiting for mercy is unnecessary when we possess the capability to meet our own requirements.

Here's the plan: Let's unite and focus on a segment of our village comprising **200 homes**. Our task involves gathering essential details from these households: names, addresses, ages, educational backgrounds, property information, and more. The specifics are meticulously outlined in the forthcoming pages for your reference.

Keep in mind that these **200 homes** collectively represent **1,000 members**. Our calculation treats each home as a member, thus limiting our membership count to 200.

As you delve into the subsequent pages, you'll find step-by-step instructions on compliance.

**Message to the Achievers:** Dear community members, you hold the power to effect change. Refuse to squander time. Instead, channel your efforts toward addressing pressing issues such as poverty and water scarcity. Identify the negative forces impacting your lives, prioritize them, and tackle them systematically. You are the architects of transformation!

If you observe closely, you'll notice numerous scenes that may not be new, but you hadn't noticed them earlier. Your neighborhood is under the influence of a few anti-social elements. Despite their small numbers, they wield significant control over the majority of the area, including your house. Their unity is their strength, allowing them to prevail.

Now, consider this: You are part of a larger unit, more than 1000 strong. Together, you have the capability to face any threat. Your primary challenges include unemployment, alcohol, drugs, and prostitution— issues that plague your surroundings.

To reclaim control, you must harness the collective strength of your 200 selected homes. Remove the hindrances that hold you back and create a safer, more empowered community."

1.  **Breaking Free from Negative Thoughts**: – Negative thoughts can be like weeds in a garden, choking out the potential for growth. They spoil our outlook and hinder progress. Instead of

nurturing these thoughts, consider replacing them with positive affirmations.

## FOR INSTANCE:

- "I welcome positivity into my life."
- "I abandon old habits and choose new, positive ones."
- "I am gentle with myself and others."
- "I control my thoughts."
- "I release all thoughts that don't serve me and empower me."
- "I choose peace."
- "With each breath I take, I release negative thinking."
- "Comparison is the thief of joy; I release comparing myself to others."

**Challenges Faced by Drunkards and Drug Users**: – Many individuals caught in the cycle of addiction lead lives marked by inertia. Whether they have food or not, they prioritize their substance of choice. Their stories will be explored further in the upcoming pages.

Looking back at their ancestors, we find a history of struggle. Despite limited resources and harsh conditions, they persevered within an imaginary boundary. As subsequent generations emerged, they pushed against these limits yet still grappled with finding practical solutions to their hardships.

The lack of financial means can make one feel trapped, as if fate has dealt an unchangeable hand. Alternatives seem elusive, and creative solutions remain out of reach.

**Hope for Improvement**: – But is it possible to elevate our lives from the existing level? Absolutely: *Even in the most neglected corners, change is feasible. Consider the village situation—a place marred by waste and overlooked by outsiders. Yet, hidden within lies potential waiting to be unlocked. A few influential figures hold sway, while others* *silently consent. Perhaps it's time to break free from this cycle and envision a brighter future.*[2]

Remember, *our thoughts shape our reality. By reframing negativity, we can pave the way for transformation and progress.*

**Unity among the Few: A Tale of Gangsters and Anti-social Behavior** – As our narrative unfolds, we encounter a small but tightly-knit group. These individuals wield their unity as a weapon, instilling fear in others to further their business interests. The gangsters enforce their rules within their territory, often resorting to sacrifices to maintain their dominance. Meanwhile, the anti-social elements dutifully follow their boss's orders, trapped by circumstance and familial ties.

**Turning the Tide: A Chance for Redemption** – Consider this: criminals, weary of their boss's tyranny, seek an escape. Extend a lifeline to these disillusioned members, and they will rally to your cause. The very gang that once supported the anti-social forces will abandon their allegiance, finding solace in an alternative path.

**Challenging Tradition: A Call for Reason** – Our ancestors, staunch in their beliefs, imposed their systems upon the new generation. Yet, blind adherence to tradition isn't always wise. They *pushed youngsters into marriages without considering financial stability, maturity, or earning potential*. The result? A cycle of poverty perpetuated, leading to a pitiable existence.

**Challenging Traditional Customs: A New Perspective** – Instead of blindly adhering to age-old customs, perhaps it's time to question their relevance. The notion that certain events must occur at specific ages serves as a rigid parameter. But is there a better way? Rather than pressuring young individuals into marriage without considering their financial stability or personal circumstances, perhaps we should prioritize their well-being and safety within the family structure. After all, adamant adherence to outdated ethics can perpetuate an unsustainable system, leading to increased birth rates and exacerbating poverty.

**Unlocking the Potential: Utilizing Idle Manpower** – Imagine harnessing the untapped potential of idle manpower in rural areas. We've been losing precious human resources day by day. What if we could reinstate this force into action? Enter the solution: an independent body—the unit—for the welfare of its members. Once formed, this unit ensures that no one remains idle. Members actively monitor and engage, preventing laziness. By running at full production capacity, these units can transform lives, lifting individuals from zero to prosperity and contributing to a well-occupied economy. Dreams fulfilled through collective effort

**100% Manpower Utilization: Paving the Way for Progress** – For years, the skills and potential of rural manpower remained hidden, obscured by neglect. But now, a dynamic force of energetic individuals has emerged, leading the charge. By organizing into units, two-thirds of our nation is becoming active and productive, with the ambitious goal of achieving **100% manpower utilization**. The implementation of this unit system control inflation, promises to transform the countryside, propelling our nation toward prosperity and self-sufficiency.

Gone are the days of idle existence. Our people have learned how to harness their abilities for personal and collective benefit. No longer will we suffer from wasted potential. Instead, we are poised to elevate our nation economically. Our ancestors, too, faced hardships—often sacrificing their own well-being for the greater good. Their struggles were poignant scenes etched in time, unimaginable to us today.

Now, through each unit, we unlock the full potential of our manpower—a beacon of hope for our youth and a testament to our national achievement. No more struggles, no more suffering. We forge a new path, one that leads to progress for our families and ourselves.

We acknowledge past mistakes and take an oath to succeed, embracing a future where every day counts toward our collective ascent.

**Empowering Self-Motivated Teams** – Historically, neither governments nor organizations have fully harnessed the vast reservoir of untapped human potential. Each day, countless individuals contribute their skills and efforts yet often remain unrecognized or underutilized. The rural population, in particular, has long endured a struggle for survival, merely existing rather than thriving.

However, a transformative shift is needed. Instead of mere subsistence, the goal should be to provide every family with an independent home—a place where new cultural norms can flourish. To achieve this, we must divide rural areas into smaller units, each with its own purpose and vision. By channeling 100% of available manpower toward productive endeavors, we can unlock the anticipated growth of these regions. This, in turn, will bolster the nation's financial stability.

The impact of revitalizing dormant areas extends beyond economics. It positively influences mental well-being, physical health, and overall quality of life. When individuals work together as a motivated team, their collective efforts yield immediate results. Confidence and sincerity thrive, and the entire community benefits. With a systematic approach devoid of unnecessary obstacles, progress becomes inevitable.

**Discover Your Resources** – As previously mentioned, you may have observed how birds like roosters and crows diligently gather their sustenance after scavenging through discarded waste. Similarly, you possess valuable human resources that you've perhaps underutilized for years. These resources are more than sufficient to help you endure and lead respectable lives. To uncover your livelihood, consider clearing away the debris that obstructs your path.

Imagine if an educated team were to collaborate with you, not from external sources but within your own community. *Their focus would be to transform a small area of your village into a thriving hub, elevating it to world-class living standards. This ambitious goal is at the core of our unit's agenda.*

In the rural landscape, subdividing into smaller units serves multiple purposes. It ensures that the population can access their daily sustenance and welfare. Additionally, it provides *a mechanism to manage community affairs effectively*. As part of your team's mission, combating poverty should be your primary objective, and you have the freedom to choose how best to achieve it.

**Unlocking Potential: The Power of Self-Motivated Teams** – A self-motivated team possesses the ability to achieve remarkable feats. When fueled by ambition and a resolute mindset, they can overcome seemingly insurmountable challenges. It's essential to recognize that relying on others to accomplish your goals is a fallacy. Instead, channel your inner drive and passion to propel you forward.

Consider the legacy of our ancestors. For generations, they harbored ambitious dreams yet often *lost their potential due to untapped manpower*. This dormant workforce remained unnoticed, neither benefiting themselves nor contributing to the nation's progress. Imagine if we had harnessed their skills—the tireless efforts of these unsung heroes could have transformed our countryside.

Our mission is clear: utilize every resource at our disposal. By providing meaningful employment opportunities, *we can elevate individuals from grassroots positions to white-collar roles*. Let us honor the hard work of those who came before us and build a future where ambition thrives.

**Empowering Transformation: From Addiction to Productivity** Unemployment plagues our youth, often by choice. Some deliberately shun work, citing various reasons. Yet, hidden within their seemingly carefree lives lies an enigma—an enjoyment that eludes outsiders. Perhaps it's time to unlock this mystery.

Consider drug addicts and drunkards—the marginalized souls who wander aimlessly. What if we could redirect their energy toward productivity? Imagine the transformation if we channeled their potential into meaningful work. Let us not dismiss them; instead, let us uncover the hidden joy that fuels their existence.

**Remember**, *every individual possesses untapped potential. It's our collective responsibility to nurture it, transforming lives and shaping a brighter future for all.*

**Drugs and Slow Poisons:** Substance abuse, whether it's drugs or alcohol, can have devastating effects on individuals and their families.

**Poisons**, in general, are substances that can harm or kill through their chemical actions. They can enter the body in various ways, including ingestion, inhalation, skin contact, or injection.

**Loneliness, isolation**, and **lack of interest** can contribute to substance abuse. Reconnecting with others and finding purpose can be essential.

Efforts should focus on turning dormant individuals into productive members of society, benefiting both their families and the nation.

**Remember:** *seeking professional assistance and support is crucial for anyone struggling with addiction. If you or someone you know is facing this challenge, consider reaching out to a healthcare provider or a helpline for guidance and resources.*

Due to unemployment, many individuals fall into the clutches of drugs and harmful substances, leading to dire consequences regardless of their age group. The prevailing trend among rural communities is to celebrate every occasion with excessive drinking. Our mission is to rescue these individuals from their addictions.

Moving forward, we must refrain from hosting parties with alcoholic beverages at home or within our community. We bear significant responsibilities toward our families, neighbors, and our nation. The allure of drinking has ensnared numerous young people, even those from disadvantaged backgrounds like yours.

Perhaps you were once new to this lifestyle, but now addiction holds you captive. Whether it's your father, mother, sister, or wife who provides for the family, your lack of awareness prevents you from appreciating their efforts. You've become aimless, living without purpose.

Your isolation and indifference have transformed you into a solitary figure, detached from others. Our collective effort should focus on reawakening dormant potential, making you a valuable contributor to both your family and our nation.

**Self-Improvement and Collective Responsibility** – You are not meant to squander your potential; instead, you must illuminate your future. As members of this unit, your skills and abilities surpass those of others. The unit relies on your growth to benefit not only your families and local area but also the entire nation. We are the solution to reclaiming valuable manpower that has been lost for years due to addiction to alcohol and drugs.

**Colonialism: A Historical Perspective** – Colonialism, an age-old practice among nations and even families, aimed to exert control over others and establish settlements. In our context, we are not battling tangible enemies but rather combating the shadows of starvation, scarcity, and poverty.

The past is behind us. Let us convene a meeting with all 200 members (Homes) and share this idea for their well-being. They must recognize that any expenditure is an investment in their own wellness. Together, we can forge a brighter path.

**Empowerment and Responsibility: A Call to Action –** Remember, you're not just working for others; you're working for yourself and your family. As unit members, it's our collective responsibility to act as moral guardians. Let's identify the lazy and inebriated individuals within our ranks—whether they're ladies or gentlemen—and encourage their active participation in our unit.

*The first crucial step is to translate the bylaws into regional languages*. Once done, we'll narrate and explain the content to all members. Our goal? To engage 1,000 members selected from 200 households. This is our agenda, and it's time to put it into action.

**Detecting Anti-social Behavior: A Collective Effort –** We assume that our members won't engage in theft within the unit. After all, this unit is our shared property, and we've overcome the hardships of starvation and poverty. But let's not be selfish. If you were to steal, you'd find that <u>our system is adept at detecting malpractices</u>. So, why risk it?

The unit employs various technologies to uncover theft and trace its usage. Even though the unit protects you and your family, maintaining a selfish mentality could lead to severe consequences. Remember, we're all in this together, and extreme punishment awaits those who defy our collective purpose.

**Enhancing Security Measures in Our Area –** The neighborhood faces several security challenges, with theft being a prominent concern. In the event of any suspicious activity affecting a family, it is crucial to promptly notify the unit office. We have devised a solution: all interactions with strangers within our unit area must occur through the unit office. This ensures that the office maintains detailed records and monitors movements via the surveillance system.

*To mitigate risks, we must strictly adhere to this protocol. Whether it's a guest, friend, or regular visitor, everyone should follow the designated route through the unit office. For strangers or those with official business, additional details should be recorded in the visitor's book.*

Furthermore, each entry—regardless of frequency—must include a timestamp and signature. To bolster security, we propose installing CCTV cameras around the unit office and nearby establishments. Additionally, fencing the entire unit perimeter will provide an added layer of protection for our community.

*Let us collectively safeguard our loved ones and maintain a secure environment.*

"Our members, being well-acquainted with one another, can readily identify third-party entries into our area. In the unfortunate event of theft attempts by outsiders or gangs, we must confront the situation head-on. When our members are found to be involved with external parties, they will face the consequences and penalties imposed by both the unit and government authorities.

All members are accountable to the unit, and those who act against its interests will bear the consequences alongside their family members. The unit reserves the following punitive measures:

**Suspension of Family Connections**: The unit may suspend family members from all interactions with other unit members, including the withdrawal of concessions and benefits.

**Restriction on Supplies**: During this period, no groceries or other supplies will be provided to the implicated family.

**Eviction**: If guilt is established, the unit will evict the member, settling their assets. The entire process must be completed within 90 days of the unit's decision.

The severity of the punishment is outlined in subsequent pages. Additionally, the membership of the implicated household will be suspended for one year, and all concessions or discounts previously enjoyed by that home will be withdrawn."

**Membership Reinstatement**: Membership can be reinstated only after confirming that there are no pending police cases or unit-related issues against the member. Typically, this reinstatement period is one year, during which the member must pay double the membership fee for a 12-month period. After recording and passing a resolution in the meeting, similar to other such cases, reinstatement can occur.

**Accountability for All**: Not only members but also all officials and staff of the unit, including those who authenticate daily accounts, must be accountable. If they assist or engage in malpractices related to accounts, purchases, sales, or any other matters, they will face the same consequences.

**Lapses and Responsibility**: While some members may escape punishment for their lapses, they remain accountable. Let us reiterate that our collective purpose is family welfare, growth, and well-being through hard work and self-motivation.

**Upholding Integrity in Our Unit** – In our unit, where all our basic needs are met, we must remain steadfast in our commitment to honesty and integrity. Reflect on your past—before this unit came into existence—and recognize the progress you've made. You've grown significantly, haven't you?

Consider the daily necessities: food, clothing, education for our children, and healthcare. Why, then, would anyone contemplate deceit within our own community? Such actions warrant no sympathy; <u>they are the result of one's fate.</u>

The responsibility of running this unit lies squarely in our hands. Let us not resort to unscrupulous practices merely to survive. Instead, let us keep our hands clean and refrain from dipping them into the beggar's pot.

Remember, *this unit serves as a voluntary organization for impoverished rural populations. They strive to live with dignity, realizing that indecision often costs more than making a wrong choice. They learn from their mistakes and move forward with regret as their guide.*

This marks their final endeavor to exist as human beings; kindly grant them this privilege. They have grown weary, much like you, of circumstances that have led them to their current state.

No one has extended a helping hand thus far, but we believe that this collective effort can alter our destiny. Even if you choose not to assist us, refrain from pushing us back into the abyss of suffering. Consider this our plea to you, a solemn vow to embrace a tranquil existence.

Life's conflicts have left every soul disheartened, and all we yearn for is a glimmer of hope. *True wealth lies not in material possessions but in the intangible treasures that money cannot purchase.*

This initiative is exclusively designed for rural populations, aiming to eliminate the adverse effects that have plagued their lives. By embracing hard work and sacrifice, rural residents can bridge the gap between their traditional lifestyles and the allure of urban existence. Let go of animosity and forge new connections.

# CHAPTER V

# THE TECHNICAL FUNCTION OF A UNIT

As previously mentioned, an office is essential for the unit's operation. It should include a manager's cabin, a staff office hall with stationery storage, attached washrooms, and other facilities. Ideally, this office space should be adjacent to the storage area where stocks are kept.

To streamline operations, ensure that the required computers and trained staff from your area handle printing needs. Rather than bulk printing, focus on producing materials with the unit's name, emblem, registration number, and other relevant details. These materials will be used from the very next day, and sales of products will contribute significantly to the unit's daily account. Effective accounting practices will safeguard your finances.

In today's digital age, most printed formats and hard copies can be replaced by soft copies stored on computers. Statutorily required formats can be customized as needed, and maintaining backups is crucial for future reference.

The unit members need not worry about expenses during the locking period (which can extend to 36 months or more). All costs are covered directly by the unit.

For financial transparency, each entry of receipts and payments should be physically verified against the ledger maintained on the computer. Vouchers and receipts must be duly authenticated by unit officials. Implementing a system where one person enters data and another authenticates it helps identify any errors. Responsible management ensures that expenses remain controlled without unnecessary extravagance.

## MEETING YOUR NEEDS THROUGH THE UNIT

Members have the convenience of obtaining essentials from the unit's shops. Both units and individual members should maintain a transaction record, including dates and details such as grocery purchases and other utilities. During the initial months, typically within the lock-in period, these disbursements should adhere to a limit set by the unit manager. To prevent confusion, communication between the shop in-charge and the home is essential. While the unit bears the expenses for crop cultivation and other activities, it is the responsibility of the allocated member to oversee and care for these resources.

## BEING DUTIFUL AND RESPONSIBLE

As a unit manager, you will delegate responsibilities to one or more members or households to oversee specific crops within the unit. Initially, they share both individual and collective responsibility for the assigned crop or task. Regular progress reports are crucial; communicate with the manager based on the established schedule (daily, weekly, etc.). For special assignments, maintain a detailed daily record, noting tractor usage, manure application, fencing, watering, harvesting, and related expenses. Provide timely updates to the unit office, which oversees your work. Before transitioning to the computerized format, submit a handwritten record to your higher-up, complete with your signature, seal, and mobile phone number. Follow the instructions diligently, especially if you are responsible for managing expenses.

# THE ROLE OF ACCOUNTING SYSTEMS

An efficient accounting system plays a crucial role in organizational operations. Let's explore how it contributes:

1. **Record Keeping and Updates**: With accurate details, the office can maintain up-to-date accounts and related records. These records serve as a valuable resource for decision-making and financial analysis.

2. **Timely Access**: When needed, you can promptly collect the accounting book for further processing. This accessibility ensures smooth workflow and informed decision-making.

3. **Authentication**: The book entries must be authenticated by the officer in-charge of your section. Each daily entry receives the official seal, ensuring accuracy and reliability.

4. **Allocation of Responsibilities**: After interviewing staff members, the manager allocates responsibilities to crop and business units. This process ensures that capable individuals handle tasks independently.

5. **Acknowledgments**: Obtaining signed acknowledgments from concerned members solidifies their commitment to their assigned roles.

6. **Skill Assessment**: Properly documenting interview details helps assess individual skills. Managers can determine whether additional training or skill enhancement is necessary.

7. **Individual Ratings**: Managers should individually rate team members during reviews. This information aids future decision-making within the unit.

8. **Reporting Losses**: If entrusted work results in losses, promptly inform higher-ups. A detailed report, including the cause of the loss, allows for timely corrective actions.

9. **Accountability**: Negligence or irresponsibility by an in-charge should be recorded in their bio-data. Such marks remain part of their records indefinitely.

Remember, a robust accounting system not only ensures accurate financial data but also contributes to organizational efficiency and accountability.

10. **Handling Uncontrollable Situations:** If a situation is beyond your control, it is essential to provide evidence and promptly report it to your superiors. By doing so, you can avoid carrying the burden alone. It is more effective to address such problems immediately rather than allowing them to persist.

1.  **Project Origins and Responsibilities:** All team members are acutely aware that we embarked on this ambitious project from a financial standpoint of "zero." Consequently, we must accept the consequences. The unit will cover essential needs such as food, but it is crucial to minimize any additional and unnecessary expenses until the locking period concludes.

## BE LOYAL TO THE UNIT

You are well aware that this joint venture exists for the welfare of your families. From day one, you've been battling poverty and hunger. Consequently, none of the members take the management's decisions lightly; they adhere to them and follow the regulations. The unit is committed to **your** agenda, not its own.

Discipline may be challenging to embrace initially, but it eventually becomes an integral part of life. With unwavering self-discipline and confidence in every action, you must work. Only then can the unit effectively execute the members' agenda, working to benefit all of you. Loyalty to the unit ensures smooth management.

Remember, you are the management of this unit. Consider that the unit implements your stringent decisions to enhance productivity. Therefore, cooperate with your management—they exist solely for your benefit.

Our agenda is to familiarize all members with work across all sections of the unit. Tomorrow, each of you will gain experience in a specific section. □

**Punishment Is Not to Destroy Members, But to Change Their Aggressive Mindset against Life** – When it comes to punishment, our approach is not severe; rather, it aims to transform aggressive mindsets. Let me clarify the details.

1.  **Limited Duration**: Punishment is outlined in a few chapters and is not overly harsh. It is restricted to a maximum of **two instances**, each lasting **12 months**

2.  **Continuity or Departure**: During the punishment period, you have two choices: continue with the unit or leave. The decision rests with you. I encourage you not to be combative; instead, recognize that the unit is here to support you and your family.

3.  **Third Offense**: If any member is found guilty a third time, especially in financial matters, they must provide evidence to the management. Any actions against the unit will result in permanent membership dismissal and eviction.

4.  **Property Considerations**: Your property's value will be returned to you within a reasonable timeframe. However, beyond that, you cannot claim anything else from the unit. If you wish, you can sell your property to the unit at the prevailing market rate or a mutually agreed-upon rate. A **10% fee** will be levied to cover expenses incurred by the unit in developing the property.

5.  **Unity and Hard Work**: Remember, our collective hard work is the remedy for overcoming poverty. You are no longer alone in this struggle; many are here to support you. The entire unit stands by you, expecting your honest cooperation and diligent effort to achieve our common goal.

1.  **Locking Period and Financial Growth**: We have already decided on a **36-month locking period** during which we must assist

the unit in achieving self-sufficiency and financial growth. Our challenging times are behind us, and moving forward, our focus will be on unit development. It's important to note that the unit is not obligated to pay salaries or wages. However, we should maintain a provision at the unit-level to allow for tax claims.

2. **Property Appreciation and Ownership**: The appreciation of property and the income contributing to the unit's capital are considered your immovable and movable assets. These assets, along with others under the unit, make you the owners.

3. **Advantage of Computerized Records**: The use of computerized records allows us to assess the unit's assets at any given time, providing a significant advantage.

**RESULT**: This unit could be the long-awaited solution for the issues faced by rural communities over the years. Its potential impact is immense, covering two-thirds of the world when fully realized. We anticipate wholehearted cooperation from concerned countries and their political support to uplift the poor from the outset. Implementing this unit system across the countryside represents the dreams and aspirations of suffering people—a chance to break free from the chains that have bound them for years.

As we move forward, abundant resources, health, power, and strength wait, complemented by government support for self-help groups. Let your mind revel in the pursuit of a lavish lifestyle.

## "EMPOWER YOURSELF: OVERCOMING CHALLENGES"

Each one of us possesses the strength to confront life's challenges head-on. We are the masters of our own destiny, and it's crucial not to underestimate our abilities.

**Remember**: *you're not working for others; you're working for yourself. You have the power to seize opportunities and achieve success.*

*In the past, you may have faced difficulties when you were alone. But now, you are part of a larger community—a collective force. This newfound strength allows you to lead a life filled with mental peace, satisfaction, and physical resilience. You've shed many burdens and illnesses, emerging stronger than*

# CHAPTER VI

# SUCCESS BEHIND THE UNIT

Actively participate in shaping the unit's destiny, and your engagement is pivotal to its success. Let's explore the limitless possibilities that lie ahead:

Empowering Wellness and Well-Being: The unit operates under the motto that "the sky is the limit." Every conceivable business endeavor, every task, finds its roots within the unit. Our primary goal is to eradicate poverty in the countryside, ensuring a lavish and secure life for all.

Leveraging Diverse Abilities and Skills: With a diverse membership, each possessing unique talents and capabilities, the unit can harness these strengths for collective empowerment. Unity allows us to tap into the full potential of our members, fostering growth and resilience.

Exploring New Avenues: Unity brings forth exciting possibilities. As individuals, you have the chance to initiate new projects by leveraging your skills and abilities. These openings pave the way for the unit's expansion and prosperity.

Business, Industry, and Agriculture: Whether it's negotiating bulk purchases or sales, the unit can engage in fruitful transactions. Small-scale industries, agricultural ventures, and related activities align seamlessly with our vision.

The First Step: Bylaws and Consensus: Begin by explaining and discussing the unit's bylaws among the selected members from the 200 homes. Seek their approval, for it is through collective understanding and agreement that we forge a path toward success.

Remember, *as a united force, we can achieve remarkable feats. Let's think differently, act boldly, and transform our community for the better!*

1. Fundraising and Unit Formation: The second step involves raising funds, specifically through membership fees. Determine an appropriate amount to be collected as working capital for establishing and running the unit. Next, register the unit by assigning it a name that reflects the local area, with the village name as an extension. This naming convention ensures easy identification, especially for government officials and the public. A distinctive and appealing name will leave a lasting impression and facilitate recognition of your products both in the market and online.

2. Membership Considerations: When it comes to memberships and fundraising, anticipate that approximately 5% to 10% of potential members (households) may not be able to afford the membership fee immediately. In such cases, other members should temporarily cover their costs. Encourage active participation from all members in unit activities.

3. Important Rule: No Free Memberships: It is crucial to prohibit free memberships. Instead, recover membership fees by compensating members through wages. These wages can then be adjusted toward their membership dues. Within one or two months, members should be able to pay their membership fees. Remember, their hard-earned money should serve as their investment in the unit.

The Initial Years: Nurturing the Unit: The first three years pose a significant challenge for all member families—the infancy stage of the unit. Beyond this point lies the unit's growth, contingent upon our unwavering commitment. Even seemingly minor issues demand our attention. Avoiding hard work when it's necessary is unwise. Dedication to the unit means embracing not only our own family but also our neighbors. As we engage in various projects, we encounter inevitable challenges, but these hurdles contribute to the unit's gradual development.

Why opt for 200 Families? Managing and controlling a group of 200 families has distinct advantages. Dealing with a smaller, tightly-knit community simplifies matters. Familiarity fosters deep understanding and lasting relationships, especially during difficult times. Moreover, this cohesive unit facilitates efficient communication. By exchanging ideas and bringing them to the management's attention, we collectively contribute to the unit's success. Additionally, implementing government rules and announcements becomes seamless through such organized units.

Effective Management at a Smaller Scale When it comes to managing, controlling, and protecting, smaller groups often prove more efficient than dealing with large crowds. Their understanding is deeper, and their ability to adapt to situations is heightened. As you observe them in action, you'll notice several advantages.

In the past, these groups were typically overseen by elected or selected individuals. *However, a refreshing change has occurred. Now, unit members collectively shoulder responsibilities according to their capacities, all on equal footing. This collaborative approach fosters a sense of shared purpose and accountability.*

Embracing Classic Growth: They gained a valid insight into their strength and weakness. *They focus on the present, unburdened by regrets or excessive worry about the future.* Survival today takes precedence over amassing wealth for tomorrow. Their path is one of practicality and resilience.

Empowering Rural Governance: Remarkably, this shift also benefits rural governance. With fewer officials or staff, the government can efficiently manage countryside affairs. Tax collection and levies are streamlined through these units, offering a more effective system with all related documents. The advantages extend beyond what meets the eye.

Unit Simplifies Census with Comprehensive Details: *The unit office provides a treasure of information to its members, including property details, tax payments, levies, family demographics, education levels, income data, and even insights into pandemics' impact on birth and death rates. This comprehensive approach ensures that details about remote areas are clearer than ever before.*

For rural populations, the unit acts as a panacea. Members work for themselves, reaping the benefits of this system. Over time, they gain self-confidence and a sense of safety for themselves and their families. The present system, though disciplined and systematic, doesn't impose undue hardship.

Effortless Revenue Collection: *The government can now collect revenue seamlessly through the unit. Members pay taxes without involving government staff or incurring additional expenses. These lump-sum payments are directly credited to the government account under the specified category. Furthermore, the unit meticulously maintains records of tax payments and other levies, which serve both official government purposes and the census.*

1. Efficient Revenue Management: *All unit-related revenue records are meticulously maintained by their office, ensuring accessibility for the government at any time. This streamlined approach not only saves administrative staff but also reduces infrastructure costs, conveyance expenses, and other related outlays. By centralizing these records, the government can achieve significant savings.*

2. Effective Collection of Outstanding Dues: *Numerous outstanding tax payments and levies often require decisions on whether to*

*collect or write them off. However, with the establishment of a dedicated unit, these dues can be efficiently recovered. The unit's focused efforts enable targeted collection, benefiting both the government and the taxpayers.*

3. Enhanced Rural Development Funding: *The unit becomes a conduit for rural development funds, surpassing previous practices. By directly undertaking government projects, it eliminates corrupt practices and substandard work. Consequently, the quality of public infrastructure in rural areas improves significantly.*

4. Assured Revenue Collection: Once operational, the unit assumes responsibility for government taxes and levies. This ensures a 100% revenue collection rate. Moreover, a lean team can efficiently manage affairs across nearby units, transforming the system into <u>an incorruptible point of administration</u> with consolidated outstanding amounts.

5. **Empowering Rural Communities: Enhancing Skills and Communication** In the past, rural communities lacked the means to develop essential skills and effective communication. However, today, there is a positive shift. *Consider a group of 1000 rural members who now exhibit educated behavior, engage politely with others, and efficiently accomplish tasks. This transformation is crucial for their overall well-being.*

6. **Strategic Unit Naming: Connecting with the Local Context** When naming your unit, think beyond mere functionality. Incorporate the local flavor of the countryside area into your unit's name. Doing so not only helps market your unit effectively but also ensures that it resonates with the community. A memorable and catchy name will leave a lasting impression.

7. **Banking and Financial Strategy:** To raise capital, deposit funds in a local bank. Approach the bank manager, clearly explaining your intentions. Consider using available properties owned by

the members as collateral for an overdraft limit. This strategic approach ensures financial stability and growth for your unit.

## BANK ASSISTANCE

1.  **Overdraft Account for Business Efficiency**: An overdraft facility allows a business to access additional funds beyond its account balance. This amount is available at any time to support the unit's operations. The overdraft account comes with a predetermined limit, which is advantageous for the unit. When funds are withdrawn, interest is charged on a daily basis. This flexibility helps the unit manage cash flow effectively and save costs.

2.  **Creating a Savings Mindset**: By regularly remitting surplus funds or daily collections into the account, the unit can cultivate a savings mentality. When the account balance is positive, no interest is payable. Additionally, this account can serve as a current account for day-to-day transactions.

3.  **Understanding the Overdraft Limit**: The overdraft limit represents the available balance that can be utilized as a drawing power. It determines how much the unit can withdraw beyond its actual account balance. Detailed information about the overdraft limit can be obtained from the bank and through practical experience.

4.  **Strategizing for Growth**: Before receiving the overdraft limit from the bank, it's essential to plan how these funds can be used profitably for the unit's growth. Consider each aspect carefully during your general meeting and explore implementation strategies.

**Remember**, *thoughtful utilization of the overdraft facility can significantly impact the unit's financial health and expansion.*

# PLAN AND PROJECTS

**Project Considerations**: When planning a project, several factors come into play. First, we need to assess the available resources, including tools, machinery, and manpower. Additionally, we must consider the area to be covered and other relevant aspects based on the land and facilities within the unit. These considerations are crucial for effective project management.

**Liability and Repayment**: The second point of consideration is how easily the liability associated with the project can be repaid. It's essential to evaluate the financial aspects and ensure that the project remains financially viable.

**Developmental Works**: Apart from constructing necessary buildings like offices and warehouses, there will be various developmental works within the unit. Each aspect should be addressed separately in project reports. By doing so, we can avoid unnecessary constraints related to bank limits. Instead of requesting an enhancement in the bank limit, we can submit new project reports for each work. Approval from the unit engineer and the bank can then be obtained during the members' meeting.

**Office Accounting**: Transparency is crucial in financial transactions. To prevent fraud in bulk sales and purchases, consider rotating the sales and purchase team members. This way, the hard-earned money of unit members remains secure, and any irregularities can be promptly detected and addressed.

Sales Accounting Procedures All sales transactions must be meticulously recorded through the sales section in the accounts. The resulting proceeds should be credited to the sale account, which should be established as the head of the account within the unit office.

Each sale should be documented separately, including essential details such as product name, weight, and date of supply. These records are based on the acknowledgments received during product receipt.

**Remember**: *Prompt remittance of sales proceeds to the bank is essential.*

1. Product Records and Validity: Comprehensive records for every product are crucial. This includes maintaining invoices, delivery notes, and gate passes.

Only items that have been sold should be transported from our unit's premises.

All documentation must bear the seal and signature of an authorized signatory or the responsible section head to be considered valid.

## OPENING A CURRENT ACCOUNT:

To access loans or overdraft facilities, members must open a current account with their nearest bank.

A resolution to open the account and authorization from the unit manager are necessary.

Once formalities are complete, the loan or overdraft proceeds should be credited to the unit's account as a debit balance, reflecting the liability to the unit.

Consider requesting an overdraft on your existing current account, emphasizing this preference to the bank branch manager.

## ACCOUNT TRANSACTIONS AND CASH HANDLING:

Every transaction should be conducted through the designated account. Minimizing cash transactions is crucial to prevent malpractices. Avoid handling cash directly whenever possible.

However, in business, sales proceeds often involve cash. To maintain accurate records, promptly deposit this cash into the bank. Note the denominations on the receipt for easy reconciliation.

**Funds from Members and the Government: –** The funds raised from members and the government serve a specific purpose. Success lies in your hands. Remember that these funds are essentially loans or overdrafts, and repayment is expected.

Leverage support *from fellow members to maximize your impact.*

**Recording Receipts and Payments: –** Maintain meticulous records. All receipts and payments must be documented in a way that can be verified during inspections or audits by the unit or government.

Whether manually maintained or in a computer system, entries are essential. These accounting practices ensure the safety of your money.

## AVOID DEPENDENCE ON SCHEMES:

Understand that there are no magical schemes providing small amounts annually. Relying solely on government assistance for years can hinder progress.

Reflect on this experience and choose a different path—one that leads to self-reliance and growth.

## UNLOCKING THE POTENTIAL OF GOVERNMENT ASSISTANCE

Imagine receiving financial aid from the government—an unexpected windfall. However, the amount is meager, barely enough to cover daily necessities. It's a common scenario: funds that fall short of making a significant impact. But what if we could channel this assistance more effectively?

Every category, whether large or small, should yield tangible results. Unfortunately, government schemes often fail to reach the grassroots-level where they are most needed. People either lack awareness of these programs or lack the capacity to claim their rightful benefits.

Self-Reliance and Collective Action: Now, consider a different approach. Imagine a unit—perhaps a cooperative or community initiative—starting its operations. Instead of waiting for government support, this unit is determined to work toward its own betterment. The initial goal is simple: secure moral backing from the government to kick-start the endeavor.

As the unit grows, it becomes self-sufficient. Rural development schemes, once essential, can gradually be phased out. The funds allocated for these programs can then be redirected for the greater good of the nation.

Empowering Communities: But there's more. This unit isn't just about survival; it's about empowerment. Beyond its regular functions, it negotiates with government authorities for civil works. By doing so, it creates additional opportunities for its members, addressing unemployment and fostering growth.

Honesty and commitment drive this unit. In return, it propels individual progress, elevating living standards within months.

## A MINDSET SHIFT

Meanwhile, in the countryside, villagers persist in their simple existence. Basic needs remain unmet, and opportunities are scarce. Yet, their mindset—"it's enough for us"—is commendable. It reflects contentment and resilience, even as society hurtles toward a new era.

Remember: This revised version emphasizes self-reliance, community empowerment, and the transformative potential of collective efforts.

Our primary goal must be to create significant change for the future, especially for our children. *Among rural communities, some individuals enjoy a slightly better standard of living either due to their ancestors' earnings or their unique perspectives on life.*

*Unnecessary protests and demonstrations demanding government support for basic necessities like drinking water can be avoided. We have progressed beyond that stage; we now possess the means to address such issues efficiently. By centralizing solutions through community units, we can tackle problems like water scarcity, ration distribution, and electricity delays.*

For instance, during the scorching summer months, areas suffering from water shortages can purchase water through these units to meet urgent needs. This approach minimizes the magnitude of the problem. Additionally,

if the government allows ration distribution or other benefits, it can seamlessly route them through these units, eliminating complaints and ensuring prompt delivery. It helps the government from the rumors and bad effects at the public level.

Furthermore, this system reduces the government's administrative burden and transaction costs. By maintaining proper accounting practices, community units can efficiently handle bulk transactions, benefiting both the government and its citizens."

These units serve as self-reliant entities, contributing to various aspects of government support. As independent bodies, they focus on the welfare of rural populations, undertaking developmental projects and providing voluntary assistance to their members.

The government relief funds allocated to these units can be distributed to member's satisfaction and government requirements. Detailed reports and statements are submitted promptly. The unit's services, including payment processing with beneficiary receipts, are provided to the government at no cost.

By introducing transparent records of real beneficiaries, these units help combat malpractices. When distributing monetary benefits, the government can easily identify deserving recipients through these channels. A comprehensive payment record is maintained by the unit.

Anticipating that poverty among unit members can be eradicated within a few months, these citizens will rise above average in status. Consequently, the government does not need to provide direct financial support. Instead, tax revenue and other levies from these citizens will be an additional benefit without significant effort. The government's moral support during implementation is expected through its officers and officials.

1.  Environmental Improvement and Infrastructure: The overall environment and infrastructure can evolve alongside improvements in lifestyle, including adopting clean and orderly habits. *As individuals enhance their attitudes and behaviors, these positive changes will manifest through their daily routines and cultural practices, setting them apart from the rest of humanity.*

2.  Guidelines for Participation: Please review the bylaws carefully, and feel free to suggest any necessary additions. This unit exists for your well-being, so actively engage in all activities, including simple tasks. When encountering someone working within or outside the unit (whether in government or other public enterprises), please refrain from disrupting their efforts. Allow them to continue their work undisturbed.

3.  Encouragement and Support: I urge everyone to participate wholeheartedly in unit activities. Kindly seek support from your peers to motivate fellow members. Their words of encouragement

and assistance will inspire a positive mindset, paving the way for a brighter collective future.

4. Protecting Our Dream Project: Let us remain vigilant against any rebels spreading unwarranted propaganda about the unit. Our vision is a corruption-free, cheat-free dream project, created by members and intended for members. These unique opportunities are open to all—let's make the most of it.

Unit Self-Reliance and Growth Units that yield substantial monetary benefits continue to generate regular income until they achieve self-reliance. The growth trajectory of each unit hinges on the skill and competence of its manager, as well as their influence within the public and government spheres.

Bank Assistance Consider inviting the bank manager to your temporary unit office. Banks actively seek opportunities to allocate their surplus funds for financing. *If the government extends moral support to each unit and instructs banks to provide financial assistance, numerous units can be established across the nation, particularly in neglected rural areas. It is a proud movement from the dormant section now by involving every household in the region as a unit member, a new network of interconnected self-help units can thrive.*

Despite being small components of the countryside or village, these units—comprising around 1000 individuals—can collaborate for mutual welfare. Their individual efforts, guided by improved moral ethics, will contribute to their growth, ultimately becoming a source of pride for the entire nation.

## BANKS AND PRODUCTIVE UNITS: A MUTUAL BENEFIT

Banks play a crucial role in financing various units, *channeling billions of dollars into their operations. This influx of funds transforms surplus and idle money into productive assets. Remarkably, both banks and these units reap equal benefits from this symbiotic relationship.*

As these units take charge of their members, encouraging positive habits and productivity, the nation's economy experiences a significant boost. *Dormant resources spring to life, contributing to a richer and more modern lifestyle for all involved.*

Members of these units swiftly transition from the surplus stage to enjoying a lavish life, thanks to their hard work. Moreover, corruption and black money (*The entire transactions of mass member groups are routed through banks will help the government to maintain a different banking style and can insist anywhere they wish to implement as this is a 100% member involvement system*) under government control within these units, requiring minimal intervention.

A unique aspect of these units lies in their meticulous cash flow management. Members actively avoid keeping their money idle, fostering a different mindset. Formerly detrimental habits now lead to health and wealth, transforming idle individuals into productive contributors.

Furthermore, these units alleviate the government's burden by addressing development needs in rural areas. Long-standing issues can be resolved with ease, and the funds allocated can propel progress across the nation. These achievements, coupled with robust national economic growth, position the country on the worldwide.

## ENHANCING RURAL DEVELOPMENT THROUGH UNIT FORMATION

When establishing new government units, there is an opportunity to reallocate funds originally earmarked for the development of specific areas. By doing so, these resources can be redirected toward modern developmental projects in other regions.

Often, substantial amounts of government expenditure in rural areas are associated with administrative costs. However, once the necessary infrastructure and related developments are in place within each unit, the government can gradually reduce financial support to the countryside.

The envisioned units will operate independently, fostering growth and capacity-building. In return, the government can collect a steady stream of revenue through taxes and other levies. *This shift from dependency to self-sufficiency is crucial for rural areas, which often struggle to generate income sufficient to meet their needs.*

To facilitate this transformation, unit members can collaborate to secure loans from local banks. Armed with project reports and all necessary documentation, they can approach specialized bank officials who cater to sectors like agriculture and small-scale industries (SSI). By leveraging the collective properties of unit members as informal collateral, banks may grant an overdraft facility in the unit's name. Once the bank liability is settled, the documents can be released.

This approach empowers rural communities, enabling them to thrive economically and contribute to overall development.

The unit is collectively formed by all of you, and your rights within the unit are equal. It's important to reiterate that there is no distinction between big and small; everyone is on an equal footing.

Before commencing any government or other project, ensure that all unit members are informed in detail and obtain their consent through signed agreements. If there are multiple projects, separate consents should be obtained during member meetings, specifying which project each consent pertains to.

## THE CAPITAL & FUND

The raised capital and bank finance should be utilized to cover various expenses, including agricultural implements (such as water-related equipment, farming tools, tractors, and other necessary items), seeds, watering, manure, fencing, warehousing, and even a shopping complex.

These expenses should be met in the initial phase. Additionally, *the agricultural implements must remain within the unit premises at all times—strictly avoiding any removal from the unit. The stock of produce should be stored adjacent to the unit office or shopping complex, with robust night security and surveillance measures in place."*

1. Building Strong Bonds within a Community of 200 Members: When a community consists of 200 members, they naturally become attuned to each other's lives. This closeness fosters intimacy akin to that of a single-family. It is essential to maintain these relationships. Rather than deferring issues to a later date, members should address problems promptly. After all, they reside within the same unit, making timely resolution feasible.
2. A Harmonious Living Environment with High Compliance: A remarkable 90% of the population adheres to rules and remains

free from violations and crimes. Once the decision to form a cohesive unit is made, members commit to living harmoniously. They embrace the unit's regulations, enjoying a serene environment with essential facilities and protection. Breaking this unity is unthinkable.

3. Empowering Transformation for the Remaining 5-10%: While the majority effortlessly follows the unit's principles, a small percentage may need guidance. Encouragingly, converting their way of life need not be daunting. Politics has no place in our welfare-focused unit. We are confident that collectively, we can address our challenges, including poverty and hunger.

Remember, *unity and shared purpose are our greatest assets in overcoming adversity.*

## NONE OF YOU DREAM THIS CHANGE SO FAR

None of the countryside villagers think about a permanent solution for their poverty and its consequences for many years.

Being drunkards and influenced by drinks and drugs, they cannot think about how to free their families and nation from this pitiful situation. It is narrated somewhere else.

We are not running this unit as a political or religious hub; both are man-made constructs. If handled perfectly, they can benefit individuals, but if misused, they can turn against them on many occasions.

Although our community comprises diverse populations with varying beliefs and interests, our primary duty is to safeguard individuals without regard to their politics, religion, or caste. The unit's purpose is to alleviate human suffering and overcome poverty.

While we respect the rare groups interested in politics or religion, we must ensure they do not exceed limits that harm the majority of people living in our community. *Their interests and beliefs should be sacrificed as we are well aware of the results of the alliances with these groups.*

Remember, this unit is your home, and all of you are part of one family. Let that be your fundamental consideration.

## INTRA-FAMILY BEHAVIOR AND CIVIC RESPONSIBILITY

Within a family, our conduct extends to interactions with other unit members. While we maintain our individual beliefs and values, we refrain from engaging in political activities that could disrupt harmony. Similarly, religious functions should never harm or offend other groups.

Our approach is amicable, prioritizing relationships above all else. As members, we have the freedom to cast our votes, respecting our personal convictions. Whether individual or joint, we make necessary arrangements without impacting others' lives within our unit.

In cases of tension among family members, reporting to the unit manager is essential. Prior permission is required for voting or taking leave from duties. It help the unit to know how many voted were casted. While we exercise our right of vote, we refrain from participating in any political functions beyond this.

Our family unit remains apolitical, driven by the collective goal of alleviating poverty and ensuring our well-being. Together, we stand united to safeguard our shared interests.

## BANKING PRACTICES

- **Fund and Bank Account**

In our operational system, securing funds is essential for running the unit. We must source and raise the initial capital collectively. To facilitate this, we open a bank account in the unit's name, using the funds contributed by our members. The individual contribution amount is determined by the members and collected accordingly.

We appoint three members to jointly operate the account. These representatives span different age groups: one should be a youth aged at least 30 years and educated, another within the 40-year age bracket, and the third around 50 years old with an educational background. The account operates under the condition that any two out of the three signatories can authorize transactions.

For transparency, every credit or withdrawal from the account must be promptly communicated. Withdrawals are strictly in accordance with the unit manager's instructions and require the approval of these three designated members. Additionally, any internal vouchers prepared should bear the signatures of at least two of them.

Importantly, the signatories are not permitted to issue checks or make direct payments from the bank without the manager's knowledge. Furthermore, the unit manager should refrain from collecting pre-signed blank checks, even in emergencies.

Managing Financial Transactions: Best Practices

When it comes to handling financial matters, there are several key considerations to ensure smooth operations within your unit. Let's delve into some guidelines:

Cash Withdrawals and Fund Transfers: While any of the three authorized individuals can collect cash from the bank, it is advisable to minimize cash withdrawals. Instead, prioritize fund transfers or utilize net banking facilities.

All payments should be routed through the designated account. This practice serves as evidence and helps prevent misunderstandings among unit members in the future.

The bank acknowledges the unit's daily transactions, so maintaining a clear trail of payments is essential.

## PAYMENT VERIFICATION AND DOCUMENTATION:

When making payments, ensure that they align with the relevant voucher or contra document. This documentation substantiates the purpose of each payment.

Only after preparing the necessary vouchers and recording entries in the books of account should you issue a check or initiate fund transfers.

Responsibility for these transactions lies with the unit manager or the authorized official.

## SUPERVISION AND ACCOUNTABILITY:

Especially when significant amounts are involved, the unit manager must oversee and authenticate all bank transactions.

Set limits for subordinate staff based on their capabilities. Define the extent to which they can handle financial matters.

Regularly review the entries before closing accounts to verify their accuracy using supporting vouchers and other relevant documents.

By adhering to these practices, your unit can maintain financial integrity and transparency, fostering trust among team members and ensuring efficient operations.

## VOUCHER PREPARATION AND RECORD KEEPING:

Creating a valid voucher and entering it into the unit's records do not impact payments directly. However, if the voucher amount exceeds your authorized limit, it's essential to seek approval from the unit manager.

Remember, *the final authority lies with the manager, so avoid making payments without their consent.*

Additionally, the unit manager should retain custody of bank documents, even though they are not directly involved in signing or operating the account.

## BANK ACCOUNTS FOR MEMBERS:

The unit office should proactively establish a bank account in the name of all families and their members. By raising awareness among members, you can facilitate banking practices through this account. Inform them about potential fraud risks and any funds owed to them by the unit.

Bank officials can participate in member meetings, providing explanations, and conducting informative sessions. When the officer is available, they can collect relevant forms based on their capacity or preferences.

Before opening accounts, seek guidance from a bank official. Members can also transfer existing accounts from other banks to this one for added convenience.

Bank Assistance for Account Opening: The bank is pleased to assist you in opening a large number of accounts. During this process, they will guide you through all the necessary procedures and provide insights into fraud prevention and remedies.

Account Usage by the Unit: These accounts come in handy when the unit office needs to transfer funds to members' bank accounts. These accounts are established in the respective names of the recipients.

Ensuring Accuracy and Caution: It's crucial that the office cash book and each member's account align with the bank's counterfoil or statement for every transaction. Given that public funds are involved, vigilance is essential to avoid any discrepancies.

Reporting Additional Amounts Received: Members should promptly inform the manager in writing about any additional amounts received from external sources. This allows the manager to record such transactions separately. Beyond this, members cannot receive extra funds apart from those allocated by the unit.

Account Accumulation and Verification: Over time, funds will accumulate in both the unit's and members' accounts. An authorized inspector should verify the unit account regularly. When authenticating the day's statement, the inspector's name (if there are multiple inspectors) and the member number can be affixed using the unit's round seal.

## AUTHENTICATION AND CONCURRENT AUDITING PROCESS

The authentication process serves as the final step in closing the day's accounts. Subsequently, the accounts remain open solely for auditing purposes. When transaction volumes exceed the expected level, the unit manager has the authority to initiate concurrent auditing.

To facilitate this, the unit manager can assemble a team of inspectors who diligently oversee daily transactions. Their role is to ensure the integrity and fairness of the unit's financial records. Regular concurrent audits, conducted at intervals of 7 to 15 or 30 days, allow for prompt identification and rectification of any errors that may arise.

It's essential to recognize that each authentication holds significant value. As a responsible manager, you are accountable not only to the unit but also to its members. In addition, interested members can apply for the position of inspector by submitting their qualifications. Based on their recommendation, the unit manager can approve these appointments. Furthermore, resolutions related to vacancies within the member's meeting can also be addressed.

Lastly, a prudent practice is to minimize the presence of hard cash stock within the office. Instead, promptly remit available funds to the bank. If an excess cash balance is identified, document the reason in a note or comment, ensuring that the unit manager is aware and provides their countersign.

## EFFECTIVE CASH HANDLING AND PAYMENT PROCEDURES

### 1. Cashier/Officer/Manager Responsibilities:

The individual responsible for handling cash should always include a comment when there is an excess amount of cash. This comment should explain why the excess occurred. Transparency in documenting such instances is crucial for accountability and audit purposes.

### 2. Timely Payments from Stall Members:

Stall members are encouraged to make payments as early as possible. This practice enables the office to promptly remit the collected amount to the bank within the designated time frame.

### 3. Advance Remittance to the Office:

To streamline the process, a portion of the cash can be remitted to the office two hours before the bank's closing time. This proactive approach ensures smoother transactions.

### 4. Alternatives to Cash Transactions:

In cases where multiple payments need to be made, consider using net banking or providing a list of payees. Instead of individually remitting cash, consolidate the total amount along with a check (check) and entrust it to the bank.

### 5. Routine Implementation and Documentation:

As this procedure becomes routine, it will prove more practical. Maintain a copy of the payment list within the office for future reference.

Emphasize that no payment or receipt should occur without a proper voucher or receipt.

Keep meticulous records of all cash, check, and fund transfer transactions in written form to prevent confusion or misunderstandings.

## PAYMENT PROCEDURES:

When making cash payments to individuals, whether they are members or outsiders, it is essential to follow proper procedures. Here are the steps to ensure clarity and accountability:

1.  Obtain a Voucher: The person receiving the payment should obtain a voucher. This voucher must include their signature, mobile phone number, and relevant details such as the purpose of payment, recipient's name, and address.
2.  Avoid Cash Payments to Illiterates: While cash payments are permissible, it is advisable to avoid making them available to illiterate individuals. Misunderstandings can arise, so exercising caution is crucial.
3.  Accounting: Regardless of the recipient's literacy level, all payments should be reflected in the individual's account. This ensures transparency and accurate record-keeping.

Each member needs to acquire the ability to sign documents, even if they are currently illiterate. Learning to sign is essential."

4. Consent from Family Members: If you are paying a member in cash, seek consent from their family members. Remember that the

money belongs to the entire family. Written consent is preferable over verbal agreements.

5. When withdrawing money from the bank or unit, it is crucial for household members to maintain meticulous records. These records should accurately reconcile the withdrawn amount with the actual cash on hand at any given moment. *Additionally, it is strictly forbidden to retain any surplus or unaccounted money within your home.*

6. Fortunately, with available facilities, homes no longer need to store large amounts of cash on their premises. The manager will determine an appropriate higher limit for the amount allowed to be kept at home.

7. Bank Transfers: Whenever possible, consider transferring funds directly to the bank account. This method is safer and provides a clear trail of transactions.

## DEPOSIT POLICY

The office accepts cash deposits directly from members, even if there is no specific deal involved. These deposits contribute to the unit's development. Here are the relevant guidelines:

Receipts: While no formal receipt is issued, the office acknowledges cash deposits.

Overdraft Account: The amount received should be remitted to the overdraft account. This action can reduce the account's limit accordingly.

## REVISED PARAGRAPHS

The unit engages in various purchases and expenses related to tractors, agricultural tools, and other relevant products. Additionally, they undertake construction work, fencing, and bore well digging. To facilitate these transactions, the unit sets the payment terms with interest rates. Specifically, the interest rate is aligned with what banks offer for their deposits, with an additional 2% applied.

When a customer deposits an amount, the unit manager issues a deposit receipt. This receipt includes essential details such as the interest rate payable, the deposit period, and the due date. These particulars are meticulously recorded on the receipt and also in the unit's records as a liability.

To ensure authenticity, the deposit receipt must be signed by the second officer of the unit who is available on that particular day. Any officer subordinate to the manager can verify the receipt, which the manager has duly authenticated. This internal process ensures accuracy and transparency within the unit.

In the event that a depositor wishes to withdraw their funds before the due date, an alternative arrangement exists. Instead of the standard 2% penalty, the depositor can opt to pay a reduced penalty of 1%. Additionally, the unit may allow a partial withdrawal, treating it as a temporary loan until the deposit matures.

**Agriculture and Allied Activities**: Agriculture plays a crucial role in meeting the basic needs of our community members. It provides essential food and resources. Additionally, it offers a quick return on investment within 3-4 months, addressing food scarcity.

## CLEANLINESS OF UNIT PREMISES

**Implementing the Dust Bin Culture**: From the outset, maintaining a clean environment is essential As we modernize our lifestyle, consider creating an eye-catching area within our premises. Each member should actively contribute to cleanliness and safety, And dustbins and necessary cleaning materials throughout the unit should be supplied to ensure a hygienic environment.

To achieve cleanliness and safety, adopt the "Dust Bin Culture" throughout the unit. This involves providing necessary dustbins, cleaning materials, lotions, and other accessories to maintain a pristine environment. By collectively embracing this culture, you'll create a healthier and more pleasant space for everyone.

**Engaging with Government Offices for Dustbins and Accessories:** If you're local government office has a system for supplying dustbins and related accessories consider reaching out to them They might be willing to share necessary items with your community. By doing so, you contribute to lightening their daily workload. Additionally, taking responsibility for this task can reduce the need for additional cleaning staff.

**Effective Waste Classification and Recycling:** When introducing a dustbin culture, it's essential to classify waste properly. Categorize it into different types: general waste, plastic, glass, and other recyclables. Dispose of general waste as compost or immediate manure. Plastic, glass, and iron parts can be sold. Even in rural areas, we can take steps beyond existing cleaning methods.

**Enhancing Rural Care and Discipline:** Units can play a crucial role in ensuring extra care for rural populations. By educating members about discipline, we can avoid the lapses we faced previously. Cultivating good habits and promoting a cleaner culture can be achieved with awareness, especially since many areas still lack proper dustbin usage, leading to scattered waste around bins in both cities and rural regions.

Unit Coordination for Environmental Awareness: The unit actively collects views of well-maintained environments through short films and other media. This serves as motivation for fellow unit members and the public. Subordinates and officials under the manager efficiently handle these tasks by allocating specific areas to designated members with clear instructions.

**Immediate Response to Litter Issues:** When unit members come across scattered waste near bins, they promptly take corrective action. They diligently follow instructions or, if the issue falls within their unit's jurisdiction, capture a photo and report it to the relevant official or manager. A cohesive team collaborates for this purpose. These photographs are then displayed on the notice board, serving as a visual reminder for everyone. Unlike supervisory staff that may lack familiarity with the local context, the unit system swiftly addresses such concerns because its members are residents of the area.

Promoting Responsible Bin Usage: Despite the installation of dustbins in various localities, only a few people utilize this facility. Many do not consider it an integral part of their lives or a serious requirement. *Through the unit's efforts, awareness can be raised among members, encouraging responsible waste disposal and elevating their quality of life to a higher level.*

Taking Responsibility for Well-Being: The responsibility for caring seriously and ensuring well-being lies with the unit members. It's essential to shift the current perception that the government-provided dustbins are merely a policy. This thinking must be changed, and cooperate with the government to implement their policy among unit members.

Rural Areas and Maintenance: Unlike cities, rural areas often lack government-implemented plans. Regular cleaning is not a standard practice. However, the unit can transform its surroundings to match world-class standards. While costly in the past, maintaining the area is feasible for rural units if approached with seriousness.

Unit Formation and Purpose: Local area members come together to form the unit, aiming to enhance member homes' welfare and development.

Empowered Unit for Development: Going forward, the unit will directly oversee comprehensive development and implement government schemes more effectively. Each member's personal growth is a priority.

Vigilance and Immediate Corrections: Unit members diligently monitor their area, promptly addressing any work defects. Additionally, access to drinking water, a critical issue, can be successfully resolved through various available sources.

The manager can allot the area to the unit homes.

Efficiency as the Sole Criterion for Staff Recruitment: When recruiting the initial set of staff and officials for the unit, it is crucial to limit their roles to responsible positions within the organization. Avoid any interference from external groups, members, or influential teams. The primary selection criteria should revolve around education, efficiency, and honesty. In case disputes arise among members, decisions should be made by majority consensus.

Careful Selection of the First Staff Cohort: *The initial team of staff members holds a crucial position responsible for managing the unit and safeguarding its assets. Each member's suitability undergoes thorough evaluation. Should any issues arise with a staff member, the unit manager promptly intervenes to resolve the situation. However, the team is granted a maximum of six months to prove their effectiveness.*

**A Competent Team for Effective Management**: *While no employee is above being a member, the manager may encounter situations that are challenging to address alone. In such cases, consider forming a skilled team comprising individuals from different age groups—youth, middle-aged, and seniors. These team members should possess the cleverness and tact to handle various matters.*

**Remember:** *employees work for you, and in return, they must demonstrate loyalty and commitment to their entrusted responsibilities.*

1.  Respectful Interaction: When working alongside colleagues, it's essential to avoid unnecessary interference or harassment. Give due consideration to any reasonable delays they may encounter. Additionally, when a colleague from another section seeks your assistance, treat them with importance and respect. By doing so, we can prevent any lingering animosity.

2.  Dealing with Arrogant Members: *If the committee is unable to handle an arrogant member, it's crucial to communicate the consequences. Let them know that they will face a minimum 30-day suspension from duty. Afterward, they can continue as an ordinary member without any official capacity for at least 90 days. Arrogant members should have the opportunity to apologize either to the committee or directly to the manager. The manager can then consider the situation from a humane perspective and provide guidance to both parties.*

3.  Addressing Allegations: *When members or teams raise allegations against employees, it's important to approach the situation delicately. Rather than perpetuating the issue, focus on identifying solutions to ensure smooth operations within the unit. Avoid repeating such incidents.*

4.  Handling Greed and Loss: If any member is found to be acting greedily or causing financial losses to the unit, they should bring forth evidence to the manager. However, it's essential not to waste time on trivial matters. Only genuine facts or significant losses should be addressed rather than allowing personal ego to negatively impact the unit in the long run.

1.  **Voluntary Commitment to the Unit:** We have collectively decided that each member's household will contribute voluntarily to the unit's functioning until it becomes self-sustaining. The surplus

generated by the unit directly benefits its members. As the unit grows, envision it like a Banyan tree, where all of us can shape its future.

2. **Annual Chart and Lock-In Period:** To monitor progress, we will prepare an annual chart. Additionally, we anticipate a lock-in period during which we'll assess the unit's development. As part of this process, let's create an alphabetical list of members, including their membership numbers, for approval in our next meeting.

3. **Initial Sacrifice and Future Prospects:** The first three years represent our collective sacrifice for the unit's success. Beyond this period, we expect smooth operations. The unit manager must consider various factors—such as education, capacity, skills, experience, and other parameters—while assigning positions to members within the unit. Together, we'll build a strong foundation for our shared future.

## EFFECTIVE WORK ALLOCATION FOR ALL

Through the equitable distribution of tasks, each member is required to work across all sections of the unit. This practice ensures that everyone gains familiarity with various responsibilities, allowing them to step in seamlessly in case of any absence. It's essential to set aside personal ego during this process.

Remember: *this unit belongs to all of us—you are both the boss and the servant.*

## WORK DISTRIBUTION FOR ALL MEMBERS

Initially, we did not differentiate based on qualifications. For the first 36 months, everyone is treated equally. Consider this: you are not working for someone else; you are working for yourself. All of us collectively own this unit.

## AGRICULTURE AND ALLIED ACTIVITIES

Agriculture plays a crucial role in meeting the basic needs of community members. As a first step, it's essential to address any urgent requirements within the unit. Agricultural products can be harnessed not only for food but also for other personal necessities. Additionally, the relatively quick returns from agriculture (within 3-4 months) can help alleviate food scarcity among members.

## AGRICULTURE AND BEYOND

Approximately 50% of our members can be accommodated in agriculture-related roles. Another 10-15% can contribute to the shopping mall as staff and officials. With 350 members remaining, we can allocate roles as follows:

Initially, all members can participate in agriculture and assist with loading, unloading, storage, and canteen duties.

The remaining 350 members should focus on land development, including digging tanks for fish rearing, setting up tents and sheds for animals, and other necessary projects. Each project should be overseen by members residing nearby.

## ALLIED ACTIVITIES AND EMPLOYMENT OPPORTUNITIES

As part of our commitment to agriculture and allied activities, consider venturing into fish rearing. Building tanks and sheds for animals and birds will be crucial. The manager will create employment vacancies based on available resources.

Remember, *our collective efforts shape the success of this unit. Let's work together to make it thrive!*

## ENSURING SKILLED MEMBERS FOR THE WORK

Our approach involves relying solely on our members for workmanship without seeking external sources. To achieve this, comprehensive training is essential. During the selection process for member houses, we should prioritize including skilled workers. In the initial phase, consider replacing up to 5% of member houses with skilled masons, carpenters, and other workers.

## INSPECTORS AS EFFECTIVE SUPERVISORS

Our inspectors should begin by working alongside supervising staff in various unit tasks. This hands-on experience will equip them with practical skills to detect mistakes promptly and find solutions. The selected inspectors must submit daily reports to the unit manager.

The manager or assistant manager should acknowledge these reports promptly and issue directives for corrective actions. Before reporting to the unit manager's office each day, inspectors should receive allocation letters detailing their assigned duties, including the following information: Serial Number, Name, ID Number, Allocated Area, and space for their signature. This streamlined process ensures efficient operations without unnecessary delays.

Without written allocation letter don't send the inspectors to the spot – It easy you tomorrow to find the result through him/her.

## WORK ALLOCATION AND REPORTING PROCESS

Work allocation within the area should rotate on an alternating basis, either weekly or monthly. Any changes initiated by officials must be implemented without disrupting the existing work shifts. The completion of assigned tasks should align with the officer's report. The manager's role involves studying and verifying the work after inspection, ensuring full satisfaction.

All inspectors are required to maintain a diary. In this diary, they should document suggestions for improving work efficiency within their respective areas. The manager or other officials must prioritize reviewing these reports daily and provide comments.

Valuable suggestions from the reports can be disseminated to other team members through circulars or discussed during meetings. Additionally, daily account-authenticating inspectors should report to the unit manager at least one hour early.

The manager communicates work allocations in writing, either directly in the work diary or through separate letters. These communications include comments related to the submitted reports. As inspectors proceed with their tasks, they sign against their names on the office list.

From small stalls to every shop within the unit, the workplace encompasses the entire mall. The manager plays a crucial role in guiding inspectors on a day-to-day basis.

## MONITORING AGRICULTURAL DEVELOPMENT AND INSPECTOR RESPONSIBILITIES

As part of your duties, it is essential to closely monitor the progress of agricultural fields within the unit. Beyond other ongoing tasks, the inspectors must be well-versed in the land area they oversee. Collaborating with the unit manager, they can accurately identify specific areas requiring attention. When additional workloads arise, consider allocating more inspectors accordingly.

**Remember:** *The unit members – the manager and staff – should know the unit area very well.*

## INSPECTOR COMPETENCE AND TIMELY EXECUTION

Inspectors play a crucial role in ensuring the successful cultivation of crops, including paddy. Within 90 days, they should become proficient in tasks such as fixing irrigation systems, managing manure applications, and overseeing plowing activities. Expertise is key, and they can seek guidance from specialists through the unit manager.

## SUPERVISION AND DAILY PROGRESS REPORTS

The manager has the flexibility to utilize inspectors as on-ground supervisors. By doing so, they can obtain daily progress reports on various agricultural tasks. Inspectors should diligently sign and authenticate each page of the submitted reports using an official seal.

## MAINTAINING THE MOTHER DOCUMENT

The documentation of these activities is vital. *Each page should be meticulously maintained, with only one report per page. Consider procuring diaries with ample pages from printing presses, bookstores, or bookbinding shops. Personalize them with the unit's name and opt for durable, class-bound versions.*

1. **Daily Priorities and Account Inspections**: Every day, members should arrive at the unit office at least one hour before closing time to prioritize their tasks. Among these members, the manager has the authority to select the most efficient individual to inspect the unit's accounts in their entirety.

2. **Allocation and Duty Changes**: Given the possibility of duty allocation changes, there should be no objections from anyone. The opportunity to participate will be extended to all eligible members.

3. **Responsibility and Honesty**: It's essential to consider your responsibility to the unit, fellow members, and your family.

4. **Official Cadre Waiting List**: As an official cadre, your position is on the waiting list within the unit. All official recruitments are impacted by this category exclusively.

**Remember** *that the funds involved are hard-earned contributions from our members, including yourself. Honesty in handling these resources is crucial.*

# CHAPTER VII

# MEMBER SELECTION PROCESS

This process involves some sensitivity, as it requires bringing together neighbors while avoiding any existing enmity or misunderstandings. Consider the brevity of life; there's no precise measuring instrument to determine its length. Your primary concern is to select members whose houses fall within a specific area. The unit limit is determined by the chosen area and is unrelated to financial status. Your initial task is complete.

Next, focus on the necessary formalities and processes. Begin by meeting neighbors personally, discussing the matter, and convincing them. If they agree, accompany them to meet other neighbors.

Create a list of the 200 houses and their occupants, ensuring no gaps between houses. We treat each home as a member, strictly adhering to the rural boundary. The maximum allowed number of inmates per unit is 1000, regardless of economic or age considerations. Adjust the number of homes to maintain this limit.

Navigating this process requires a delicate touch, as it involves bringing together all your neighbors while avoiding any potential enmity or misunderstandings. Remember, life is shorter than we often calculate, so let's proceed with care.

Your first task is to select a member from a specific area—one who won't leave any neighbors behind. The proposed unit limit isn't determined by financial status; rather, it hinges on whether they fall within the chosen area. With this step completed, we now turn our attention to the necessary formalities and processes.

Next, arrange personal meetings with your neighbors. Convince them of the importance of this endeavor. Once they are on board, gather a list of the approximately 200 houses and their residents. Together, we'll move forward toward our shared goal.

**Division of Unprivileged Members:** If more than 10% of the total members fall into the unprivileged category, consider dividing them into two or three units equally. For instance, if there is an unprivileged member's colony with 50 homes, it's better to form three units by dividing the colony rather than handling them as a single unit. However, avoid exceeding 200 homes in any group/unit.

1. **Initial Membership: As part of the working capital for the unit, each house (considered** a member) should contribute. Let's assume a fixed membership fee of Rs. 20,000 per member, resulting in a total of Rs. 40 lakhs. These funds can cover initial expenses such as paperwork, unit registration, and other necessary costs. While the suggested amount is arbitrary, the key is to ensure that all members can comfortably contribute. By doing so, the scheme can be successfully implemented, leading to prompt results. However, be cautious about expanding the number of homes beyond 200 within a single group/unit, as it may become unwieldy and challenging to manage.

2. **Trust Formation**: Members can establish a trust or unit under a specific name. The trust should be formally registered, with all members signing appropriate forms and adhering to the bylaws. In this context, consider dividing the countryside area into several units, each functioning as an independent corporate office. Remarkably, there's no upper limit on the number of

trustees, allowing the unit to form a trust even with all 200 member homes.

**Remember** *the wise sayings: "Everything is easy when you are Crazy for it" and "Nothing is easy when you are Lazy for it."*

# EMPOWERING RURAL COMMUNITIES: A CALL TO ACTION

The rural population, often marginalized and overlooked, has endured a fate of feeling insignificant—both to themselves and to others. They seldom recognize their own humanity, unaware that the challenges they face reverberate through their lives. Why did their ancestors not seek solutions for their future? Perhaps it's time for change.

**Uniting for Transformation** Rather than individual efforts, a sincere collective can catalyze significant shifts. Our unit aspires to form a cohesive group, working collaboratively toward shared goals.

**The Power of Practical Support:** Speeches and advice alone cannot transform mindsets. Real tools are essential for positive change. For years, these tools were absent from the lives of rural communities. Now, within our unit, mutual support fosters wellness. We stand together, committed to each other's growth.

**Paving the Way for Livelihoods:** Consider your future—a permanent livelihood for you and all humankind. Graduation may not be a priority for others, but it's your decision. While words alone won't alter your physical reality, financial backing, proper guidance, and self-motivation play crucial roles.

**Strength in Unity** A small family faces practical challenges, but a sincere group can transform lives. Follow this guide, seize the limited opportunities, and shape your existence as you envision it.

In the quiet embrace of the countryside, the rural population often finds itself relegated to the margins—deemed well for nothing, both by society and by their own self-perception. They seldom recognize their intrinsic humanity, unaware that the challenges they face reverberate through their lives. Why, then, did their forebears not seek solutions for their future?

Yet, within this seemingly forgotten landscape, a beacon of hope emerges the power of collective effort. A sincere group, working in unison, can wield transformative influence far beyond the impact of individual endeavors. This unit aspires to coalesce, to form a cohesive force that transcends mere intention.

## "IT IS YOU TO DECIDE"

Speeches and advice, while well-intentioned, often lack the tangible tools necessary for genuine change. For years, these rural lives have languished, caught in a cycle of well-meaning words without practical implementation. Anyone can dispense counsel, but it is only when practical possibilities align that true transformation occurs. Here, within this unit, mutual support blossoms—a shared commitment to wellness and progress.

As we look ahead, consider the path toward lasting livelihoods. No one champions your graduation with fervor; that decision rests squarely on your shoulders. Words alone cannot reshape your physical reality, but financial backing, sound guidance, and unwavering self-motivation form the bedrock of transformation.

A small family or a handful of individuals may struggle against practical obstacles, but a sincere group—a united front—can wield immense influence. Let this guide be your compass, steering you toward the life you envision. Opportunities are scarce; seize them with purpose and determination.

"The concept of 'the unit' encompasses not only the individual but also their family. It is a collective entity with shared rights and responsibilities. By recognizing and supporting this unit, we can unlock prosperity and positive change.

In rural areas, there exist dormant lives—individuals who have been overlooked or deemed 'good for nothing.' However, our mission is to transform them into active, productive, and valuable members of society. By doing so, we contribute not only to our families but also to our nation and the world.

Supporting this unit can yield remarkable results. Within a few months, you may witness miracles in your own life and community.

Governments allocate funds annually for the welfare of rural populations, particularly at the grassroots-level. Unfortunately, there's a common perception that these funds don't reach the intended beneficiaries. Going forward, we propose a systematic approach: channeling government and organizational assistance through the unit to ensure it directly benefits those in need."

**Remember,** *positive change begins with collective effort!*

1. **Equitable Utilization of Funds**: The union, representing all rural members, ensures that funds are utilized for the benefit of the entire population. Each unit member receives an equal share, which contributes to the growth and development of the unit. These funds are directed toward the unit's capital fund.

2. **Immediate Focus on Food Security**: Recognizing your expertise in agriculture and allied activities, we propose an immediate focus on ensuring sufficient food for 200 households. Within the next 3 months, prioritize cultivating various crops across all available land within the unit's boundaries.

3. **Eradicating Poverty through Agriculture**: Our primary objective is to lift member households out of poverty. Leveraging the

advantage of a 3-6 month harvest cycle, active participation in other activities will follow. As confidence grows within the unit, joint efforts will yield positive outcomes.

4. **Optimal Resource Utilization**: By sharing surplus manpower between units, we ensure that no talent goes to waste. Idle employees can be put to productive use elsewhere, contributing to overall efficiency.

5. **Cost Savings**: <u>Instead of hiring new employees, exchanging workers</u> allows us to utilize existing resources effectively. This reduces recruitment costs and training expenses.

6. **Skill Enhancement**: Employees gain exposure to different work environments and processes. *This cross-training enhances their skills and broadens their expertise.*

7. **Improved Flexibility**: *Manpower exchange enables quick adjustments to meet fluctuating demands. Units can borrow or lend workers as needed, maintaining operational flexibility with other units.*

8. **Collaboration and Networking**: Interacting with colleagues from other units fosters collaboration and knowledge sharing. It builds a sense of unity within the organization.

9. **Reduced Workload Pressure**: During peak periods, units can borrow manpower from others, preventing burnout and ensuring timely project completion.

10. **Enhanced Learning**: Younger employees benefit from exposure to diverse tasks. They learn about various roles and processes, contributing to their professional growth.

<u>In summary, manpower exchange promotes efficiency, cost-effectiveness, and skill development while fostering a cooperative work environment.</u>

1. **Unit Collaboration and Ownership**: The unit's practical experience has propelled its members into top management

positions. It's essential to recognize that each member isn't merely a worker or an employee; rather, all are co-owners of the unit, sharing equal rights. Consequently, any loss of an hour's manpower affects the entire unit.

2. **Addressing Labor Scarcity**: Casual laborers and skilled workers, such as carpenters and masons, are scarce commodities in the global market. Leveraging their services based on demand is crucial. When our unit lacks such members, we're compelled to seek assistance from neighboring units. To mitigate this scarcity, strategic planning should include skilled workers when selecting member houses.

**3 Unit Identity and Financial Assistance**: A unit's name plays a pivotal role in public and government recognition. It should be both attractive and distinctive. By establishing a recognizable identity, the unit becomes a conduit for government financial assistance, benefiting all its members.

**Enhancing Your Unit's Identity: A strategic approach when naming your unit is to** consider a blend of practicality and allure. The unit's name should resonate with the rural landscape it represents, capturing attention and leaving a lasting impression. A touch of elegance can work wonders, especially when marketing your products or engaging with stakeholders.

**Navigating Administrative Waters** Maintaining meticulous records and fostering positive relationships with government officials are essential. These efforts contribute to your unit's reputation and facilitate smoother operations.

**Remember**, *fame and goodwill go hand in hand*.

**Diverse Lands, Varied Cultivation** Recognize that not all members possess equal land holdings. Factors like water availability and topography influence land suitability. Transform idle properties into revenue generators by utilizing them effectively.

**Starting with Agriculture.:** Begin your journey by addressing agricultural challenges. In rural areas, wastelands often result from water scarcity or owner neglect. Leverage collective strength to overcome these obstacles. Convert so-called wastelands into high-yield agricultural plots. With ample resources—financial, human, and mechanized—you can rent earth-moving machinery or use your own to rejuvenate these lands.

**Remember,** *unity empowers transformation. Let your unit's actions speak volumes, turning barren patches into thriving landscapes.*

**8 Empowerment and Possibility** As part of the countryside or rural population, you and your ancestors harbor a wealth of ideas waiting to be put into action. Begin by selecting land that is easily accessible to the public, complete with roads and essential facilities. This land can serve various purposes: a commercial unit's office, a residence for members, and storage sheds for crops and other products. By doing so, you'll save valuable resources.

However, alongside these opportunities lies the responsibility to clear away the debris of outdated beliefs and practices. These remnants have lingered for years, hindering growth. Now, as you form a cohesive unit, remember that nothing is insurmountable when tackled collectively. Rest is a luxury you can't afford; instead, focus on systematically overcoming obstacles one by one.

Consider this: just as you wouldn't rely solely on your strength to remove oil from your body through massage instead of using soap. Facing life's challenges requires more than sheer force. Seek out apt solutions, apply them diligently, and witness transformation unfold.

**Remember,** *unity and purpose can turn seemingly impossible tasks into achievable ones.*

**Shared Purpose and Vision**: Clearly define the purpose and goals of your unit. What do you want to achieve together? Having a shared vision will help align everyone's efforts.

**Effective Communication:** Regularly communicate with each other. Share ideas, concerns, and progress. Active listening is crucial for understanding different perspectives.

**Trust and Respect**: Trust is the foundation of any cohesive group. Build trust by being reliable, honest, and respectful toward one another.

**Roles and Responsibilities:** Assign roles based on individual strengths and interests. Everyone should contribute their unique skills to the unit.

**Collaboration and Cooperation:** Work together on projects, tasks, or initiatives. Collaboration fosters creativity and problem-solving.

**Conflict Resolution**: Conflicts are natural. Address them openly and find solutions. Avoid personal attacks and focus on the issue at hand.

**Celebrate Successes**: Acknowledge achievements, no matter how small. Celebrate milestones and progress as a team.

**Remember,** *unity is not about uniformity; it's about diverse individuals coming together for a common purpose.*

Instead of relying solely on physical force, consider using soap or a similar product. To wash the oil from your body. When faced with critical situations apply common sense and seek appropriate remedies. Utilize the collective knowledge of all team members—anyone can suggest a solution.

Overcoming laziness is crucial. Each individual must transition to hard work. In the past, there may have been little to do, but the current situation demands more effort. Strive for a better life for yourself and your family.

Remember, *no one is imposing tasks upon you forcibly. Voluntarily accept responsibilities that align with your physical and mental capabilities. Commit to working diligently until favorable circumstances arise.*

**Unite** against adversity: combat hunger, poverty, water scarcity, and poor living conditions. Together, we can overcome these challenges.

**Embrace Responsibility:** As a member of this unit, it's essential to shift your mindset and work collectively toward achieving our shared goal. Begin by transforming yourself—discard unnecessary egos, unproductive behaviors, and negative attitudes. Pass on your skills and experiences to fellow members, empowering them to rise alongside you.

This shift in lifestyle promises a permanent improvement—a manifold betterment compared to your previous state. Gone are the days of waiting for someone else's assistance; now, you feast on the fruits of your own labor. Your unity with neighbors has unlocked this capacity. Perhaps you once considered them enemies, but circumstances have shifted, and you now join hands for the sake of your children and families, altering your lifeline irrevocably. You've learned how to lead your life.

No longer fixated on mere survival, you envision a new existence: nourishing meals, quality education for your kids, and decent clothing. Shedding laziness and unhealthy habits, your mindset transforms. Instead of chasing fleeting pleasures, you focus on securing a better future before the next setback.

**Remember,** *each step you take contributes to a brighter path ahead.*

The days slipped by, leaving no discernible impact on you. It was as if you were under the influence of ancestral heritage—a legacy of drugs passed down through generations. These substances cast shadows over your life, leading to struggles: hunger, inadequate clothing, substandard living conditions, and a lack of education for your children.

You harbored hope that perhaps the government or some benevolent force would transform your existence. Yet, in reality, you squandered your precious days, achieving nothing. Despite harboring lofty ideals, the shackles of poverty held you captive, stifling any progress.

But here's the turning point: <u>a platform awaits you—a stage where you must perform selflessly and tirelessly</u>. Collaborate with others, harness the situation, and strive for collective well-being. Your ideas, once confined to your mind, can now be shared with thousands. Through this platform, you can breathe life into them, secure funding, and witness immediate implementation as fellow members rally behind your vision.

Embrace this opportunity, for it holds the promise of transformation—a beacon of hope in a sea of limitations.

**Remember**, *your ideas have the power to ignite change.*

## CAPITAL AND UNITY

To establish a solid foundation, consider opening a bank account for the capital. This account will cover initial expenses such as unit registration and other related costs. Day-to-day necessities like agricultural tools (such as tractors, seeds, watering equipment, and fencing) will also be funded from this account.

**Unity as One Family:** As unit members, forge strong bonds akin to a single-family. You're embarking on a new journey together, facing life's consequences collectively. While the unit represents a single home, remember that you are many—capable and resilient. Together, you can confront any challenges that come your way.

**Ownership and Responsibility:** You jointly own the unit, agricultural land, and various other properties across 200 homes. Safeguarding these assets is crucial—they belong to all of you. As you walk this path, clarity will emerge regarding your rights, roles, and duties within the unit. Idle moments are scarce; every minute counts.

**A Positive Outlook:** Banish negativity. You bear responsibility, and there's no room for pessimism. Your minds brim with positivity and joy, ready to take action. Anticipation fills the air as you envision new lives fueled by dreams and ideas for the future.

**Remember,** *this journey is about unity, responsibility, and optimism.*

## DEAR MEMBERS,

As we move forward, it is essential to recognize that each of you bears significant responsibilities. The management of the unit's assets and financial matters is now a collective duty. No one is exempt from their share of responsibilities and accountability.

"Every member is equal; no one is above or below another. Even though someone may be younger, elders should maintain a give-and-take approach. <u>This will benefit your children, allowing them to lead a different life than yours.</u>"

These assigned tasks serve as a constant reminder, keeping you vigilant and focused on executing your roles within the unit. Under the guidance of the unit manager and other officials, strive to carry out your work systematically and efficiently.

Should any challenges arise, whether minor or significant, as a member, you are encouraged to promptly communicate with the unit office. Whether through oral communication or written correspondence, addressing issues promptly is crucial, especially during this initial phase of the unit's establishment.

Our ultimate goal is to foster a sense of intimacy among members—a feeling akin to being part of a close-knit family. These connections, previously unexplored, will strengthen your bonds and instill newfound confidence. Let us embrace this journey together, building upon yesterday's progress.

**Unity and Purpose**:: Your initial achievement lies in having companions; you are not alone. Together, your collective goal is to combat poverty, and immediate fulfillment of your needs is the aim. Through a collaborative effort, you will find success.

**Exploring Resources**: Beyond your immediate surroundings, there exist abundant resources in your land and properties. Explore these, along with neighboring areas.

**Strength amidst challenges and** past difficulties, you now possess greater resilience to confront obstacles and threats.

Rather than waiting for an uncertain future, many unorganized individuals worldwide can follow this path.

**Path to Prosperity: With dedicated hard work over some years,** you can ascend to a position of wealth.

**Conversely,** *your efforts can also benefit the government in various ways through this collective endeavour.*

# CHAPTER VIII

# THE INFERIORITY AMONG MANY

There exists a timeless adage: "A smile can unlock a heart faster than a key can open a door." Let this wisdom illuminate not only your own existence but also the broader world. Your fellow members endure myriad struggles, and their burdens become intertwined with yours. By sharing these hardships and confronting them collectively, you can surmount the challenges that beset you all.

Transparency is paramount. The problems you face must be laid bare to discover remedies and effective solutions. While immediate resolution may elude us, gradual progress is attainable. Begin by identifying individual members' issues and seeking remedies. Only then can your unit function harmoniously and serenely.

Avoid sowing discord among your ranks. Within your close-knit community, diverse personalities have coexisted for years. Now, as a united family, refrain from uttering words that wound others. Instead, focus resolutely on shaping a brighter future.

**Remember,** *some may have strayed from the conventional path due to life's circumstances. Extend forgiveness and support, guiding them along the new trajectory that defines our collective journey. Together, you forge a path—a unit bound by shared experiences and unwavering compassion.*

1. **Avoid Hurtful Words and Reminders**: Refrain from using abusive language or bringing up someone's past, even in jest. Words that

highlight weaknesses or impact individuals and their families can have lasting effects.

2. **Remember** *that your words can affect their skills and abilities, especially when they come from friends or relatives.*

3. **Self-Reflection and Imperfections**: Recognize that nobody is perfect, including you. We all have shortcomings. Instead of contributing to mental distress, let's practice empathy and kindness.

4. **Reporting Abusive Behavior**: If anyone within the group uses abusive language, it's essential to report it to the manager. Every member has the responsibility to maintain a peaceful environment within the unit.

5. **Embracing Imperfection**: Many individuals join groups to hide their vulnerabilities and present themselves as flawless. However, acknowledging imperfections fosters growth and understanding.

6. **Moral Support and Rural Remedies**: The unit's mission is to improve the lives of rural populations. With government support and moral guidance, we can save lives and empower people through awareness programs and moral classes.

**In the heart of rural areas, Empowering Rural Communities through Unit Systems**, the government and political parties have a unique opportunity to initiate a transformative change—the establishment of unit systems. These systems, once implemented, can become an enduring lifeline for the impoverished population. Their impact is profound, and the gratitude they evoke lasts forever.

For rural residents, these units represent more than just an experiment; they are a last chance—a beacon of hope in the face of adversity. To political parties, they serve as a perpetual vote bank, a strategic move that pays dividends over time. The countryside and village lives, once touched by these units, are forever grateful. Their loyalty to the government remains unwavering.

Consider the essential services—daily necessities, rural funds, and pension schemes—that reach these communities. They are lifelines, lifelines that politicians are keenly aware of. Some visionary leaders experiment with these grassroots initiatives, reaping impressive results. As elections approach, they continue to fine-tune their strategies, knowing that tangible outcomes matter.

Imagine the impact of a small kit—a mere one or two days' worth of food or a modest sum of money—on election results. Now, envision a permanent solution like the unit system. The results would be nothing short of fantastic—a testament to the power of thoughtful intervention and sustained support.

Let us champion these unit systems, for they hold the promise of a brighter future for our rural brethren.

## ADDRESSING THE SOARING BIRTH RATES

The unprecedented surge in birth rates has exacerbated poverty, pushing it to alarming levels. Particularly in rural areas, the uncontrolled population growth far exceeds expectations, plunging communities deeper into the abyss of destitution. As time passes, the government must proactively assist these rural regions.

## RESOURCE SCARCITY AND CONFLICT

Enmities among rural inhabitants stem from the fixed and limited availability of resources. The relentless rise in birth rates demands more than what is currently accessible, resulting in dire situations and conflicts. It's a battle for survival.

## CHANGING MINDSETS AND INTRODUCING SOLUTIONS

To address this crisis, a paradigm shift is essential. Confidence must be instilled in every individual that the government will enact protective laws and establish new units to safeguard the rights and properties of rural populations. These units will play a crucial role in curbing the birth rate.

## REMEDIES THROUGH AWARENESS

Awareness classes targeting parents across all categories are imperative. Parents who bring children into the world without adequate facilities face daunting challenges. By strictly limiting support from units or the government, we can prevent births where parents cannot ensure their children's well-being. The focus should be on achieving financial stability within the units before allowing further births.

## UNIT RESPONSIBILITY FOR BIRTH RATE CONTROL:

The unit must diligently monitor its members to reduce the controllable birth rate. This responsibility should extend beyond the initial stages and become an integral part of unit management. Failing to do so will adversely impact the lives of our members.

**Awareness and Consequences**: The unit must educate its members about the consequences that parents and children may face. Without proper awareness, our nation cannot progress beyond its current state, and our efforts may yield negative results. Members should recognize that their negligence affects their entire family, especially in rural areas where suffering is widespread.

**Parental Responsibility and Legal Measures**: Parents should not evade their duty to protect their children. Legal measures are essential to enforce this responsibility. However, implementing laws among illiterate and impoverished populations poses challenges. Therefore, focusing on unit members during formation is more feasible. This approach benefits our members and curtails harmful practices like child labor and anti-social behavior.

**Remember,** *collective efforts lead to positive change!*

## ENHANCING ACCOUNTABILITY AND EFFECTIVENESS: A ROLE FOR THE UNIT

In the labyrinthine corridors of government systems and the intricate machinery they employ, tracking down culprits is no straightforward task. Many evade capture, slipping through the cracks. Incarceration alone isn't the panacea; instead, we must address the root causes that lead individuals down such paths. The unit members, uniquely positioned, can wield more influence than any other tools currently in use.

## VIGILANCE FROM WITHIN: LEVERAGING INSIDER ADVANTAGE

As part of the system, you possess a distinct advantage: the ability to observe. Regular, persistent efforts allow you to monitor closely. While the government initiates various welfare activities, their implementation often falters due to staff limitations—relying on the sincerity of those who execute them. Outsiders, constrained by their roles, can only do so much. Herein lies the unit's strength: it can swiftly allocate resources to the deserving and take decisive action, ensuring optimal utilization and follow-ups.

## TURNING THE TIDE: EMPOWERING UNIT MEMBERS

Among the unit, individuals with chickened pasts are a rarity. With encouragement and support, they can transform into valuable assets. As a compact team, the unit can maintain vigilant oversight, each member assuming the role of a moral sentinel. Together, they hold the power to reshape outcomes and foster a more just society.

**Ensuring Integrity within the Unit**: We remain vigilant and resolute, never allowing anyone to deceive the unit or its members once again. Our commitment to the unit's principles should be unwavering, and we must not compromise on this matter.

**Marriage and Financial Considerations**: Marriage is a common custom, especially as one reaches a certain age. However, many young individuals, even among the educated, fail to consider their financial stability before embarking on this significant life journey. While families often insist on marriage, only a few exhibit maturity and actively shape their future.

**Traditional Customs and Poverty**: In rural areas, illiterate communities adhere strictly to old customs, compelling their youth to marry without any specific criteria. Unfortunately, this adherence perpetuates poverty rather than ensuring a secure life for married couples and their future generations.

**Beyond Age: Financial Strength Matters**: The parameter for marriage should extend beyond age alone. It should also encompass the financial stability of the family, particularly the prospective couples. A home should receive a certificate of financial capacity before being allowed to marry, ensuring that no child suffers needlessly.

**Challenges with Reclaiming Wayward Youth**: Some children receive training in theft and other anti-social activities during their formative years. Bringing them back into a positive path is no easy task.

**Unit Intervention for Safety and Transformation**: Our unit plays a crucial role in curbing criminal behavior. By closely monitoring all members, we create a safe environment. Let us focus on the present and provide necessary support, including awareness classes, to facilitate positive change.

A Call for Reflection

*We must adopt a stern stance toward those who have experienced vastly different lives in the past compared to their present circumstances. The unit emphasizes self-control, recognizing that they have inherited numerous mistakes from their ancestors.*

*While these lessons once guided their existence, times have changed. Now, they lead respectable lives alongside their families and neighbors.*

*However, a warning echoes: should they persist on the ancestral path, no force can shield them from the consequences. Such a journey guarantees immense suffering. Our rural communities harbor no illusions of opulent lifestyles or cutting-edge technology. Their aspirations revolve around sustenance—daily bread. Born into anticipation, they endure years of underprivileged existence, lacking even the most basic necessities: proper shelter, clothing, food, and water. Hope persists, waiting for a brighter day to dawn.*

**Unity and Fulfilling Dreams**: When individuals come together with sincerity, they can swiftly realize their basic dreams. Unity among people leads to more pleasant lives. Although external forces cannot alter your mindset, it is within your power to do so. Begin this journey as a united unit and embrace the positive changes.

**Prioritizing Relationships**: Often, we fail to recognize that our suffering stems from a single mistake: not realizing the value of certain relationships. Following others blindly based on their mindset won't lead to a fulfilling life. True friends won't stay up all night replacing wet napkins on your forehead during a fever—only your mother would. She deserves the top spot in your priorities.

**Choosing Wisely:** When someone insists on interfering and dictating your life, it adversely affects a significant part of your existence. Recognizing mistakes and avoiding them becomes crucial. Take the time to think twice before making decisions.

## THE TALE OF JOSEF STALIN AND THE CHICKEN:

Legend has it that Josef Stalin once plucked a live chicken in front of his followers. Whether fact or fable, it's easy to imagine the brutal Soviet dictator doing just that. He forcefully stripped the squawking bird of its feathers, leaving it bare. The lesson? Sometimes, power reveals its true nature when wielded without empathy.

## STALIN'S LESSON

"Watch," Stalin said, sprinkling small grains onto the floor. The bird immediately followed him, pecking up the scattered food. "Do you see how that chicken follows me for sustenance?" he asked his followers. "People are similar. Even if you cause them great pain, they will continue to follow you, seeking nourishment throughout their lives."

Some politicians still experiment with these practices today, distributing food and money among their supporters to gain favor. Are we becoming Stalin's chickens?

## THE POWER OF UNITY

In their expressions, you'll often notice sorrow or struggle. The solution lies in unity. Membership in a collective effort becomes an obligation—one where sincere work helps lift everyone from their sinking state. Remember, while you may be doing everything right, others play a role in your hardships. Change this mindset, align the wheels, and move toward a smoother path—the right destination awaits. Your efforts not only benefit you but also countless others.

## THE GENTLE TRAPS

Anti-social activities ensnare those who struggle to face life's challenges. They accept offers merely to survive. Both ancestors and the new generation have lost control, drifting from poverty to destitution. It's time to gather and unite—the remedy for your future. Many exploit your vulnerabilities, but together, you can rise beyond their traps.

**Stalin's Insight**: "Watch," Stalin instructed, sprinkling small grains onto the floor. The bird trailed him, eagerly pecking up the scattered food. "Do you observe how that chicken follows me for sustenance?" he queried his followers. "People exhibit similar behavior. Even if you inflict great pain upon them, they will continue to follow you, driven by their basic needs throughout their lives."

**Politicians and Their Tactics**: Some politicians persistently experiment with these practices, distributing food and money among their supporters to curry favor. But are we, too, becoming akin to Stalin's chickens—unquestioningly following those who provide for us?

**The Unit as a Solution**: Written across their faces, you'll often discern sorrowful expressions. However, a remedy exists—the unit. Your membership and sincere contributions within the unit becomes your lifeline. While others may not directly assist you, collective efforts buoy you from despair.

**Changing Perspectives**: Recognize this: You execute everything flawlessly, yet others contribute to your melancholic existence. Shift your mindset and steer your efforts onto the right track. The wheels, once aligned, will propel you toward the desired destination.

**Remember,** your endeavors benefit not only you but also countless others.

## THE GENTLE TRAPS

In the quiet corners of existence, where shadows linger, and desperation thrives, there exists a web of **gentle traps**. These snares are not made of steel or barbed wire; instead, they are woven from the threads of circumstance and vulnerability.

**Anti-social activities** cast their insidious influence upon those who struggle to face life head-on. These souls, burdened by inefficiency and hardship, find themselves at a crossroads. They are forced to accept offers—sometimes dubious, often desperate—simply to survive. The weight of ancestral legacy and the expectations of a new generation bear down upon them, pushing them from poverty to the brink of begging.

But there is a glimmer of hope—a remedy hidden amidst the chaos. **Unity** becomes the beacon, the sole path forward. All who share this plight must gather, their collective strength a shield against exploitation. Many misuse their suffering, capitalizing on their vulnerability. Yet, these weary souls remain trapped, unable to break free or elevate their lives.

The truth is stark: there is no work, no avenue for change. Self-help and joint programs seem distant dreams. The world conspires against them, orchestrating their entrapment. The very air whispers strategies to ensnare them further. And so, when weariness consumes their resolve, glittering offers emerge—a lifeline in a sea of struggle. With little hesitation, they accept, binding themselves to terms and conditions. Their sinking families, desperate for safety, become collateral in this delicate dance of survival.

**Your Youth and Their Motives**: Their focus lies squarely on your youth. Your future and safety barely register in their calculations. Their hidden agenda unfolds through your children. You may believe your kids are secure, but unwittingly, you place them in their snares. When the realization dawns, you'll find yourself powerless, merely suffering the consequences.

**The Youth's Dilemma**: The youth—your children—are caught in a bind. They have no alternative but to accept offers that straddle life's two extremes. Most of them aren't inherently criminal; rather, they seek to protect their families. The unit presents safety measures, demonstrating how to transcend your current situation. Within this unit, no external control exists; instead, mutual self-help fosters growth. The choice is yours: accept or decline the offer.

**Breaking Free**: You possess the option to break free. Abandon your current existence, even if it seems comfortable, like "Stalin's chicken." Liberation from their influence lies within the unit—the sole remedy to regain control.

## SEEKING SAFETY FOR YOUR LOVED ONES

Many of you tirelessly toil, driven by an unwavering commitment to your families' well-being. Your involvement in less savory endeavors promises substantial returns, tempting you with the allure of adventure. These gains, though meager, help put food on your children's plates and support your aging parents. Yet, deep down, you recognize that this is not a lasting solution—a mere bandage on the wound of financial struggle.

Consider this: there exists an alternative—a permanent escape from the shadows of illegality. Imagine a life where safety isn't a fleeting illusion but a steadfast reality for you and your family. The path to such security lies within reach.

## THE ANTI-SOCIAL INFLUENCE

Among you, certain individuals—men with persuasive tongues—embrace an anti-social approach. They canvass others, particularly the youth in rural villages, who remain tethered to their families. These young souls bear the weight of familial burdens, their present circumstances overshadowed by hunger and desperation. In their plight, they are willing to sacrifice everything for their loved ones, accepting whatever comes their way.

Yet, beware: this path is no mere survival—it's knowingly stepping into traps, trading one hardship for another. Seek permanence, not mere existence. Choose wisely, for your family's future hangs in the balance.

## BREAKING THE CYCLE OF ANTI-SOCIAL BEHAVIOR

In a short span of time, numerous young individuals and their networks will mobilize. These anti-social activities will rapidly permeate every nook and cranny of the nation, fueled by sheer muscle power.

The agenda of these anti-social elements often exceeds their initial expectations. Driven by the allure of money, they swiftly engage in activities that yield financial gains. Whether they are unaware or knowingly complicit, they begin minting money.

Unfortunately, this path leads to bondage. Many of these boys end up sick or physically impaired within a brief period. As their health deteriorates, they gradually withdraw support and seek replacements. However, during this transition, their own children remain vulnerable due to their tender age.

Consider this: seeking a permanent solution for your family's well-being is crucial. Becoming an anti-social activist doesn't yield any real benefits; instead, it perpetuates the same cycle for future generations. Safety and contentment elude your entire family, affecting not only you but also your children and their descendants.

Rather than contributing to a harmful cycle, channel your efforts toward building something positive—an empire that benefits not just others but also ensures your own well-being.

**Rescuing Vulnerable Populations from the Clutches of Anti-Socials,** It is remarkably straightforward to save vulnerable populations from the clutches of anti-social elements. These individuals eagerly await helping hands to guide them out of their predicament. However, the anti-socials, driven by cunning and business-minded motives, abruptly withdraw their support from those who yield no further benefit. The assumption that their old gang will perpetually provide assistance is a fallacy. As fellow members, it is our responsibility to reveal this truth to them. Despite their handicaps, they mistakenly believe they remain free and secure even after leaving the gang.

**Empowering Lives: Offering a Safe Livelihood** Our unit must play a pivotal role in molding these individuals. We aim to provide them with a safe livelihood—one that not only sustains them but also supports their families. By articulating the benefits of this transformation, we can successfully reintegrate them into society.

**Addressing Rural Poverty: Controlling Birth Rates** To combat the poverty prevalent in rural areas, we must prioritize controlling birth rates. Your abilities should not be stretched thin by supporting large families with numerous members, which ultimately leads to impoverishment. Many parents neglect their responsibilities toward their children, exacerbating the nation's poverty crisis. The well-being of these children hangs in the balance, and it is our collective challenge to address this pressing issue.

**Remember**, our actions can shape lives and uplift communities.

1. **Legal Responsibility and Compassion**: While laws exist, their enforcement remains a challenge due to various reasons. Stricter implementation is difficult for the government as it involves many staff and it is very much expensive, but it becomes more manageable at the grassroots-level.. Units—whether communities, organizations, or individuals—can play a crucial role in ensuring compliance.

2. **Plight of Vulnerable Populations**: The sight of children begging for a single meal is a stark reality across our nation, leading to the proliferation of orphanages. Similarly, elderly individuals suffer without proper care from their near and dear ones. It's a heartbreaking situation.

3. **Empowering Units to Protect Relatives**: Units can make a difference. When these units achieve financial stability, they

can safeguard their members' relatives from ending up in such homes. By doing so, they contribute to the government's efforts to eliminate such institutions.

4. **Parental Accountability and Responsibility**: Neglecting children due to parental negligence should never be tolerated. Parents must be held accountable, legally passing on all responsibilities. Even if units step in to care for children and the elderly, relatives or parents cannot evade their duty.

5. **Implementing Stringent Measures**: Units should introduce a robust punishment system. They are uniquely positioned to address issues like unwanted births and mistreatment of elderly parents and relatives within their communities.

6. **Aging Population and Responsibility**: The plight of the elderly is evident everywhere—whether in the countryside, towns, or cities. Who bears responsibility for their well-being? Parents, relatives, and society as a whole must reflect on this question.

7. **Ensuring a Bright Future**: In their twilight years, many seniors suffer mistreatment from their own children. However, every child deserves a promising future. Adequate support during childhood can pave the way for a disciplined and fulfilling life.

## CHANGE OF MINDSET

1. **Changing Our Mindset**: We must shift our mindset away from expecting the government to provide everything and take responsibility for all aspects of our lives. Instead, let's recognize that we also have a role to play. Self-help and personal responsibility are essential for living independently.

2. **Individual Responsibility**: Each of us, as individuals, should embrace our moral responsibilities toward ourselves, our families, our neighbors our nation, and the world. By doing so, we contribute to a stronger collective unit that can achieve great heights.

3. **Unity and Infrastructure**: When our community or unit requires infrastructure or other public services, we can approach the government for support. However, an alternative exists in our unity. By coming together, we gain strength and develop a resilient mindset to tackle challenges effectively.

4. **Addressing Unwanted Births**: Unplanned births have a significant impact on society. The unit has to explain to its members about the merits and demerits of this system. From childhood onward, individuals suffer due to circumstances beyond their control. This feeling of isolation and inferiority can dampen enthusiasm. While government-sponsored schemes exist, many real beneficiaries remain overlooked due to bureaucratic limitations.

*Let's strive for a society where everyone's needs are met and no one is left behind.*

Changing the mindsets of inmates within the prison system is a formidable challenge. Their experiences, often marked by trauma and adversity, can shatter their sense of self and leave them feeling shapeless. As prison administrators, it is crucial to intervene sincerely in their lives, engaging with individual members and guiding them toward positive transformation.

Traditional methods alone may not suffice to reshape their outlook. The walls that confine them also bind their spirits as they share sorrowful stories with fellow inmates. Breaking through these emotional barriers requires concerted effort. Here are some strategies to consider:

**Create a Supportive Environment**: Rather than dwelling on their past mistakes, foster an environment that encourages growth. Provide opportunities for education, skill development, and self-improvement. When inmates feel valued and supported, they are more likely to embrace change.

**Empowerment through Responsibility**: Assign meaningful tasks and responsibilities within the prison community. When individuals contribute positively, they gain a sense of purpose and agency. This can be a powerful catalyst for mindset shifts.

**Counseling and Therapy: Regular counseling** sessions can help inmates process their emotions, confront their past, and envision a different future. Therapeutic interventions can address trauma, anger, and self-destructive patterns.

**Peer Support Programs**: Encourage inmates to support one another. Peer mentoring and group discussions allow them to share experiences, learn coping strategies, and build resilience. Knowing they are not alone can be transformative.

**Mindfulness Practices**: Teach mindfulness techniques to manage stress, anxiety, and impulsivity. Mindfulness helps individuals stay grounded, regulate emotions, and make better decisions.

**Education and Skill Building**: Offer educational programs, vocational training, and workshops. Learning new skills provides a sense of achievement and opens doors to employment upon release.

**Restorative Justice**: Shift the focus from punishment to rehabilitation. Restorative justice practices involve dialogue, accountability, and repairing harm. Encourage inmates to take responsibility for their actions and make amends.

**Positive Reinforcement**: Acknowledge progress and celebrate small victories. Positive reinforcement reinforces desirable behaviors and motivates further growth.

**Remember** that changing mindsets is a gradual process. It requires patience, empathy, and a commitment to human dignity.

By creating a supportive and empowering environment, we can help inmates rebuild their lives and find hope beyond the prison walls.

1. **Government Welfare and the Countryside:** The rural areas remain largely untouched by the positive impact of government welfare initiatives. Despite the best intentions, sincere efforts to extend a helping hand have been scarce. Consequently, progress toward establishing cohesive community units has been slow. Members, however, persistently inch forward, hoping for better days.

2. **Lack of Clarity and Expectations:** While many have stepped up to assist, the core issue lies in the lack of a clear focus. The rural population struggles to identify viable paths or make informed choices. Their futures remain uncertain, and this uncertainty weighs heavily upon them.

3. **The Ultimate Disadvantaged:** These individuals are the epitome of poverty, exploited by those who take advantage of their vulnerability. The prevalence of criminal cases and unsavory situations further dampen any positive outlook they might harbor.

4. **Contentment amidst Struggle:** Despite the odds, they find solace in the limited facilities available. Their mindset adjusts to accept their circumstances, even if it means convincing them that they are akin to orphans. Their lives unfold with minimal care, navigating countless adjustments.

5. **Survival Strategies:** Daily life involves enduring abusive language from society. They've become adept at cleverly navigating their way through survival, even if it means deceiving others. Unfortunately, there's little to learn or seek from their families, neighbors, or surroundings, as negativity pervades their environment.

## BREAKING CYCLES AND CREATING CHANGE

In the midst of their challenging circumstances, many individuals find themselves trapped without a glimpse of escape toward a better life. These are people who hail from the most difficult family backgrounds yet harbor a deep desire for transformation. They yearn to break free from the shadows of their family's past, seeking a path toward decency and self-improvement. However, lurking in the shadows is someone even more malevolent, ready to wield the weapon of painful reminders.

Within the confines of our unit, it falls upon the management to take decisive action. We all carry hidden histories, back-office secrets we'd rather keep buried. The inmates share common origins and similar life situations. Their childhoods were marred by an insidious inferiority complex, isolating them from social interactions and participation.

But the stories of those who have suffered abuse are far worse than the abuse itself. These individuals live in constant fear that their painful narratives will be exposed within the unit, prompting them to take precautionary measures.

Moving forward, we must find a remedy. In any of our units, we cannot allow the birth of children without proper parental care. It is our collective responsibility as unit members to prevent such situations. Let us refrain from allowing the birth of bastards—children left vulnerable due to parental neglect. During our general sessions, we must candidly discuss the consequences these kids endure because of their parents' negligence.

**In 2019,** there remains a concerning lack of awareness among our population. Many continue to grapple with the haunting specter of tragedy, yearning for its eventual resolution.

However, distressingly, some parents persist in abandoning their children on the streets. These actions, akin to criminal behavior, stain their hands with the blood of their own kin. Such individuals deserve neither pity nor a place in our society.

The unchecked growth of our population fuels animosity among rural communities. They perceive a threat, believing that their rights are being pilfered. This enmity reverberates beyond local boundaries, affecting our entire society, nation, and even the global landscape.

Regrettably, violence has become commonplace. Gangsters and individuals, leading lives of hardship in the countryside, engage in lethal conflicts. But there is hope. Each of us possesses the power to quell these malevolent forces, much like dispelling poisonous smoke. By observing the transformation and progress of our collective unit, we can contribute to eradicating harmful beliefs.

Implementing rules, especially in rural areas, proves both costly and time-consuming for the government. Instead of merely seeking opportunities to levy fines on the public, let us shift our mindset. The responsibility lies with us—the unit—to educate members about commonly known laws and foster understanding.

1. **Eliminating Unknown Violations and Imposing Fines:** The practice of allowing violations due to lack of awareness and subsequently imposing fines should cease permanently. Our primary objective should be to familiarize every unit member with the relevant subject matter. Introducing a minimum knowledge policy will ensure that they are well-informed.

2. **Public Awareness and Communication:** The rules must be disseminated widely to the public. The Road Transport Authority should utilize available media channels for advertisements. Additionally, government authorities can leverage these units to freely share essential information that the public must be aware of.

3. **Efficient Communication Channels:** Leveraging mobile phones, the public relations officer of the unit can efficiently relay

messages to all members. This streamlined approach ensures immediate implementation of government rules and regulations, surpassing traditional methods.

4. **Daily Updates for Informed Members:** By utilizing the unit structure, the government can swiftly enforce rules. The management ensures seamless communication to members, providing them with comprehensive daily updates to enhance their knowledge base.

5. **Government Unit and Public Awareness**: The government unit serves as an intermediary, ensuring that a significant portion of the population possesses the necessary knowledge about their country. While implementing rules poses challenges, the unit aims to streamline this process. By spreading awareness and imposing fines judiciously, the government can achieve its goal. However, uncertainties persist despite these efforts.

6. **Unit Members and Fines**: Unit members, well-informed through regular classes and meetings, need not pay fines. Instead, their hard-earned money can benefit the unit. Rather than coercion, the unit focuses on explaining the advantages and disadvantages to its members.

7. **Strength in Unity**: Although anti-social elements exist, their impact is limited. The unity among criminals once posed a threat to rural communities. However, our unit now stands stronger, with thousands of members committed to safeguarding the population.

8. **Unit for Anti-social Control**: The specialized unit swiftly neutralizes anti-social elements. Our converted members, well-versed in the enemies' strengths and weaknesses, adeptly confront any threat. As a formidable team, we possess strength, resources, and discernment. Our ability to overcome obstacles is the unit's primary advantage and central mission.

**Revolutionizing Care for the Elderly and Orphans**: The archaic system of old-age homes and orphanages must be eradicated globally. No elderly person or child should suffer without proper care. Each individual deserves an address, guidance, and protection throughout their life journey. If unit members can care for their parents, why maintain separate facilities? Let us advocate for change within our governments and ensure that no one, whether a "bastard" or an elder, wanders the streets in search of sustenance. Our intention and agenda should prioritize their well-being.

1. **Marriage and Parenting Responsibilities**: When a couple decides to marry, it's essential to consider their readiness for parenthood. Rather than rushing into having children, they should first mature in all aspects of life, including financial stability. Skipping out on responsibilities to their kids should be avoided.

2. **Financial Preparedness before Parenthood**: While allowing couples to marry, it's crucial for the government to assess their financial strength. Couples should demonstrate their ability to provide for a child's needs, including food, education, and other essentials. This approach benefits not only individuals and families but also contributes to the well-being of nations and the world.

3. **Addressing Begging and Financial Sufficiency**: Many people from economically disadvantaged backgrounds struggle without any purpose. To address this, restrictions should be in place. Even though there were no such restrictions earlier, the situation must change. Couples who choose to marry should be financially self-sufficient before considering having children. Waiting until they attain the capacity to support a child is essential.

4. **Unit Responsibilities and Life Skills**: The unit anticipates responsibilities from its members, emphasizing practical life skills. Through mingling with other members, study classes, and

awareness programs, everyone can progress in life. Financial stability and preparedness are key factors in this journey.

1. **Education and Societal Security**: Education need not be the sole determinant of leading a secure, society-oriented life. Instead, let us become models for others by demonstrating our worth through collective efforts. Our mindset plays a pivotal role in shaping our growth and modernization.

2. **Unity as Shelter**: Consider our unit as a shelter for thousands of members. Together, we create a pleasant environment where everyone works not only for themselves but also for their families. Our shared purpose is to lead decent lives, fostering a high society, rich culture, and desirable lifestyle.

3. **Transformation within Three Years**: Within a maximum of three years, we can transform our present circumstances. During this period, we'll facilitate positive changes within the unit. As financial stability grows, we'll gradually enhance our income and manage expenses wisely.

4. **Freedom from Poverty**: Poverty need not persist among us. Each member can live life on their terms, free from financial constraints.

5. **A Vision for the Future**: In light of rising birth rates, let's take decisive steps. Our goal: eliminate orphanages and old-age homes within 5 to 10 years. Every unit should become self-sufficient, capable of managing its members effectively. This is our shared agenda.

## STRENGTHENING BONDS ACROSS GENERATIONS

In any family unit, children and the elderly share a special connection. As members of the same family, it is our responsibility to support and care for one another. When the family unit becomes self-sufficient and can cover the expenses of its members, it paves the way for a better life for both the elderly and the young. Children thrive when surrounded by relatives who can provide guidance and love.

Life often takes unexpected turns, leading family members to part ways. However, there comes a time when we can reunite and invite our loved ones back into our lives. These reunions can create lasting memories, especially during the twilight years of our elders. Similarly, young adults can reconnect with their parents after long separations due to fate or circumstances.

In the past, financial disparities among family members sometimes caused strain. However, the family unit worked together to overcome these challenges. Our collective goal should be to ensure that no family member suffers from hunger or deprivation. By supporting one another, we can create a life where everyone feels cherished and valued.

Moving forward, let us strive to eliminate any gaps that lead to sorrowful lives within our family. Every child is wanted, and every elderly member deserves respect and care. Together, we can achieve a harmonious family unit that protects and uplifts all its members.

1. **Marriage Considerations**: In rural areas, there exists a tendency to push young girls and boys into marriage once they reach a certain age. Unfortunately, factors like maturity, financial stability, and the potential challenges of married life are often overlooked.

Consequently, many individuals suffer needlessly. It is crucial for governments to prioritize eligibility criteria beyond mere age and take steps to eradicate organizations that support child marriages globally. This way, people can lead happier lives.

2. **Breaking Harmful Practices**: The practice of treating humans like caged animals by donating money and rearing them in confined

spaces must cease permanently. Our goal should be to eliminate this dehumanizing approach.

3. **Empowering the Next Generation**: To improve the existing situation, we need to focus on nurturing maturity and financial independence in young men and women. They should start earning early, plan for their own families, and ensure their children receive proper education. Community support systems should provide resources to help young people generate regular income.

**Remembe**r: *these changes can lead to a more equitable and fulfilling future for everyone.*

1. **Parental Accountability and Responsibility**: It is crucial that both parents, as indicated on the birth certificate, promptly acknowledge their roles. Along with this, the child's blood group should be recorded. After DNA testing, the unit should transfer the responsibility for the child to the parents. The kids should either be cared for directly by their parents or, if necessary, the parents should provide financial support for their upbringing.

2. **Addressing Accidental Births**: Accidental births can occur unexpectedly. These cases should be verified through tests to determine whether the girl is indeed the mother. Once confirmed, the unit becomes the responsible guardian, ensuring that the child receives all necessary facilities and care.

3. **Abolishing Monetary Payments to Children**: The practice of paying a certain amount to a child based on parentage should be abolished by law. Instead, the government should mandate that parents jointly bear the entire financial burden. This ensures that children do not suffer due to their parents' negligence.

4. **Challenging Unwanted Birth Rates**: To combat unwanted birth rates, the unit must adopt these measures. By doing so, we prevent a cycle where children labeled as "bastards" face

hardships from childhood until their final journey. Let us prioritize the well-being of every child, regardless of their circumstances.

The straightforward practice of providing compensation has inadvertently led to a surge in unwanted births. In an attempt to gain tax exemptions, many individuals donate to orphanages and old-age homes without fully considering the implications of perpetuating this system.

Consider this: Someone's careless actions or thoughtlessness result in the birth of an innocent child who then faces a lifetime of suffering. It's high time we reflect on why, as a society, we continue to support a system that confines lives within the metaphorical cages of orphanages.

The care of vulnerable children, including strengthening family-based care, preventing unnecessary family separation, and ensuring quality care alternatives, remains a low global priority despite its impact on lifelong health and well-being. Initiatives like "Changing the Way We Care" aspire to strengthen government systems, build social worker capacity, and transition orphanages to community-based services.

1. **Individual Responsibility and Government Accountability**: The responsibility lies with concerned individuals, and the government can enforce accountability. However, despite the severity of the situation, there seems to be no effective remedy. Issues like begging, theft, and prostitution are on the rise, and many parents remain indifferent. Some children end up choosing these paths due to their circumstances. As a society aiming for peace and discipline, we must address this problem proactively. Rather than compensating the child, we should focus on holding parents accountable for their role in the child's upbringing.

2. **Shared Responsibility and Parental Accountability**: Parents should not limit their involvement in their child's life to financial support alone. In existing cases, parents must actively

participate in their child's day-to-day affairs and education. After all, both parents share responsibility for bringing the child into the world. We should refrain from protecting those who mistreat their elderly parents or send their kids to old-age homes or orphanages. Such actions do not warrant protective measures.

3. **Urgent Change and Safeguarding Innocent Lives**: The government can take swift action to address these issues. Regardless of existing laws, we can create a system that regularizes and safeguards innocent children from miserable lives. Let's work toward a drastic change that benefits our society as a whole.

**Controlling birth rates** is a crucial aspect of ensuring a sustainable and equitable future for our society. Let's delve into the paragraphs you've provided and explore how we can address this issue.

1. **Preventing Unwanted Births**:

It is indeed essential to prevent unwanted births. No one should suffer needlessly due to circumstances beyond their control. Ensuring that every child has a chance at a fulfilling life is a collective responsibility.

Families should consider their financial capacity and status when planning for children. Responsible family planning can lead to better outcomes for both parents and children.

The role of local units (such as community organizations or government bodies) is critical. They can actively engage in promoting awareness about family planning and birth control methods.

If there are existing laws related to family planning, these units should actively implement them. By doing so, they contribute to safeguarding the well-being of many children.

2. **Beliefs and Reality**:

The belief that "God gives children" is prevalent across various religions and cultures. However, we must also recognize the practical realities of our world.

In the past, natural resources were more abundant, and families could share them sufficiently. But times have changed. Overpopulation strains resources, leading to hardships for children.

Children are suffering due to lack of food or basic necessities, a stark reality. It's essential to bridge the gap between belief and practicality.

3. **Awareness and Action**:

*Members of communities should be well-informed about the need for birth control. Education and awareness play a crucial role.*

Understanding the drawbacks of an uncontrolled system is the first step toward positive change. When we recognize the challenges, we can work toward solutions.

Implementing birth control measures is relatively straightforward, yet it requires collective effort. Let's break down barriers and prioritize the well-being of future generations.

**Remember**, *birth control methods are available and effective. They empower individuals and families to make informed choices about family planning. Let's work together to create a world where every child has a chance to thrive.*


## FAMILY UNITY AND FINANCIAL MANAGEMENT

Some of you are acutely aware that you bear the responsibility of planning and managing your family or families. However, due to limited access to external resources, maintaining unity within your family unit becomes essential. Unfortunately, the sheer size of your family often exceeds your ability to control it effectively, resulting in financial constraints.

The burden of expenses surpassing your income leaves you with little control over family maintenance. You find yourself borrowing excessively, creating a cycle of debt that becomes increasingly unmanageable. While some of your creditors may empathize with your situation, others turn adversarial, causing tension and unease in your life.

To confront these creditors, you may resort to desperate measures, perhaps even escaping through self-destructive behaviors like substance abuse. Regrettably, this path leads to a life devoid of purpose, where existence persists without meaningful contribution to yourself or your family.

Therefore, consider this: Why squander your precious life without truly enjoying it? Reflect on the cause of your existence. Even in the face of tragedy, there lies an opportunity for growth. Just as rose bushes bear thorns, we can choose to focus on the beauty that emerges from adversity. The decision to be positive or negative ultimately rests with us.

**Remember:** *our choices shape our lives, and embracing unity within our families can lead to a brighter future.*

## TAKING CONTROL OF BIRTH RATES: A FAMILY'S DILEMMA

In the quiet corners of our family home, where dreams and responsibilities intersect, the issue of birth rates looms large. The situation demands change, intervention, and a candid assessment of our circumstances. Let me share how the rising birth rates have impacted our family's economy and what it means for our future.

1. **The Economic Strain:** As the number of family members grows, so do our financial burdens. The relentless increase in birth rates has stretched our resources thin. We find ourselves

juggling expenses—education, healthcare, and daily needs—like tightrope walkers on a precarious wire. The dream of living lavishly and luxuriously in our modest unit seems elusive.

2. **Rural Realities:** Our roots are firmly planted in rural soil. Here, expenses often defy control. The fields need tending, the livestock require care, and the seasons dictate their terms. We don't choose the expenses; they choose us. Yet, we grapple with the reality that each new addition to our family exacerbates our struggles. The once simple life now feels like a maze of financial constraints.

3. **Responsibility and Sacrifice:** Amidst this turmoil, I realize that my role extends beyond mere existence. I am not just a member; I am a guardian. The newborns look to me for sustenance, guidance, and a chance at a better life. The facilities we deny them—better education, nutritious meals, and a safe haven—are painful sacrifices. Poverty casts its shadow, and I am torn between providing and withholding.

4. **The Burden of Choice:** Why should the kids suffer? The question echoes in my mind. My partner and I share the weight of responsibility. We are architects of our family's fate. Doubts creep in—did we choose wisely? Could we have managed with fewer children? The answer lies in pragmatism. One child for a family is manageable; more than that, when income is scarce, it becomes an unwieldy burden.

5. **A Future Re-imagined:** As I pen these thoughts, I resolve to understand our position better. We must chart a course that balances dreams and reality. Our family's future hinges on deliberate choices. Perhaps, in the quietude of our home, we can redefine prosperity—not in opulence, but in love, resilience, and shared dreams.

May this reflection guide us toward a path where our dreams and responsibilities find harmony and where our children's future is shaped by both compassion and practicality.

1. **Comparing Egos and Financial Struggles**: The ego often leads us to compare ourselves with our neighbors. Striving to match their level can plunge us into deep financial liabilities, affecting us profoundly. Instead of concealing your struggles, consider opening up to your family. They understand your financial status, even when your pocket feels empty. Their support can be your path to recovery.

2. **Neglected Rural Populations**: Imagine a rural population akin to a lost boy in a home—no livelihood, no one to guide. When they lose control over their family, they lose everything. Anti-social activists exploit their vulnerability, luring them with tempting offers. These individuals, trapped and desperate, accept terms they can't avoid. Eventually, they turn anti-social. But there's hope—a unit exists to rescue those ensnared. It breathes life back into them.

3. **Desperate Measures and Extreme Consequences**: The fight against fate drives anti-social to extremes. They jeopardize their existence and their families. Consuming alcohol and drugs, they muster the courage to engage in criminal activities. Each act push es them closer to the edge, where life takes a perilous turn.

4. **Remember**, seeking help and opening up can be the first step toward healing and transformation.

**When Prostitution Becomes a Lifeline** For some, prostitution becomes a lifeline—a means to fulfill their needs. Once entrenched in this life, returning to normalcy seems impossible due to their circumstances.

**The Population Burden and Neglected Children** As the population grows, everyone plays their part, yet few consider how to raise and care for children. Even beggars find themselves responsible for large families. Addressing this challenge is a critical agenda.

**Parental Responsibility: A Lifelong Impact** Newcomers often bear the weight of their parents' choices throughout their lives, a silent criminal offense that goes unnoticed. Despite realizing their mistakes, parents continue down the same path, even when they struggle to provide basic necessities for their children. Loneliness pervades the childhoods of these kids, who often go without food and other essentials, creating a pitiful existence.

1. **The Silent Crime: Neglecting Vulnerable Lives** The gravest crime transcends borders and legal systems—it is the silent tragedy of young lives brought into this world without due consideration. Whether legally or illegally, when two young individuals become parents without assessing their financial stability, they inadvertently set the stage for a multitude of criminal situations. These innocent children, born into uncertainty, deserve better.

2. **Beyond Orphanages and Old-Age Homes: A Call for Accountability** Rather than relegating these young parents to orphanages or old-age homes, we must hold them accountable for their actions. Separating children and elders from their families, often without regard for their emotional well-being, perpetuates a cycle of trauma. Instead, we can create a protective unit—one that shields vulnerable lives, ensures safety, and offers a chance at a good life.

3. **Population Control and Responsibility** By controlling birth rates, we can mitigate the strain on resources caused by population growth. Simultaneously, we must rethink our approach to caring for elders. Entrusting their well-being to related family members rather than old-age homes can foster a sense of responsibility within our communities.

4. **The Unseen Suffering of Tomorrow's Hope** Across the globe, countless children suffer silently. They are the hopes of tomorrow, yet they endure hardship due to circumstances beyond their control. This situation breeds a criminal mindset—a desperate search for solutions, even if it means cheating others or resorting to desperate measures.

5. **A Call to Action**: We cannot ignore reality. Many offer money and food to those in need, but few raise their voices against this pervasive crime. Is it because society fails to recognize it as such? Let us collectively acknowledge this issue and work toward a world where every life is valued and protected.

**"Addressing Unwanted Births: A Collective Responsibility"** While many nations have laws in place to regulate birth rates, compliance remains low. Those who disregard these laws should be held accountable, not through imprisonment, but by assuming responsibility for the child until they reach adulthood.

Unplanned childbirth leads to a host of problems for both children and their parents. These children often face challenging circumstances, and their futures may be marred by poverty or unfavorable living conditions. Some even turn to anti-social behavior, becoming a burden on society.

To combat this issue, local units can take action independently in their unit. By raising awareness among their members, these units can collectively implement measures to control unwanted births. Marriages within the unit should be based not solely on age but also on the financial capacity of the couple, ensuring a stable environment for the child."

**Responsibility and Family Planning:** Young individuals should prepare to shoulder responsibility for their own families once they reach the age of majority and decide to marry. This responsibility extends to caring for their spouse and children, rather than the entire extended family. Neglecting this duty can adversely affect their children, and the relevant authorities will take action if necessary.

**Global Vigilance and Reporting:** According to established norms, a comprehensive network covers every nook and cranny of the world. No area remains unnoticed. Any activities occurring within this network should be promptly reported to the authorities.

**Support and Decision-Making:** As young adults mature, they become capable of managing their families. While they are part of this network, decisions are made collectively, and assistance is provided to them and their families. The network takes precautions to prevent hardships similar to those faced by the parents.

**Marriage and Childbirth:** Although there are no restrictions on marriage, the birth of a child should be postponed until the network is prepared to safeguard the family's well-being.

*Safeguarding the Nation: Implementing these measures through the network contributes to the nation's wellness and financial stability.*

**Youth Vulnerability and Criminal Exploitation:** Unfortunately, some children are exploited for criminal activities from an early age. Even adults, after rigorous training, are drawn into anti-social behavior. Often, lack of education and dire life circumstances force them to accept attractive yet dangerous offers.

Like the rural population, the kids are not capable of fighting against their fate. The government is doing many supports, but most of the time, it is reaching the wrong hands than the deserving.

Many malpractices are happening every day in the part of rural in its nook and corners are a well-known truth and are knowingly passing on their way. Many are starting orphanages and similar organizations for the sake of the poor rural population but it is benefiting very small sections that start that.

By the time the kids are grown up and start to be involved in many crimes, many are using their services to mint money. Such practices can possibly be stopped by the strong interference of unit management if the government supports them.

100% of inmates of the unit say 200 homes and its inmates turn to modernize and change the country basics to live in a calm and quiet way that lead a pleasant life among all.

Though there are many laws pertaining to childbirth and their protection none of the irresponsible are bothered. It is affecting the growth of kids until they matured they are just living without food, clothes, home and are totally in financial difficulties.

1.  **Challenges Faced by Rural Children:** The rural population, including children, often lacks the means to overcome their challenging circumstances. While the government provides support, unfortunately, these resources frequently end up in the wrong hands rather than reaching those who truly need them.

2.  **Malpractices in Rural Areas:** In the nooks and corners of rural regions, malpractices persist. Some individuals establish orphanages and similar organizations ostensibly to assist the impoverished rural population. However, these efforts often benefit only a small fraction of those in need.

3.  **Exploitation and Crime:** As these children grow up, they become vulnerable to exploitation. Some individuals exploit their services for personal gain, leading to involvement in criminal activities. To curb such practices, strong intervention from unit management is essential, supported by government initiatives.

4.  **Unit Inmates Striving for Change:** Remarkably, 100% of the inmates in our unit—approximately 200 homes—aspire to

modernize and transform the fundamentals of our country. Their vision is to lead peaceful, fulfilling lives.

5. **Neglected Child Welfare:** Despite existing laws safeguarding childbirth and child protection, irresponsibility persists. These neglected children face hardships, including hunger, lack of clothing, homelessness, and financial struggles, hindering their growth until they reach maturity.

**Remember:** *addressing these issues requires collective effort and a commitment to ensuring a brighter future for rural children.*

"This is a cross-section of the world – unwanted births are giving problems to entire homes and to the world as a whole. The pity stage without care from the parents really affects their childhood. Their experiences from situations mold them, and they live accordingly."

"In this cross-section of the world, unwanted births pose challenges for entire households and the global community. The absence of parental care during the vulnerable stages significantly impacts children's upbringing. Their life experiences are shaped by the circumstances they encounter."

"The economy of the nation/world is affected. It is not wrong to assert that parents who are incapable of properly raising their children should refrain from giving birth. Such situations bring sorrow to their lives, and the repercussions extend to the children who suffer throughout their existence."

"The economy of nations and the world at large bears the consequences. It is reasonable to argue that parents who lack the capacity to provide a proper upbringing should reconsider having children. Such decisions lead to personal anguish and perpetuate lifelong struggles for the offspring."

"Our population has increased significantly, surpassing what charitable efforts can handle. While there are numerous homes designed for orphans (including children, the elderly, and disabled individuals) worldwide, individualized care remains elusive due to the distinct functions of these institutions."

"Our population has surged beyond sustainable levels, straining the capacity of charitable initiatives. Despite the existence of various homes catering to orphans (including children, the elderly, and the disabled), personalized attention remains scarce, given the diverse roles these institutions serve."

"Insufficient funding for food and other essential needs exacerbates the plight of these homes. They resort to begging within their premises, entirely dependent on donations. Unfortunately, the collected funds often fail to directly benefit the inmates, a distressing reality."

"Inadequate financial resources for basic necessities compound the challenges faced by these homes. Residents resort to begging within their confines, relying solely on donor contributions. Regrettably, the funds collected do not always translate into meaningful welfare improvements for the inhabitants."

"Some high-level management oversees these organizations, yet the experiences of the residents remain strikingly similar. Despite varying circumstances, the outcomes persistently fall short of protective measures. Perhaps addressing the root causes from the outset is essential to achieving lasting change."

"Even with high-level management overseeing these organizations, the residents' shared experiences remain remarkably consistent. Regardless of situational differences, the outcomes consistently lack adequate protection. Perhaps a focus on identifying and addressing root causes early on is crucial for achieving meaningful transformation."

1.  **Responsibility and Care for Children**: Instead of merely forming organizations and protecting them, we should delve into the root

causes of the allegations. If the allegations are valid, real parents must take action without evading their responsibilities. Utilizing modern technologies and reintegrating children into society should be our primary goal.

2. **Shared Burdens and Systemic Challenges**: Why should the general public bear the burden of others' abandonment? The lack of a robust system leaves some individuals suffering since childhood. This perpetual problem forces many onto the streets daily, creating a heartbreaking scene.

3. **Protecting Children's Precious Years**: If someone wishes to handle this matter in a sacred way, that's a different perspective. However, we must not allow anyone to play with children's lives. They deserve proper care during their precious childhood years, even if they lack biological parents.

4. **Addressing Abandonment and Neglect**: Sadly, babies are sometimes discarded like trash or subjected to violence. Rather than focusing on parental fame or reputation, let's encourage responsible actions. Parents can deposit necessary funds and entrust a unit to care for their child. The child will grow up within the unit, receiving education, employment opportunities, and safety. The unit can request financial support from parents until the child reaches adulthood, ensuring their well-being.

**Ensuring the Welfare of Vulnerable Individuals** In order to promote the well-being of children, it is essential for the responsible unit to directly contribute to their benefit. These children should grow up alongside their peers, free from any sense of loneliness. Regular progress checks are crucial to assess the actual impact of these efforts.

However, a concerning trend has emerged: old-age homes, orphanages, and similar institutions are proliferating, such as mushroom huts for begging. The underlying poverty and helplessness have become news, evoking sympathy across the nation. Unfortunately, some unscrupulous individuals exploit these vulnerable situations for financial gain, disregarding the dignity of our society.

To address this, self-respecting and well-managed units must step forward. By doing so, they can take charge of substandard organizations within their localities. Despite existing laws meant to safeguard the rights of children and the elderly, these rights are often neglected. Instead of prioritizing legal entitlements, we should value their lives. Even properties designated for the elderly are sometimes taken away, leaving them without shelter.

The lack of an effective system to address such cases perpetuates the suffering of those in need. Sons and daughters, who owe their lives to their parents, sometimes abandon them during their most vulnerable moments without waiting for their final call.

This revised version emphasizes the importance of safeguarding vulnerable individuals and highlights the need for responsible action to protect their rights and dignity.

If any case related to any of our homes, we should collect and arrange to provide them shelter along with that home. This unit can protect such old-age and kids, handicapped, and autistic affected not directly but through their homes. The home is directly responsible to them, not the unit.

All necessary assistance with much responsibility will be extended by the unit including their medical expenses, etc. When the home to which they are related should be responsible to them, they will be happy and have a safety feeling than others take care of them.

The unit can give them maximum help and make them feel safe and should inspect their affairs periodically will feel much more security. To ascertain the progress and keep a record of that effect in their file whether it is positive or negative. If it is negative, the unit should entrust their neighbors more than once to watch the progress. You will get a correct result.

In any situation related to our homes, we should promptly collect and arrange to provide shelter for those affected. While this unit may not directly protect the elderly, children, handicapped individuals, and those with autism, it can indirectly support them through their homes if they are related to them.

The primary responsibility lies with the home itself, not the unit. However, the unit will extend all necessary assistance, including covering medical expenses. When the home to which they are connected takes responsibility for their well-being, they experience happiness and a sense of safety.

The unit strives to offer maximum help, ensuring their safety and periodically inspecting their affairs for added security. Keeping a record of their progress—whether positive or negative—is essential. In cases of negative progress, the unit should entrust multiple neighbors to monitor the situation, leading to accurate outcomes."

## "CARE FOR ABNORMALS AND BRING THEM BACK

*Every day, no matter how busy you are, someone must create opportunities for individuals to gather and interact with others or similar groups. If any of them are considered normal, they can be entrusted with tasks within the unit. By assigning simple responsibilities, we can enhance their IQ and develop their personal skills and abilities, freeing them from unwanted thoughts."*

## "CARE FOR INDIVIDUALS WITH SPECIAL NEEDS AND REINTEGRATE THEM

*amid daily business, it remains crucial to create opportunities for people to assemble and connect with others. For those who fall within the normal spectrum, entrusting them with unit tasks can serve as an ideal way to enhance their IQ and foster personal growth. By assigning simple responsibilities, we empower them, allowing them to break free from unwanted thoughts."*

Similar to addressing poverty, we must consider various vulnerable groups: children, the elderly, unmarried individuals, the sick, those affected by autism, and people with disabilities who require assistance. However, rather than exerting direct control, the unit should collaborate with related homes to provide support. If these individuals seek help through the unit office, the manager can facilitate assistance to their families.

It is essential not to assume responsibility for outsiders who are not directly connected to any member household. Such actions fall outside our established agenda.

*Unfortunately, the neglect of these marginalized lives significantly impacts the nation's image. Many of them roam the streets, exposed to hunger and deprivation, while others exploit their vulnerability. To address this, the unit can exercise full control when assisting its own member households. Additionally, periodic visits by doctors and nurses can enhance their sense of security, following the physician's recommendations.*

"Similar to addressing poverty, we must consider various vulnerable groups: children, the elderly, unmarried individuals, those who are sick, affected by autism, or dealing with mental health issues. The organization should take into account these individuals who require assistance from others. However, rather than exerting direct control, the unit should collaborate with related homes to provide support.

If these individuals seek help or assistance through the unit office, they can make requests. The manager can then facilitate necessary aid for needy families. Importantly, the unit should refrain from assuming responsibility for outsiders who are not directly connected to any member household. Such actions are not aligned with our agenda.

**Unit Governance and Responsible Practices** The units operate in accordance with local laws and regulations, ensuring that their members adhere to respectful conduct. These units play a crucial role in overseeing the lives of the underprivileged, safeguarding them within their own homes.

One of our primary objectives is to prevent births in families lacking responsible parents. These unplanned births not only impact the nation's integrity and prestige but also hinder its growth. Tourists and travelers visiting the area contribute to its development, and by addressing the root causes of unwanted pregnancies, we can allocate resources more effectively.

**Mercy Killing Implementation** If the government wish to implement the mercy killing very few of suffering horrible pain and sufferings can be avoided. In cases where the unit operates under a Mercy Killing system, patients suffering immensely are allowed to seek assistance. This compassionate approach, guided by medical advice, unit members, and relevant government departments, aims to alleviate severe suffering.

By applying logical thinking and practical solutions, we can create a healthier and more harmonious environment within our homes and the entire unit.

**Financial Considerations** While orphanages rely on public donations and other funding sources for their operations, the unit operates differently. As voluntary members, our financial stability remains unaffected by the types of expenses incurred.

# THE DILEMMA OF ORGANIZATIONAL FUNDING

Organizations often accumulate substantial funds through sympathetic appeals, but the utilization of these resources significantly impacts their growth and the well-being of their members or beneficiaries. Unfortunately, decisions regarding fund allocation are often made by a select few, sometimes leading to questionable practices.

Unlike individual units, where inmates or members directly participate in decision-making through discussions and meetings, larger organizations rarely involve their beneficiaries. Religious and political leaders, as well as wealthy individuals from the surrounding community, should not interfere in determining the needs of the inmates.

The fundraising methods employed by religious and political organizations often expose the vulnerabilities of their beneficiaries. Public sympathy is sought by highlighting the weaknesses and disabilities of these individuals, all in the pursuit of financial gain.

However, your organization takes a different approach. It avoids creating situations that resemble begging, preserving the dignity and respect of its members. Instead, consider exploring alternative avenues, such as engaging staff, volunteers, and maintaining proper financial records.

Furthermore, when forming a new unit, consider tracing the roots of relatives involved in similar orphanages. Their involvement could contribute significantly to the cause and help save those in need.

*If any individual were to come back to life, our unit would provide them with assistance and treatments through their related home.*

Many of the inmates in charitable organizations find themselves without work, confined to a limited area. Their lives become restricted, leading to idleness and a decline in health, rendering them inefficient.

Unfortunately, this approach doesn't foster growth; instead, it perpetuates laziness. Our unit operates differently. Each member actively contributes based on their health and abilities.

## UNIT'S ROLE IN CONTROLLING BIRTH RATES: UNDERSTANDING THE IMPACT

We the unit directly engage with our members to raise awareness about the risks associated with increasing birth rates. The unit emphasize the lifelong challenges a child may face. Additionally, the unit highlight parental responsibilities. Despite our efforts, if any member's household violates the unit's decisions, The unit allow reconsideration only once the unit achieves financial stability. Our struggle against poverty leaves us with no other recourse.

"We find ourselves already at the poverty level, and it is crucial that we do not burden our unit further by allowing excessive childbirth until we achieve financial stability—perhaps within the next 2 to 3 years. Additionally, we advocate for a one-child policy among our members.

When any member violates the established norms of our unit, they must face the consequences outlined in our punishment protocol. During this time, they cannot expect any support from the unit; this stance is non-negotiable. Their suspension remains in effect until the unit attains self-sufficiency.

Our unit diligently provides for its members, but the rising birth rates have strained our resources, making basic necessities like food increasingly scarce. To address this, we must actively work toward reducing the birth rate and hold parents equally accountable.

Parents must wholeheartedly embrace each child's responsibility; there can be no evasion. The unit will devise effective laws for implementation within our community. Otherwise, we risk bearing the consequences of someone else's reckless actions, jeopardizing both the unit and our children. We must prevent this tragic outcome.

*As for orphans—whether children or the elderly—they should no longer resort to begging or seek refuge in orphanages. Our shelter provides for all their needs, and henceforth, we shall care for these vulnerable individuals without burdening the unit further.*

Old-age parents and children related to our unit members should never suffer hunger or deprivation on the streets or in orphanages. It is the responsibility of each member to ensure their well-being. Regular visits by the unit manager will assess their welfare, and any suggestions to alleviate their suffering will be implemented within our homes."

*"The safety and well-being of our inmates is of utmost importance. We are committed to protecting them from sexual harassment, and any reported cases will be handled seriously by our managers and other team members. Our unit exists to promote the wellness of rural communities, ensuring that everyone receives equal benefits.*

To achieve this, we must address certain issues. Specifically, we need to discontinue the practice of admitting children, elderly individuals, or others into orphanages. While our unit has never entertained orphanages or similar organizations, we recognize the need to take action at our level.

*There is a concerning trend where religious, political, and other leaders shed tears for these vulnerable categories, often with ulterior motives. Going forward, our unit will genuinely support and protect them. Rather than encouraging donations to orphanages, which may promise a path to heaven, we aim to remove the orphanage system from our country entirely.*

Our unit's primary goal is to enhance the well-being of our members' homes. We appreciate the sincere efforts of our members, which contribute to the unit's progress. Through our work, we anticipate uplifting those below the poverty line by addressing cultural, financial, and educational needs."

1. **After Abolishing the Orphanage System**: Once the orphanage system is abolished, there will be no facility to admit children or elderly individuals for financial gain. The cost associated with these units is high, and they demand payment for survival. Consequently, admissions are now rare and anticipated.

2. Empowering Entire Villages: *Imagine if entire villages become self-sufficient through these units. Such a transformation could account for nearly 3/4th of the world's economic growth. Eliminating harmful habits from rural areas and promoting each village to surpass many cities is the ultimate dream.*

3. **Collective Progress and Interdependence**: *The progress signs exhibited by these units fill the entire world with pride. They also teach a valuable lesson:* interdependence and self-help *can achieve remarkable outcomes*

4. **Implementing Government Rules**: *The units play a crucial role in enforcing strict birth rate regulations. Despite rural populations often disregarding these rules, they still believe that following the unit's culture will lead them to a path of progress.*

5. **Unit As A Protector And Support System**: *This Unit Takes On The Responsibility Of Protecting Each Member Involved, Offering Support To Those Currently In Dire Situations.*

## EMPOWERING AWARENESS CLASSES FOR SELF-SUFFICIENCY AND RESPECT

Awareness classes within the unit have transformed its members into self-sufficient and self-respected individuals. Their focus lies squarely on the well-being of their families, steering them away from life's threats. By practicing responsibility, they prepare themselves to face the challenges inherent in their roles.

*Many, like parents who bear responsibility for their children's lives, these unit members are equally accountable to their organization. The unit's mission is to equip them with the skills needed to confront life's trials head-on. From rural areas, this collective effort promises to bring about a significant economic shift for our nation.*

Through education and heightened awareness, we hope to illuminate the distant consequences of unchecked birth rates. Poverty remains a stark reality, and the country's populace is acutely aware of its underlying causes.

While solutions may have existed for years, some clandestine forces have thwarted the implementation of necessary rules and laws. Despite this, a resilient few have managed to overcome adversity and lead more prosperous lives.

**The Consequences of Overpopulation** As the population grows, so does the prevalence of criminal behavior. Scarce resources drive some individuals to resort to cheating or criminal acts in order to acquire what they need. However, if we establish a system where everyone has equal access to facilities and resources, the temptation for trespassing or criminal behavior diminishes.

Unfortunately, enmity among people is on the rise. Factions form, conflicts escalate, and lives are lost—all in pursuit of looting the possessions of rival groups. The stark contrast between the rich and the poor exacerbates this situation. While some live lavishly, others struggle to find even basic sustenance.

In rural areas, hardworking individuals barely scrape by with one meal a day. Yet, they persist, forming alliances to overcome adversity. However, the trend of robbing others only perpetuates poverty. By killing or looting from fellow humans, one merely shifts the burden from one hand to the other, leaving the nation's economy stagnant.

*"The beneficiaries of such a threat can mint money or wealth, but you have no life—you are just a scapegoat suffering and ending your days in jail or some other way. This behavior not only impoverishes many other groups from whom you steal, but it also lacks consideration for a permanent remedy, wellness, or a peaceful life for all."*

"This unit thinks differently. We plan to offer a peaceful life to all our members and address their current sufferings. Instead of enriching ourselves by looting others' belongings, we aim to uplift them. When you recognize this reality through our collective efforts, you will change."

"As human beings, we have very little time allotted to us. Unfortunately, we often waste it by interfering in other's lives, exerting negative influence, causing harm, and controlling others. These actions not only disrupt our own peace but also impact our families directly or indirectly. Living peacefully for even an hour or a day becomes challenging."

"Ironically, while harboring grudges and planning to teach others, we forget the lesson that we've spent significant time without truly living—a peaceful life that ultimately amounts to nothing. It affects not only us but also those who support us. Perhaps our sons or relatives have lost their lives due to our influence."

**"If You Wish to Compete With Another,**

**Remember** *that both of you end up wasting energy chasing each other fruitlessly."*

## APPLICATION FORM

*(The application is attached elsewhere and can be detached and used for the registering purpose.)*

The comprehensive nature of this application form is essential because many of our members fall below the poverty level and may be eligible for government schemes. By providing detailed information in this application, you determine your eligibility to access government rights and claims.

**Government Support and Funding**: These resources are intended for less privileged members of unit with the goal of creating assets for them.

**Asset Creation**: These funds are used to create assets until they are on par with those held by others.

**Income Fund**: Once the unit reaches a certain level, a fund can be established from the income generated every year. It will help to avoid the differentiation among members.

**Lease and Adjustments**: At that point, lease agreements and other adjustments for equalize assets of all members can be permanently discontinued.

The government supports and funds are meant for the no privileged members among you so that amount to be used for creating assets to them. Until their assets reached equal to others and a fund to be create out of the units income for this purpose. Then the lease and other adjustments can be stopped forever.

As long as your unit remains financially stable, you can benefit from government financial support. Additionally, the unit can access government assistance on behalf of its members until it achieves financial soundness.

To streamline operations, we recommend registering and classifying members based on their qualifications, work experience, and skills.

Whether they are electricians, drivers, casual laborers, or other skilled or unskilled workers, proper allocation of tasks ensures efficient utilization of resources.

Furthermore, if there is surplus manpower within the unit, consider sharing it with neighboring units. This approach not only reduces unemployment but also minimizes idle days.

## RECORDS REGARDING UNIT MEMBERS

To establish this unit, we need to complete an application in the specified format, including all necessary details. Afterward, it should be signed, accompanied by a clear explanation of the unit's purpose as outlined in the bylaws. Each household must maintain a comprehensive file containing information about family members, their status, and a copy of the bylaws. These records serve as a permanent reference.

Every member's home should maintain meticulous records, ensuring that no essential information is overlooked. Similarly, each household can maintain a similar file. Once registered, the data should be uploaded to the unit's computer on a family-by-family basis. However, these details must not be exploited by any individual for personal gain except in critical situations. The privacy policy of the unit strictly prohibits sharing this information with others.

Furthermore, it is crucial to create backups of these records, securely stored under the joint custodians' supervision. These records remain relevant for the duration of the unit's existence.

"The responsibility of managing the unit and handling its confidential matters lies with either the unit manager or a designated manager. These sensitive affairs should be accessed using a secure password and the manager's thumbprint, ensuring that access is restricted to authorized personnel only. Exceptions may arise in cases involving legal proceedings, law enforcement, or government requirements.

The unit serves as a valuable resource for its members, allowing them to access benefits based on their eligibility as recorded by the government. Additionally, maintaining concise records for each member is essential for future reference. Details related to birth, death, marriage, and other family events must be diligently documented, including event dates and relevant particulars.

While recording these details, it's advisable not to omit any relevant information. Even seemingly minor particulars may prove crucial in the future. Timeliness is essential—updates should occur promptly whenever an event takes place. If necessary, such updates should pass through the unit office, ensuring accurate and up-to-date records.

Assigning this responsibility to a designated individual is crucial. They must diligently track events, noting dates, days, and other relevant information. By doing so, the unit can maintain a comprehensive database of its members, including educational backgrounds, employment status, and other relevant details.

NOTE: Tracking members' income over time will also serve as evidence of the unit's effectiveness in supporting and encouraging its members."

## ADVANCING TOGETHER: THE COLLECTIVE PROGRESS

Within the confines of a shared roof, families coexist as a joint unit, yet each maintains their own individual homes. In this harmonious arrangement, there is no clamor for pocket money or clandestine savings. Instead, the unit safeguards its finances diligently, ensuring that every rupee remains secure within its walls. For detailed financial records, one only needs to visit the unit office.

The latent potential of idle manpower, dormant for years, now finds purpose. By channeling this resource, the unit and its members unlock substantial savings. These funds, in turn, benefit the rural populace, bolstering the local economy and ensuring the unit's financial stability.

Much like your expenses accumulate, so too does your income. Within a span of 3 to 6 months, you witness the multiplication of your financial resources. As these microcosmic units thrive, they contribute to a macroscopic boost in the nation's economy. Census data reveals the pulse of rural areas—their economic health, growth trajectories, and financial well-being—all meticulously assessed.

The organization's modus operandi, its disciplined approach, serves not only its members but also the nation and the global community. Continuous improvement, a beacon guiding progress, proves more valuable than delayed perfection.

1. **Economic Transformation and Individual Profiles**: The remarkable leap of the economy from zero to exponential growth, coupled with diverse managerial approaches by both managers and subordinates, underscores the unique attributes of each team member. Their capabilities, skills, health, wealth, and lifestyle contribute to a compelling narrative.

2. **Environmental Impact and Ambiance**: Beyond the visible commendable growth in the region, the distinct environments and premises play a crucial role in shaping the overall ambiance. The dwelling houses of team members, along with the rich developments in the area, stand as commendable achievements.

3. **Unit Records and Personal Reflection**: The narrated growth stories should also manifest in the unit records. However, upon reflection, you may find yourself disappointed by the contrast with your previous life. Nevertheless, the newfound energy fuels your enthusiasm as you compare the current results with those from your earlier experiences.

# THE DATA FOR CENSUS

1.  **Population Count**: The primary purpose is to determine the total number of people residing in a specific area. This count helps allocate resources, plan infrastructure, and make informed decisions. Being the members of this unit is disciplined and everything about them are available in their unit office the availability of Census figures about them are very easy.

2.  **Demographic Data**: Censuses collect data on age, gender, ethnicity, education, occupation, and other relevant characteristics. This information aids in understanding the composition of the population and identifying trends.

3.  **Resource Allocation**: Governments use census data to allocate resources such as funding, services, and infrastructure. For instance, schools, hospitals, and public transportation systems are planned based on population distribution.

4.  **Policy Formulation**: Census data informs policy decisions related to healthcare, education, housing, and social services. It helps policymakers address specific needs and challenges faced by different groups within the population.

5.  **Redistricting**: Censuses play a crucial role in redrawing electoral boundaries. Accurate population data ensures fair representation in legislative bodies.

6.  **Historical Records**: Censuses provide valuable historical records. Researchers, genealogists, and historians use this data to study societal changes over time.

7.  **Emergency Preparedness**: During emergencies (such as natural disasters or pandemics), census data assists in disaster response planning and resource allocation.

**In summary:** *censuses serve as essential tools for understanding and managing populations, shaping policies, and ensuring equitable distribution of resources.*

## CENSUS INFORMATION FOR ENHANCED DATA COLLECTION

The data collected through these units plays a crucial role in providing the government with real-time information about every unit on a specific date. Unlike previous census efforts, these records offer comprehensive details about our rural areas, surpassing the limited scope of oral samples.

Notably, health-related information, including details about diseases, treatments, and blood groups, proves invaluable during hospitalization or medical emergencies. Additionally, these records aid in managing pandemic outbreaks and provide insights into progressive trends.

Furthermore, when the government implements awareness campaigns, vaccinations, or medication distribution, disseminating instructions to members becomes more efficient through these units.

Beyond these practical applications, these records also shed light on the transformation of individuals. From drug-addicted and lethargic individuals to active contributors with 100% productivity, their stories can be documented and celebrated.

In summary, these census units serve as powerful tools for data collection, healthcare management, societal progress, and many others.

## "FROM NEGLECT TO RECOGNITION: EMPOWERING A SECTOR"

In the pursuit of truth, one must remain honest not only to oneself but also to others. Reflecting on the collective efforts of various units, we discover a multitude of advantages. Among these, a previously overlooked sector has the potential to ascend from its depths of sorrow to prosperity. Remarkably, this transformation doesn't hinge on government intervention or external assistance;

rather, it rests upon the unwavering determination and confidence of its members.

*Now, these individuals stand recognized by society, their nation, and the global community. They've emerged as leaders, surpassing their fellow citizens by conquering adversity and embracing novel ideas. Their resilience serves as an enduring lesson—one that transcends time.*

*In the past, they burdened the government financially, necessitating the creation of numerous welfare funds. Unfortunately, due to inefficient distribution and a lack of beneficiaries' awareness of their rights, these efforts yielded limited results. However, a new paradigm emerges a system implemented through dedicated units poised to revolutionize their trajectory.*

## EMPOWERING COMMUNITIES THROUGH SELF-HELP SYSTEMS

In recent times, citizens have taken it upon themselves to contribute to the nation's economic growth. Rather than relying solely on government support, they actively participate in various ways to assist the government. One notable approach is the implementation of a self-help system within their communities.

Under this system, community members collaborate through a central unit. Decisions made by this unit are communicated to all members, ensuring transparency and collective involvement. To streamline administrative processes, homes within the community can designate a representative. This authorized member signs documents on behalf of the entire household, eliminating the need for every resident to attend each unit meeting individually.

Initially, all members sign the necessary applications and bylaws, granting authorization to one of their peers. However, this authorization remains flexible. Others can cancel it at any time, providing a valid reason. By carefully preserving the original documents with the unit, each home maintains a copy—a record specific to their residence.

Importantly, this system prevents any resolutions from passing without the knowledge and consent of all homes and members. Even seemingly trivial matters are subject to collective scrutiny. Furthermore, if circumstances change, the authorization can be transferred to another individual through a letter signed by over 60% of the home's members. *This ensures that no resolution is adopted without due diligence, regardless of external pressures.*

In summary, this self-help system empowers communities, fosters accountability, and ensures that decisions are made collectively and transparently.

**Avoid Unnecessary Burdens:** *It's essential to recognize that certain actions may have adverse effects. Therefore, it's wise to avoid unnecessary burdens.* Why sign an old record if you weren't actively involved? Let's focus on more meaningful endeavors.

**Our Collective Goal:** Together, we will achieve success. As you read this, understand that it's meant for you and your dedicated team. No one should take a single rupee from your hard-earned money. Guard against any attempts to exploit you. Our mission is simple: **enjoy life**.

**Unleashing Potential:** As members, we must acknowledge that the world has advanced significantly in the last century. Unfortunately, inefficiencies persist in rural areas. The untapped potential of our workforce is worth millions, yet it remains unnoticed.

**Embrace Life's Brevity:** Our time on Earth is short. Let's maximize it through hard work and legal means. There are countless resources around us—some still unrecognized. We can harness these resources to our advantage, turning them into opportunities for financial gain.

**Collective Solutions:** By coming together, we've found a remedy. Through discussions and meetings, we'll uncover new avenues for earning money. Whether it's innovative businesses, agriculture, or related activities, let's explore the possibilities.

**Remember**: *Life is short—make the most of it!*

1. **Fostering Active Participation:** We actively engaged all our unit members in various activities, ensuring their full participation. Additionally, we made them well-informed about every aspect of our unit. By emphasizing that this unit is not only their dream project but also a shared family asset, we instilled a sense of ownership and commitment.

2. **Effective Communication and Updates**: To keep everyone informed, we propose implementing a news dissemination system. Announcements during meetings would serve as an effective channel for updates. Furthermore, any critical information should be prominently displayed on the office notice board, ensuring even absentees stay informed.

3. **Seizing the Last Opportunity**: This is your final chance to succeed. As a unit, we must closely monitor developments and actively identify any actions that could undermine our efforts. Let's be vigilant and protect our collective goals.

4. **Abundant Opportunities within the Unit**: Looking ahead, there's no need to seek employment elsewhere. Our unit offers ample openings. You can leverage your skills and creativity to design and shape your own roles. These positions aren't just jobs; they provide a decent livelihood.

5. **Unit as a Resourceful Hub**: By collaborating and thinking collectively, we can transform our unit into a thriving hub. Let's create opportunities for the upcoming youth based on their diverse skills and imagination. Instead of seeking external employment, let's find fulfillment within our unit—*a heavenly way to live life*.

## THE TUG OF DISTANT DREAMS

**Why, indeed, do some seek faraway lands?** Perhaps it's the siren call of adventure, the promise of novelty, or the belief that elsewhere lays a better life. The grass, they say, is greener on the other side. Yet, as you rightly point out, there's a cost to such pursuits—a sacrifice of the known for the unknown.

## THE JOYS OF PROXIMITY

**But what about the joys of proximity?** The warmth of family, the laughter shared with neighbors, the familiar streets where memories bloom like flowers—these are treasures that cannot be quantified. When life offers abundance within arm's reach, *why wander afar?*

## RURAL RICHES AND BOLD CHOICES

**Ah, the rural landscape!** It's not just a backdrop; *it's a canvas waiting for brushstrokes of progress.* Your words resonate—the countryside should thrive, not merely survive. And indeed, it can. **Imagine a BONANZA,** *where innovation blooms like wildflowers after rain.*

## IDEAS SPROUTING IN THE FIELDS

Here are some seeds of possibility ideas that could transform rural life:

**Banana Wafer Making**: Slice under-ripe bananas, bathe them in syrup, and fry them into crispy wafers. A simple venture with sweet returns

**Small-Scale Super Shops**: As village life evolves, so do its needs. A well-stocked shop could be the heartbeat of your community. – and many more.

**Pet Bottles Production**: Polymer consumption is on the rise. Tap into the demand for PET bottles—a sustainable business.

**Vending Buffalo Milk**: Carefully tended buffaloes yield prized milk. *A venture that nourishes both body and pocket*

**Iodized Salt Production**: *A pinch of progress—essential for health, lucrative for business.*

**Handicraft items –** *Numerous items can be dealt with by the members is having good demand in cities*

**Tailoring –** *Is an everlasting demand, and many*

## THE TURNING POINTS

**Bold decisions**, my friend, are the compass needles of destiny. They steer us toward uncharted waters, where opportunity dances with uncertainty. So, let's chart a course—*a rural renaissance, a symphony of solutions.*

**In the Quiet of Countryside:** Remember, the unit isn't just a place; it's a promise. *A promise to many, it nurtures, uplifts, and weaves dreams into reality.* As the sun sets over familiar fields, let's sow hope, reap innovation, and watch our lives bloom like sunflowers reaching for the sky. Your journey waits.

## WITHOUT GOVERNMENT FINANCIAL SUPPORT: A PATH TO IMPROVED LIVES

The objective of this initiative is not to provide a luxurious lifestyle for rural people but rather to offer a satisfactory existence free from hunger, poverty, and scarcity. The unit's primary focus should be on addressing immediate needs, starting from day one. When mutual assistance becomes a reality, other challenges can be more effectively managed.

**Our approach should be gradual**: Prioritizing access to clean drinking water and improving living conditions for those in poverty takes precedence. In subsequent chapters, we will delve into comprehensive solutions. While children's education remains a critical concern, our immediate priority lies in alleviating their hunger and poverty, even if it means sacrificing their educational needs temporarily.

These multifaceted issues cannot be resolved all at once. Patience and resilience are essential as we work toward a better future for those affected.

This unit is giving importance and taking it as a major issue in the lives of the members rather than their children's education. We need to consider the financial stability of the inception unit. However, we cannot address all the hindrances faced by rural populations simultaneously.

Only once the financial position improves can we focus on children's education. Detailed information about children's education will be provided on an upcoming page.

We must find a permanent solution to unemployment among villagers and rural populations. Since many of them are poor and uneducated, we should introduce work opportunities related to agriculture and other tasks that do not require advanced skills from the outset.

The unit prioritizes employment based on individuals' education levels. Even illiterate members of the unit receive offers, especially for civil works. Thus, from day one, we aim to address the unemployment problem.

During the initial stage of the unit, there are numerous unskilled tasks to be performed, including work in agricultural lands, warehouses, stores, and construction. All construction projects, such as shops, offices, and warehouses, are executed by unit members.

## EDUCATION AND EMPLOYMENT: A TRANSFORMATIVE JOURNEY

In bygone eras, education was a distant dream for the less fortunate. Opportunities were scarce, and facilities were virtually non-existent. However, times have changed. Today, educational facilities are within walking distance for many, bridging the gap between aspiration and reality.

Within our community, employment opportunities abound. Whether you're skilled, unskilled, or educated, there's a place for you. The unit not only offers a decent livelihood but also supports the education of members' children, covering related expenses.

As we welcome new members, we ensure they have sustenance and work from day one. Preparations are underway—establishing shops, storage spaces, and other infrastructure. Tools and implements are procured to maintain quality and efficiency.

Educated members play a crucial role. They share their expertise with less experienced peers, whether it's teaching the alphabet, mathematics, or other essential skills. By doing so, they contribute to the unit's growth and empower others to follow suit.

## EVENING CLASSES: UNLOCKING KNOWLEDGE ANYWHERE

In our unit, we encourage everyone who wishes to learn to participate in evening classes. These classes are not bound by location; you can attend them from anywhere. While theoretical knowledge is essential, practical experience plays a crucial role in understanding complex concepts. It's like grasping the essence of a subject through hands-on practice.

When selecting staff or members for training, consider their physical well-being after a long day of work; attending a class can be challenging. We don't want anyone to lose out due to exhaustion. Our class training personnel take care of this aspect. They assist in teaching and help each member improve their skills. The goal is to enhance the quality of our unit as a whole. Moreover, they empower individuals to handle tasks independently, even in their absence. Their capability becomes a source of pride for us all.

Now, let's talk about our collective purpose. As part of this unit, each of you will contribute to something greater. Affluence and position are not the sole motivators. Our work goes beyond serving the nation or the public—it's about safeguarding our families. Just as the affluent prioritize their loved ones, our unit members share the same intention. Education becomes our shield, allowing us to earn and protect our families. It's the path to a lavish life.

Through this unit, you'll not only save but also earn for your future needs. The education you've acquired can be put to practical use here. Consider it an opportunity to elevate your rural area, making it a place where living lavishly is within reach.

## EDUCATION AND PRACTICAL SKILLS: BUILDING A COHESIVE UNIT

If you are educated, your skills serve as a catalyst for your endeavors, contributing to the formation of a cohesive and morally sound unit. This unit, shaped by its members, becomes a vital force for individual well-being. Basic education equips members with the tools needed for a standard of living, while their inherent and acquired skills require continuous honing.

To ensure the unit's effectiveness, every member must actively participate in its practice. Regularly allocating work across all sections allows familiarity with diverse tasks. Consider the example of doctors: they are compelled to practice in rural areas for a specified period. This commitment ensures that rural communities receive quality medical care, often relying on government hospitals where treatments are free compared to urban centers.

The underlying message is clear: education doesn't exempt you from practical responsibilities. Whether you hold qualifications or not, you may find yourself working in agriculture, managing stores, or overseeing logistics. Your skill set, combined with practical experience, enables you to identify defects that an unskilled person might overlook.

Even officers within the unit should engage in fieldwork through rotational assignments. This firsthand experience ensures that everyone becomes proficient in running the unit independently when others are absent. Mere high-ranking positions without foundational knowledge hinder effective management. If someone misrepresents an issue, lacking relevant skills prevents accurate assessment.

Remember, *education isn't just about theory—it's about applying knowledge to real-world scenarios, regardless of your role within the unit.*

## EMBRACING VERSATILITY: ENHANCING SKILLS AND BUILDING A BRIGHT FUTURE

In any organization, whether public or private, there's no need to feel ashamed about attending to various tasks. The ability to handle diverse responsibilities is a strength, not a weakness. Consider your own business: you can perform any job within it. This practice not only boosts your skills and abilities but also brightens your future prospects.

## KEY PRACTICES FOR SUCCESS

1. **Work Allocation**: Regularly allocate work in alternate intervals, regardless of merit or physical limitations. Sometimes, those who face challenges may surprise us by solving issues more effectively than others.

2. **Unity and Collaboration:** Within our unit, the presence of experienced and skilled members from various sections ensures smooth operations. The collective effort of all team members ensures that the unit's business remains unaffected.

3. **Skill Enhancement**: Allocating work across different sections also enhances individual inborn skills and efficiencies. Over time, our unit can boast fully trained workers who have rotated through various roles.

4. **Expertise Across Sections**: Our Members' Expertise Spans All Aspects Of The Unit's Business. Their Familiarity With Our Operations Is Both Our Luck And Our Pride.

5. **Regular Rotation**: To foster adaptability, we should practice allocating work among all sections every three months or even more frequently. This approach equips members to handle any section independently.

6. **Molding Capable Individuals:** By embracing diverse responsibilities, our unit molds members who can confidently face any challenge—both within the organization and in their personal lives.

**Remember,** *versatility and continuous learning are the keys to success.*

## ANOTHER PURPOSE BEHIND THIS ENDEAVOR

One of the primary intentions behind this initiative is to cleanse immature minds of ego. The notion that one's accomplishments solely depend on oneself is flawed. In reality, success often hinges on the collective efforts of many. By recognizing this, we aim to foster a spirit of cooperation and mutual support.

**Ego Clash: A Detriment to Progress:** Ego clashes can be detrimental to personal growth, career advancement, and overall well-being. To combat this, consider engaging in an internal struggle against your own ego. Acknowledge that your achievements are intertwined with the contributions of others. <u>Our ancestors, lacking this awareness, endured unnecessary suffering</u>.

**Unity and Efficiency:** Regardless of size or stature, no one among you is inherently superior in their work. While someone may excel in their domain, they cannot surpass your abilities in your own field. Our unit is formed by setting aside ego and enmity. Our shared goal is collective progress.

**Avoiding Ego Clashes:** Within our ranks, ego clashes are strictly prohibited. Such conflicts not only harm individual careers and relationships but also jeopardize the very foundation of our unit—a structure built through the collective toil and determination of its members.

**Inclusion and Decision-Making:** Even if someone hesitates to join us initially, we must remain open-minded. Selecting 200 members is no small task, and allowing time for decisions ensures a thoughtful and committed group.

*Let us march forward together, united and ego-free, toward growth and success.*

We are in the process of selecting 200 members for a unit. It is customary that when someone expresses interest in joining later, we need to either rewrite the bylaws or reserve space for them. Therefore, we allow potential members a few days to consider their decision. If you find this approach useful, you can share a copy of the bylaws with them.

However, there's a caveat: once bank financing is sanctioned, we cannot add new members. Those who wish to join the unit can do so after a minimum of three years. Additionally, any properties beyond the minimum holding requirement can be considered leased, and an appropriate amount must be paid to these members.

The purpose of this process is to equalize property ownership among all members. Extra funds, whether from government sources or other funding, can be used to gradually offset the lease payments until they are fully paid off.

Why the three-year waiting period? Initially, the unit is not expected to pay lease fees due to its other commitments. The lease terms are mentioned elsewhere.

For members who choose not to avail discounts on purchases, food, and accommodations, the corresponding amount should either be paid or credited to their unit account each month. <u>If they decide to withdraw the money, they can do so through the bank.</u>"

"The funds entrusted to the unit by its members should accrue interest, as is customary for deposits. This interest rightfully belongs to the depositors and should be disbursed accordingly.

Within the unit, there may be individuals who possess substantial wealth. You can introduce the concept of the unit to them. Occasionally, there are land and property owners who lack caretakers. In such cases, you can extend an invitation for them to join the unit. However, if they decline, there is no need to persist.

Our unit operates as a voluntary association for the collective well-being of its members. We do not compel anyone to join. However, we may encounter challenges when dealing with properties owned by non-members within our unit boundaries. Maintaining and handling these properties can be complex. In such situations, the unit has two options: either purchase the property or exchange it for another.

Lease payments made on these properties serve as adjustments to balance property holdings among members. If we decide to sell a property at the prevailing market price, the unit can facilitate the transaction. If affordability becomes an issue, selling to a third-party while recovering the lease amount paid to the previous owner is a viable solution. Additionally, if the new owner chooses to join our unit, we can assist them by providing the lease amount, even for land purchases."

1. **Property Ownership for Outsiders**: If there are properties owned by individuals who are not members of our organization, they can purchase agricultural land or other types of land within the unit limit after three years. Alternatively, if the outsider is willing to lease the land, you can proceed with that arrangement and cultivate crops suitable for that specific land.

2. **Dealing with Outside Landowners**: In many cases, outside landowners either lease their property to our unit or sell it. As the unit manager, it is essential to take the initiative in such situations. Sometimes, similar cases involving our members and other units should be resolved amicably

3. **Financial Safety Measures**: Until you achieve financial stability, consider negotiating with the landowner. You can propose a lease agreement for three years or even a sale agreement, paying an advance amount. Additionally, other members who are interested in purchasing the land should be involved to facilitate the process.

4. **Land Allocation for Landless Members**: For members without land, approach the local government office to explore land allotment options. Government-owned lands can be allocated in the names of eligible landless members' households.

# THE UNIT MANAGER: AUTHORITY AND RESPONSIBILITY"

1 The **Unit Manager** wields supreme authority within the unit. With the power to oversee unit members, financial matters, and project viability, their role is pivotal. Regular member meetings, facilitated by the manager, allow decisions to be made collectively. Given the manageable size of the unit (comprising only 200 houses), convening meetings is straightforward.

2 Unit members place unwavering faith in their manager, akin to passengers trusting a captain or driver. Their lives are intrinsically tied to this leadership. However, any betrayal—whether by turning into a deceptive politician or otherwise—has severe consequences. Members won't pardon such transgressions, even if it means forsaking divine intervention.

3 Consider the magnitude of a united group—more than 1000 strong—against a deceitful manager. The repercussions could be catastrophic, affecting not just the manager but their entire family. The unit provides everything, and blind obedience to the manager's orders is the norm. But honesty and impartiality are paramount. A straightforward approach ensures a lavish life for the manager and their family.

4 Before assuming the mantle of responsibility, prospective managers must weigh the cost. While personal expenses matter little to the unit, revealing secrets or acting against its interests can irreparably harm the manager's life. Individual members, each with unique perspectives, require regular engagement. If an expensive initiative benefits all, it's worth pursuing.

**Remember,** *the journey begins with effort, but the rewards can be everlasting.*

## ASSUMING LEADERSHIP: A WEIGHTY RESPONSIBILITY

Undertaking a leadership role within a unit carries inherent risks. Honesty is paramount—both toward the unit and its members. Before assuming charge, reflect deeply on your commitment. A misguided decision could spell disaster for everything associated with you.

The post you're stepping into holds immense respect among unit members, but it demands qualities like education, experience, and sacrifice. These are non-negotiable essentials.

The unit's trust in you is profound. They've entrusted their all based on the belief that you and they are part of a family, transcending past transgressions. As you enjoy the privileges and benefits, remember that this trust is a precious gift.

## MANAGERIAL INTEGRITY AND MEMBER DEPENDENCE

The unit manager must emerge from within the unit itself. Your honesty extends beyond mere words—it encompasses treating other members as family. They rely on you, believing you'll shield them from harm. Their hard work and efforts deserve your protection. Should they find themselves at their wits' end, desperation may drive them to extreme measures.

## INFORMED CONSENT AND COLLECTIVE DECISION-MAKING

Before embarking on any project, transparency is key. Gather all members for a general meeting. Share project details openly, ensuring everyone is informed. Obtain their consent through signed agreements. If multiple projects align, consider consolidating approvals to save time. In our unit's unique context, where governance is absent, every member's signature matters.

**Remember**, *no project should favor a select few families—it's about collective benefit.*

**Responsibilities of the Unit Manager:** As the unit manager, you wield authority over the unit members. It is your duty to closely monitor the unit's finances, resources, and project viability. Never approve a project unless it directly benefits the members within a short timeframe. While you lead the unit's growth, remember that you are accountable to them. Avoid any unethical practices that might lead to legal disputes. The consequences for you and your supporters will be severe, especially now that the unit has expanded from a small family of 4-5 to a formidable group of thousands. Their collective strength ensures they won't tolerate deception, even in their last chance to thrive.

**Effective Communication and Decision-Making:** Should you wish to propose additional initiatives or implement changes through the unit, consider sharing legally acceptable ideas during general body meetings. Alternatively, convene a comprehensive gathering to discuss such matters.

**Remember**, *the manager's role encompasses many responsibilities beyond mere oversight.*

**Addressing Anti-social Behavior:** Dealing with anti-social elements within the unit can be facilitated by other members. If you offer a guaranteed solution, they will likely accept it. The unit itself serves as the guarantee you must provide to these members. Given their history of disappointment due to past deceptions, altering their mindset won't be an easy task.

## MANAGERIAL INITIATIVES

The urgency is palpable—the unit cannot afford to wait any longer. The funds, sourced from members and secured through a bank loan, serve a specific purpose. Now, the onus lies with you to transform this financial backing into success.

**Remember**, *it's merely a loan, and repayment is imminent.*

As the manager, you hold the key to maximizing support from all members. Vigilance is crucial—keeps a close eye on absentee participants from the outset. Encourage their active involvement, for within the dormant lies untapped potential. Once they engage in unit activities and contribute productively, they become valuable assets. Their unique life experiences enrich the unit far more than others.

However, there's a common tendency among men: free money often fuels extravagant spending. This phenomenon extends to rural funds disbursed by the government. Instead of channeling these resources effectively, recipients divert them for other purposes. Government schemes rarely reach the grassroots-level, and their inadequacy adversely impacts local projects.

The real beneficiaries—the deserving categories—often lack awareness of their rights and entitlements. They struggle to assert their claims. But now, this unit will champion their cause. Dormant members will be reinvigorated, and their properties will be harnessed collectively. No longer limited by individual constraints, they'll collaborate systematically. With the combined efforts of the bank's funding and the unit's initiatives, the rural landscape can flourish and progress.

**Empowering Rural Areas and Our National Growth:** Despite past challenges and instances of looting, we remain resilient. Our abundant resources are scattered far and wide, waiting to be harnessed. It's time to unite and elevate rural areas, propelling the nation to new great heights. Each piece of land, each unit, should be more than functional— it should be ornamental, adorned with infrastructure that enhances its beauty. No property shall remain barren; every inch of soil will yield a crop. Our vision includes glowing premises, pristine environments, and contented inhabitants.

**"The Crucial Role of Government:** *By facilitating the establishment of numerous units in rural areas, the governments can reap significant benefits.* Over a five-year plan*, it can harness these advantages.*

**Staff Selection: A Strategic Endeavor:** Running a business involves assembling the right team. Decisions cannot be impulsive; they require thoughtful planning. First, identify what your unit aims to launch. Based on these goals, create a comprehensive list of staff roles. But here's the challenge: we have a diverse workforce, each member possessing unique skills and abilities. Our past inefficiencies have cost us valuable manpower. Now, we must allocate positions wisely. In the inaugural general meeting, decide on plans, estimates, and who will shoulder official responsibilities. Let's prepare meticulously, ensuring every staff member finds their place in this dynamic journey.

**Uploading Member Details for Efficiency:** In the modern era, computerization has revolutionized the way we manage information. It's time to leverage this technology for the benefit of our organization. By uploading member details to the computer system, we can streamline processes and access crucial information effortlessly.

Imagine having educational qualifications, age categories, and other relevant data at your fingertips, available for each section and position within the unit. This transition from manual record-keeping to digital access will enhance efficiency and accuracy.

## RECRUITMENT AND UNIT MANAGEMENT

When recruiting for our unit, we must carefully select a principal officer and unit manager. These individuals play a pivotal role in overseeing unit affairs. They are the driving force behind the unit's development. As we consider candidates, honesty should be the primary qualification.

Honesty fosters trust among team members and ensures transparent operations.

**Moving Forward with Trust Registration:** Once we've formed our unit, the next step is trust registration. Gather all members for a meeting and pass a resolution. Prepare duplicate copies—one for the bank and the other for our unit's records. With these documents in hand, approach a local bank for financial support. Consider utilizing the overdraft facility, which aligns well with our unit's nature.

Additionally, prepare project reports and estimates before meeting with the bank manager. If any lawyers are part of our group, involve them in the compliance procedures and documentation related to the bank advance.

**Remember**, *our collective past doesn't define us; it's our commitment to honesty and collaboration that will shape our unit's future.*

**Legal Matters and Trust Registration**: Lawyers play a crucial role in preparing the registration of trusts and related documents. Once this initial step is completed, ongoing formalities must be meticulously handled in a systematic manner. Legal matters, including the submission of documents to government and semi-government offices, as well as land-related rights, need to be addressed.

Additionally, any excess land, especially government-owned parcels, should be accounted for and brought to the government's attention. If your unit is involved in such land, consider seeking regularization from the government. Legal experts can provide remedies for various legal matters.

**Responsibilities of an Assistant Manager**: The Assistant Manager position is essential for the smooth functioning of any organization. While not always required from the outset, an Assistant Manager steps in when the Manager needs support. Here are the key responsibilities of an Assistant Manager:

**Staff Management**: The Assistant Manager must be educated and capable of efficiently managing staff. This includes handling day-to-day operations, maintaining accounts, and ensuring data is accurately uploaded into the computer system.

**Qualifications and Equivalence**: The Assistant Manager should possess qualifications equal to those of the Manager. They are directly involved with unit members, staff, business clients, and customers. Maturity and politeness are essential traits.

**Promotion from Within**: Existing inspectors who meet the eligibility criteria can be promoted to the Assistant Manager role. This approach avoids unnecessary waiting periods and utilizes the experience gained within the unit to efficiently manage its affairs.

1. **Building Strong Relationships**: By fostering close relationships with each and every member of the unit, you can effectively address most of their issues directly. If necessary, seek ratification from the manager. Your dedication to helping the unit thrive is crucial.

2. **Utilizing Skills for Unit Growth**: Your skills play a pivotal role in the unit's success. Whether it's related to fieldwork, crop management, industrial production, material procurement, or sales, ensure that all processes flow through the unit.

3. **Supervision and Daily Discussions**: While there are specialized sections and officials overseeing various aspects, your active supervision ensures the unit's smooth functioning. Regular discussions with subordinates about daily business contribute to your overall success.

4. **Acknowledging Contributions**: Appreciate staff members when their actions lead to greater benefits for the unit compared to previous teams. Simultaneously, address any shortcomings or faults in their services that impact the unit.

5. **Active Involvement and Encouragement**: Engage directly with production areas and interact with third parties, including staff members and other employees. Your indirect encouragement fosters enthusiasm and motivation.

6. **Genuine Patience and Consideration**: Display genuine patience when dealing with unit members. This quality is essential for effective leadership and team dynamics.

7. **Inspectors:** All members, regardless of gender, have the authority to review the day-to-day accounts. They can do so directly or through other members or inspectors based on their qualifications and experience. The unit manager compiles a list of inspectors for approval during members' meetings.

If any errors or malpractices are detected, they should be promptly reported to the unit manager. Remember that the unit is your responsibility, and you should never attempt to shield anyone or keep secrets. Doing so could impact your career and even lead to consequences for your family.

Furthermore, eligibility for promotions, higher grades, increments, and other benefits is contingent upon your actions. If anyone authenticates an account for personal gain or causes losses to the unit, the responsible inspector must rectify the situation. In such cases, the entire family's membership may be temporarily suspended until the issue is resolved.

Honesty is the core expectation from all members—both staff and officials. Your commitment to the unit will propel you to unexpected heights.

**Remember,** *fellow members are like family, and maintaining integrity is our primary agenda.*

## WORK EXPERIENCE

The unit should utilize all members, regardless of their educational background, to gain practical experience. Assign those tasks in areas such as agriculture, shopping malls, or wherever their health permits. It is essential to maintain a record or register of their work, which should be updated promptly by the manager or supervisor.

Additionally, the unit should establish a system for recognizing and rewarding outstanding achievers among the members. Consider offering increments, promotions, or gifts based on their demonstrated skills to motivate and encourage them.

Apart from accounting, extensive qualifications are not necessary. By providing opportunities across various portfolios within the unit, all members can gain valuable experience in different sections. *This approach will enhance their capabilities and empower them to run the unit independently.*

## MEMBER PROGRESS RECORD

To ensure government support for eligible individuals and maintain comprehensive records, it is essential to document various details related to our members. These records encompass educational backgrounds, dates of birth, marital status, and any other relevant information. By digitizing this data and storing it in our computerized system, we can harness their skills for future endeavors or consider them for promotions.

Within the unit records, we must capture family-specific data about each member. Whether positive or negative, a brief description of each individual's attributes should accompany their records. Encouragingly all members are encouraged to take the initiative and register their details with the unit office.

Additionally, we need to maintain an up-to-date overview of the unit's progress. This includes tracking stock levels, purchases, sales, ongoing projects, and daily or weekly developments. While these details remain confidential, they should be shared transparently with all members.

Regarding individual members, it is crucial to document their experiences and skills demonstrated during various projects. This record will prove invaluable when utilizing their services in the future. Furthermore, whenever significant events occur, we should promptly record the abilities and achievements of each member and communicate this information to them.

## EFFECTIVE PROJECT EXPENSE MANAGEMENT

Accurate project expense tracking is crucial for successful project management. Whether it's a large-scale initiative or a smaller project, managing costs ensures that resources are utilized efficiently and that the project stays within budget. Let's delve into the key aspects of project expenses and how to handle them effectively.

## UNDERSTANDING PROJECT EXPENSES:

**Direct Expenses:** These costs are directly tied to the project itself. Examples include specialized software, contractor hours, travel expenses, meals, and mileage. Direct expenses can be either fixed (unchanging) or variable (dependent on market conditions).

**Indirect Expenses:** These costs aren't directly linked to the project but still need to be paid. They include rent, support staff salaries, utilities, and software licensing fees, advertising, office supplies, and legal fees. Like direct expenses, indirect costs can also be fixed or variable.

**Daily Records and Vouching:** Properly recording project expenses is essential. Update records daily to maintain an accurate financial trail.

Given the bulk of money involved in projects, meticulous vouching and documentation are crucial. Any questions or disputes from team members should be addressed promptly by the concerned officials or unit managers.

**Encouraging Team Members:** The success of any project lies in the collective effort of team members. Encourage them in their work, especially when they exhibit special skills.

Recognize development work that stands out. Consider giving gifts and presents to team members and their families. Maintain a special book or digital folder to record these events.

**Uplifting Inborn Skills:** Our aim is *to empower team members. By nurturing their inherent talents, we brighten their future. Let them break free from limiting mindsets and recognize their value to the unit, the nation, and beyond.*

**Remember:** *effective expense management contributes not only to project success but also to the growth of members.*

# CHAPTER IX

# THE COUNTRYSIDE WILL THRIVE

As humanity increasingly relies on nature, it discovers pathways to robust health and strength—from childhood to old-age—through the utilization of various medicinal plants and trees. These natural remedies shield us from diseases, rendering hospitals and treatments less necessary.

In rural homes and fields, people engage in activities that keep their bodies warm and fit. They devise strategies to combat pandemics, effectively containing outbreaks within specific households. By restricting entry, they safeguard themselves and others from the negative impact of contagious diseases.

The essence of a nation's freedom lies in the well-being of its citizens. Yet, the scarcity of food and even clean drinking water persists, affecting lives for years. Many openly protest against government inadequacies. Despite our independence, government initiatives aimed at uplifting rural areas and improving lives often fall short of their intended impact. The remedy remains elusive.

Amidst this struggle, unscrupulous individuals adulterate food products to profit, compromising public health. However, a new approach emerges, prioritizing healthy sustenance for all. Rather than diminishing life, we seek to enhance it—nourishing our communities and controlling population growth through mindful choices.

## THE CHALLENGES OF RURAL LIFE

In bygone days, wealth existed, but people hesitated to reveal it. Few openly acknowledged their affluence, fearing that others would scrutinize their high standard of living. Consequently, they refrained from flaunting their income, even though they worked hard to earn it.

From childhood, children imbibed the wisdom of frugality. They were taught to prioritize essentials over extravagant clothing, often handed down from older family members. Adaptability became their hallmark, and they accepted their circumstances without complaint.

Despite enduring various hardships, individuals strived to maintain their dignity. However, navigating the complex web of societal expectations and restrictions posed challenges. Those who faced adversity, especially by the age of 30, encountered numerous trials

## THE STRUGGLE FOR RURAL DEVELOPMENT

Government initiatives allocate substantial funds for rural development. Unfortunately, the implementation often falls short due to reliance on external staff unfamiliar with the local context. These outsiders lack genuine interest in the progress of areas beyond their own.

Despite the government's sincere efforts, the intended beneficiaries rarely receive the full benefits. The focus remains on remote regions where officials hesitate to work. Basic necessities are scarce, and the environment is neglected, discouraging anyone from residing there.

The lives of these secluded communities remain hidden from the authorities responsible for their welfare. Their existence defies conventional norms, offering a unique perspective on human survival.

The government wishes to implement its schemes for the development of the area and the well-being of families residing there. However, the benefits have not effectively reached them, and many remain unaware of the government's offerings. Some intermediaries are taking advantage of this situation.

Going forward, a dedicated unit will oversee everything, ensuring that all benefits promptly reach individual families. This unit has already taken charge of addressing the living conditions in these remote areas. Its unique setup sets it apart from any previous practices.

The unit's residents will be under its care from the very beginning. Another advantage is that most unit members are familiar with each other and the challenges they face due to their shared locality.

As a cohesive community, they will support one another, sharing concerns and solving problems through the unit. The intention is to foster collaboration and eliminate further issues. Each member has voluntarily joined and takes ownership of the unit.

1. The unit strictly focuses on matters related to its purpose and does not interfere in other affairs. Its formation aims to address specific issues faced by the underprivileged living in remote areas, working toward the well-being and upliftment of its members.

## TAKING CARE OF DESERVED WELFARE: A RURAL UNIT'S MISSION

The members of this unit are committed to wholeheartedly serving their community. The unit's bylaws are thoughtfully designed, ensuring that each member's rights are respected and interconnected with others who run their businesses independently. The unit's primary focus is on rural areas, where it strives to improve the well-being of the countryside population.

However, being a public entity, the unit faces challenges in safeguarding its resources. There's a risk of exploitation by those experienced in such matters, especially when funds are allocated for specific purposes like a father's medical treatment. Many rural residents have not availed themselves of government funds for their wellness, leading to stagnant lives. This unit aims to change that by utilizing resources effectively and aligning with the government's vision.

## EMPOWERING RURAL COMMUNITIES: THE ROLE OF THE UNIT

Now, let's consider a transformative approach for the countryside and its families. The **Unit** has the potential to revolutionize our country by providing numerous amenities and facilities. Imagine a team of educated individuals from the village population stepping forward, taking initiative in small areas of the countryside. By forming this unit, we can elevate our nation's standard of living to a world-class level.

**Remember**, *facing adversity is part of the journey. People may criticize, challenge, or doubt you, but your strength and resilience define your success. Let's combat the inertia in rural areas, reshaping mindsets, and leaving a lasting mark of progress.*

Please the paragraphs many politicians are born for the whole but none of them think about their house, their neighbors their area because their responsibilities are more than that vast. Now we are dependent we have no such a huge responsibility to face. Nobody realized that wellness should start with our family and neighbors, and a certain area should be yours.

If you are self-sufficient, that effect will lead to the nearest areas and others. At least a few of you think about a change in you. We can directly think about how we can uplift each of your lives with the available resources. It is our responsibility, and it leads to success.

We are well aware that none of you can make a change in the entire world at a time, but it is possible if you take responsibility for small pieces of land that can develop. A vast area that can develop through this movement is our desire for many such pieces of land in our world.

One by one, the hazards to meet, poverty, scarcity of even drinking water, and many other needy demands of the public are to be solved yourselves. We have to attain our target through the joint venture, and many small pieces of land and the inmates of that area can be developed in a possible modern way without scarcity for anything.

One of the agendas of the unit is to throw away the anti-social activists from the unit limit. The activists are very few but through their typical tricks, they frighten all the villagers. None of the rural are ready to go against them because they either to avoid a show or are afraid of them.

## "EMPOWERING LOCAL COMMUNITIES: A CALL TO ACTION"

In our political landscape, leaders often bear the weight of the entire nation, yet they sometimes overlook the smaller, more immediate spheres of influence—their own homes, neighborhoods, and local areas. These responsibilities extend far beyond their official duties. As citizens, we find ourselves dependent on these leaders, but our individual responsibilities are not as vast.

It's time to recognize that wellness begins at home, within our families and neighborhoods. Each of us should consider a specific area as our own—a place where we can make a difference. When we become self-sufficient, that positive impact ripples outward, benefiting neighboring regions and beyond. Even if only a few of us embrace this mindset, it can spark meaningful change.

Our collective responsibility lies in uplifting lives using the resources available to us. Success is born from these efforts. While we may not individually transform the entire world overnight, we can certainly make a significant impact by taking charge of smaller parcels of land. Imagine a vast network of interconnected communities, each thriving and evolving through our shared commitment.

Addressing challenges one step at a time, we must tackle issues like poverty, water scarcity, and other pressing needs. By collaborating on joint ventures, we can develop these smaller areas in modern, sustainable ways. Let's create a world where scarcity becomes a thing of the past and every community flourishes.

Within this vision lies another crucial agenda: removing anti-social elements from our midst. These troublemakers, though few in number, wield influence through cunning tactics, intimidating even the rural population. It's time for us to stand up—to reject their fear tactics and work collectively toward progress. After all, change begins at home, and it's within our power to shape a brighter future for all.

In the shadowy world of criminals, they consistently steal the limelight, perpetuating their dominance over others. Their audacity stems from honing their skills in remote corners, relying on sheer muscle power.

When dealing with outsiders, they employ a myriad of tactics to instill fear. Yet, beneath their bravado lies vulnerability—they fear reactions from those they intimidate. United by their goal of terrorizing rural communities, they boast of their formidable gang. Only when you dare to defy them do you glimpse their true strength.

The rural populace, however, remains fragmented—a fact not lost on these anti-social elements. Their enmity thrives while you, the scattered residents, rarely meddle in your neighbor's affairs. This disunity inadvertently aids the spread of anti-social behavior in your vicinity.

But now, the tide turns. With a force of a thousand strong, you stand ready to confront them and their threats.

To combat the prevailing hardship, focus on cultivating easily-grown crops in your agricultural lands. Swiftly reap the yields to alleviate hunger. Blanket the entire area with crops, leaving no idle spaces. Enhance the environment with cleanliness, orderliness, and floral beauty. These crops will sustain your community and serve commercial purposes.

You hold the power to transform your circumstances.

**Dreaming Beyond Limits**: *Imagine reaching heights beyond what seems possible based on existing resources. Picture a motivated team working tirelessly, fueled by ambition. Even if it's just for a few months, strive for financial strength that exceeds expectations. Soon, your unit can proudly declare self-sufficiency* in food production.

1. **Sacrifice and Transformation**: Embrace sacrifice for the greater good—your unit and family. As you operate in a way never before practiced, watch the entire country transform. Residents in your area will adopt advanced lifestyles, habits, and attitudes. But why wait? Change is happening everywhere, and it's time to break free from complacency.

2. **Against Laziness, Toward Purpose**: Laziness is not our fate; it's a mindset we've allowed. While some march toward rapid development, we must seek permanent, drastic changes in our lives. Every project implementation should happen swiftly. Our time is short, and life should be meaningful—let's seize it!

**Remember,** *ambition and action can turn dreams into reality.*

## "UNLOCK LEGAL PROSPERITY WITH UNIT"

Anti-social activists often resort to illegal means to amass wealth, blissfully unaware of the havoc they wreak on others' lives. Their actions impact families, children, and countless innocent individuals like you.

The selfish mindset that compels you to live at the expense of others is a silent ruler over your choices. Have you ever pondered how you arrived at your current destination—a place that once eluded you?

Many of you find yourselves ensnared by powerful criminal networks, forced to contribute your skills, youth, and strength for their benefit. But now, the UNIT offers you a lifeline—an opportunity to reconsider your path. It unveils a legal, viable source of income and a way out from the clutches of the very gangs that haunt your nights.

Why fear these gangs? They may be formidable teams, but the UNIT stands equally strong. It will liberate you from the grip of anti-social forces forever.

We all yearn for a peaceful existence, free from threats. By aligning with the UNIT, you sever ties with destructive relationships. What purpose do the ill-gotten gains from illegal activities truly serve? Isn't your family's well-being worth more than fleeting riches?

Choose a different life—one that doesn't leave you perpetually on edge. Invest in yourself, your family, your neighbors, and ultimately, your nation. Shed the arrogance that once bound you to criminal circles.

Love awaits you, and so does a secure future. Join the UNIT, where legal earnings provide comfort even in the darkest of circumstances. Here, you protect not just your boss's interests but your own family's legacy.

"Within this unit, you earn money daily—a substantial amount that you can monitor closely. You're the master of your domain, not beholden to any boss. The money accumulated through daily business activities in the unit becomes your property, appreciating over time.

Realize that there's no viable alternative. If you continue as you are for another two or three generations, neither you nor your family will achieve a prosperous life. The unit and its functionaries play a crucial role in the area's growth for now, and it's essential to engage with and follow their processes.

As we progress through the following pages, remember that despite past challenges and looting by many, we possess everything we need. By uniting, we can elevate our lives to a world-class standard within a few years. Moreover, we have the power to propel our nation to new heights, securing its position as a global leader.

When visitors arrive, let our premises speak for itself. Each piece of land within the unit should be ornamental, showcasing well-designed infrastructure, lush greenery, beautifully landscaped gardens, and even artificial mini-forests. These features captivate everyone who encounters them. Our agenda encompasses not only happiness but also pleasant surprises that others will envy.

As a small area under your ownership, entrusted to the unit for development, you have the means to effect positive change. By collaborating and working together, you can transform the area into a productive and thriving space. Despite limitations in membership and geographical scope, shared responsibilities allow you to exert control and drive progress."

When the unit attains the break-even points at the earliest with all setups in their units thereafter, they can release the commitments one by one, convincing the members to go easily. Life can improve, as well as in cities, when all the facilities are available under the unit. The difference between the city and rural will be minimized – is our **AGENDA**.

## ALL NEEDS ARE MET BY THE UNIT

The unit will work with parental responsibility to its members. All their needs are borne by the unit, and none of them are spared to live their earlier lives. The unit will arrange their daily needs and employment for all. You must realize that nothing is free in the world. The unit is part of its income source and has to start a business house within the unit limit. Its size should be a mall/shopping complex if it is a big complex attached to the unit with many shops and stalls, go-down and storage areas with many high-quality products of the unit, and also from outside for marketing them. The unit's office should function on its first floor so that the unit-related officials and staff can watch most of the activities through CCTV and directly from around them. The unit involves 200 homes, their properties, and crops; hence, harvests are in bulk, so its storage should be wide.

**Optimal Storage Solutions for Your Complex** When designing storage facilities, consider constructing three-story buildings that can withstand the weight of the products stored. Whether located on the ground floor of the complex or adjacent to it, these spaces serve essential storage purposes. For even more efficient utilization, explore the possibility of underground storage, provided weather conditions and natural factors permit. Utilizing the entire area for stock goods and similar items can lead to significant savings.

**Diverse Storage Options** These storage facilities cater to a variety of needs, including groceries, stationery, and other related items.

Additionally, they can accommodate your crops and products. To enhance efficiency, ensure that there is ample passage for vehicles to load and unload within the facility. This approach not only saves time and manpower but also reduces costs compared to transporting goods externally.

**Direct Supply of Fresh Produce** For perishable items such as vegetables, fish, and chicken, consider direct home delivery. Members can supply these goods directly to the unit office, either through the unit itself or independently. The process should be based on order slips issued by the unit office.

**Detailed Records for Accountability** Upon delivery, obtain signatures from the supplied homes and meticulously record the supply details, including quantities. While the unit oversees the needs and expenses of its members, maintaining separate records for each home, along with copies for the members, ensures transparency and accountability.

**Financial Tracking and Annual Expenses** To manage consumption effectively, maintain a passbook or statement of account for each member. This practice assists the unit in calculating annual expenses. Start by considering the maximum amount spent as a baseline and then build upon that figure.

**Reimbursement and Operational Management for a Shopping Mall Unit** In our shopping mall unit, we directly oversee the management of the entire facility. Our team includes dedicated staff, including salesgirls and boys, who handle tasks such as loading and unloading. Since these roles don't require extensive skills, we can efficiently accommodate a small team.

## HERE ARE THE KEY RESPONSIBILITIES:

1. **Cash Collection and Accounting**: Our sales staff are responsible for collecting cash from customers and maintaining accurate

records. We also manage payments from third-party vendors and outsiders. The accounts of our members are meticulously recorded. Our unit office arranges the necessary stock for the upcoming days. Regular tallying of account books and cash statements ensures transparency.

2. **Bulk Purchases and Bargaining**: We procure items in bulk for 200 families at a time. By negotiating directly with manufacturers, we secure favorable prices. All purchases are accounted for promptly, including verification of received items, invoices, and payments.

3. **Verification and Accountability**:

Our unit manager selects a team of inspectors. This team verifies inward and outward items..Movement slips, sealed and authenticated, guide their actions. Collective accountability ensures efficient operations.

4. **Efficient Operations**: We embrace automation by computerizing all sections. This streamlines processes and reduces the need for excessive staff.

5 **Stall Responsibility**: Small stalls within the mall are entrusted to individual members. They handle everyday stock-taking and ensure accurate cash tallies. The entire stall's responsibility lies with the staff collectively.

**By adhering to these practices, we maintain a well-functioning and accountable unit.** Every small unit of the business and other activities should have the proper record, which should be physically verified by a team selected for that purpose on an ongoing basis. Should not cause any lapse in doing this or postpone it until the next day. A third person who is a member selected for that purpose should authenticate the records before closing that day's account.

Never put your happiness in someone else's hands. All the team members who are related and finally authenticated are accountable for any issue related to that concern. Business and other activities planning to commence after forming the unit: You can decide what all are viable to do under this unit, which will be discussed with the members in their first general meeting.

Mainly the commodities that the members are using daily basis are the essentials so go with those items and improve the stock and the different products step-by-step. It may be our products and the items outsourced. These stocks must be limited for our members. Investing in unwanted items will be a dead stock to the unit and its members, so think twice while deciding the type of business without affecting the unit's financial stability.

If you practice a special item or many supplies according to an indent from all 200 homes, you can avoid wastage.

## MAINTAINING ACCURATE RECORDS

It is essential to maintain up-to-date records on a daily basis. A team of educated members should meticulously verify the cash ledger, bank account, and all daily transactions. These verified records, along with authenticated printouts, should be filed for future reference. Further details are elaborated in the subsequent pages.

## ROLE OF CATEGORY OFFICERS AND INSPECTORS

These category officers and inspectors will eventually be considered for roles such as Assistant Managers and other officials based on their skills and expertise.

## FINANCIAL PROGRESS AND HARD WORK

When operations run smoothly, the financial position of each member will significantly improve. This progress relies on the dedicated efforts of every family member and the unit staff. Detecting malpractices and fraud is crucial, as are factors like water sources, floods, droughts, and climate conditions, which impact the unit's growth.

## OUR COLLECTIVE DREAM

The unit represents our shared aspiration—a distant destination we aim to achieve. All tasks within the unit should be carried out using the available manpower, including both men and women, as documented in the unit office records.

## MAXIMIZING MANPOWER

The unit manager must actively engage all members from the outset, utilizing 100% of the available manpower. If there is surplus manpower, it can temporarily assist neighboring units and vice versa.

## AGRICULTURE FOR SUSTAINABLE INCOME

Initially, focus on agriculture as a short-term and straightforward means of generating income. Cultivate crops to meet the daily needs of the members.

1.  **Record Keeping and Verification**: The records must be diligently updated on a daily basis. A select group of educated members should meticulously verify the cash ledger, bank account, and all daily transactions. Their responsibility includes authenticating the ledger entries, printing out relevant details each day, and filing them for future reference. Further details are elaborated in the subsequent pages.

2.  **Role Transition for Category Officers/Inspectors**: These category officers and inspectors will eventually be considered for promotion to Assistant Managers and other official positions based on their skills and performance.

3.  **Financial Progress and Collective Efforts**: When operations run smoothly, the financial position of each member will witness significant improvement. This outcome hinges on the hard work of every family member and the dedication of the unit staff. Detecting malpractices and fraud is crucial, as are factors like water availability, floods, droughts, and climate conditions, which impact the unit's growth.

4.  **Shared Responsibility and Gender Inclusivity**: All tasks related to this unit should be executed using the available manpower within the unit. Both male and female members, as documented in the unit office records, should actively participate.

5.  **Unit Manager's Role**: The unit manager must personally engage in mobilizing participation from all member households starting from day one. Utilize the full 100% of available manpower. If there is an excess of manpower, consider temporarily allocating it to neighboring units and vice versa.

6.  **Agriculture for Sustainable Income**: Initially, focus on agriculture as a short-term and straightforward means of generating income. Cultivate crops that meet the daily needs of the members.

Remember, the success of our unit lies in collective effort and commitment toward our shared vision.

**Exploring Crop Possibilities and Financial Gains** Within our unit, members have the opportunity to explore various crops beyond mere consumption. These crops can be transformed into valuable products that are readily converted into cash. It is essential to involve as many members as possible until the unit accumulates sufficient funds.

## THE CANTEEN DILEMMA

The question of whether to rely on home-cooked meals or utilize the canteen presents itself as a secondary consideration. This decision must be made during our general meeting, and arrangements can be adjusted accordingly. If the canteen option is chosen, preparations for utensils and related items should be made.

**Canteen vs. Self-Preparation: Each member** has the freedom to choose between the canteen and preparing their own meals. Ultimately, the majority will decide. However, we cannot simultaneously pursue both options. Opting for the canteen involves significant expenses, and committing to it means a minimum three-year commitment. Initially, members can focus on unit work, while those involved in the canteen will alleviate kitchen-related responsibilities.

**A Flavorful Experience** In the canteen, members can propose daily menus to the authorities. These menus, displayed on the notice board, promise a diverse culinary experience.

**Mindset and Decision-Making** When everything is established, altering our mindset could lead to losses for the unit. Therefore, during our general meeting, let's decide with at least an 80% vote. This approach will grant leisure to all after hard work in the field and other areas.

1. **Introducing New Dishes in the Canteen:** Employees are encouraged to explore culinary creativity by proposing new dishes for the canteen. To do so, seek direct permission from the manager and formally notify your department. This approach ensures a diverse range of flavors and culinary experiences.

2. **Staff Allocation and Shifting:** While introducing new dishes, consider the canteen staff's responsibilities. Instead of shifting the entire team, the manager can strategically reassign one or two assistants. This maintains effective control over canteen operations.

3. **Fish Tanks and Sustainable Food Sources:** Each unit within the organization should maintain medium-sized, beautifully designed fish tanks. These tanks, managed by interested members, can provide fresh fish for consumption. Additionally, surplus fish can be sold in the market, either processed or raw.

4. **Healthy Food Choices:** If the decision is made to serve canteen meals to employees, consider incorporating fish, leafy vegetables, and lean meats on a weekly basis. The majority's preference for healthy options should guide the menu.

5. **Maintaining a Pleasant Environment:** A well-kept office and canteen, adorned with a beautifully landscaped garden, enhances the overall ambiance. This not only makes a positive statement but also provides an extra sense of relief to members. A hygienic system should be consistently upheld.

## ENSURING CANTEEN CLEANLINESS:

**Regular Inspections**: Managers and officials should routinely inspect the canteen, kitchen, food storage, and work areas to maintain cleanliness.

**Avoid Food Waste**: Never allow food waste to accumulate nearby, as it can create unpleasant odors. Instead, consider using it as feed for fish or other animals.

## 2. Waste Management Strategies:

**Pig Rearing**: If feasible, consider pig rearing to manage canteen waste effectively.

**Kitchen Waste**: Non-food items in the kitchen can be converted into agricultural manure through composting. – *Using earthworms, you can process the compost, which is possible without any additional investment.*

**Staff Support**: Adequate staffing in the canteen can facilitate cleaning and food supply, allowing members to relax during their breaks.

## 3. Optimal Meal Times:

**Direct Canteen Meals**: Encourage members to have meals directly from the canteen during morning and evening hours for a leisurely experience.

**Staff Well-Being**: This approach also allows canteen staff to take necessary breaks and relax.

## 4. Infrastructure Considerations:

**Quality Kitchen**: Aim for a permanent, high-quality kitchen setup.

**Temporary Start**: Begin with a temporary shed while planning for a more permanent building and additional facilities.

## 5. Choosing Food Systems:

**Home Cooking vs. Canteen**: Evaluate the merits and drawbacks of both systems (groceries, vegetables, fish, etc.) to make an informed decision during initial discussions.

# STREAMLINING FOOD SERVICES: THE CASE FOR A UNIT CANTEEN

Within our unit, we diligently attend to the needs of our members, ensuring their well-being extends beyond mere duty. However, it's time to consider a practical solution that can enhance efficiency and convenience: a unit canteen. Let's delve into the advantages:

1. **Time Savings**: By centralizing food provision, members can reclaim precious time. No more individual cooking efforts—instead, a shared canteen caters to everyone's sustenance needs.

2. **Variety and Consistency**: Management favors the canteen for good reason. Here, all members receive uniform meals, and the daily menu boasts delightful variety. Whether it's a hearty breakfast or a savory dinner, the canteen delivers.

3. **Creative Culinary Ventures**: Imagine this: members contributing their culinary flair to the canteen. Those skilled in cooking can showcase their signature dishes, adding a delightful twist to our collective dining experience.

4. **Waste Reduction**: Serving meals through the canteen minimizes food wastage. Think about the impact—200 households collectively reducing their leftovers. It's an eco-friendly choice.

5. **Empowering Ladies**: Particularly for our female members, the canteen system liberates time otherwise spent in the kitchen. They can focus on other pursuits, knowing nourishment awaits them.

6. **Currency System**: To facilitate canteen transactions, we propose issuing a unique currency to member households. A simple numbering system ensures efficient stock management.

So, let's embrace this culinary revolution—a canteen that unites flavors, saves time, and fosters camaraderie. Bon appétit!

Instead of maintaining a daily account for each home and its members with identical numbers assigned to each home, the canteen can streamline its accounting process. There's no need for a credit-based account for individual homes or members. The responsibility for accounting lies with the unit, particularly the currency-issuing section, which can be efficiently managed by a single staff member. Additionally, this approach allows home residents to purchase required items directly from the canteen or other stalls and shops within the unit.

By adopting this system, the unit eliminates the need for individual account maintenance. Only the total amount paid will be tracked through currency transactions, granting residents the freedom to spend as they wish. Essentially, there is minimal control over spending.

Usage data will be reviewed annually to assess spending patterns. This analysis will determine which homes or members spent more or less, whether on a yearly, monthly, or specific date basis.

Consider situating the canteen near the unit office, granting the office better oversight. If necessary, the office can also provide tea, coffee, and snacks to staff, visitors, and even customers. Creating a modern office space adjacent to the visitor areas adds prestige and requires a one-time investment.

1. **Enhancing Intimacy and Varied Menus**: The canteen system fosters greater intimacy among members as they interact face-to-face beyond office and work sites. An additional advantage lies in the diverse menu offerings across all seven days, meticulously crafted based on member-approved menus. Our motto: "Work hard, live lavishly."

2. **Convenient and Wholesome Meals**: Members can rely on the canteen for their meals, eliminating the need to cook after their unit duties. Similar to reputable public hotels, our canteen

ensures no adulteration or unnecessary taste additives. We prioritize health by avoiding old or wasted food.

3. **Relaxation and Efficient Staffing**: Enjoy canteen meals stress-free! Members can relax and attend to personal needs, such as cleaning premises, tending to clothing, and caring for children. Adequate staff—comprising cooks, suppliers, helpers, and cleaners—ensures smooth canteen operations.

4. **Essential Machinery and Future Plans**: Our canteen utilizes machinery for efficient food preparation, including cutting vegetables, fish, and meat. Essential equipment like grinders, cooking ranges, fridges, storage racks, and utensils are readily available. As our financial position improves, we'll consider dining tables and chairs, but for now, comfortable floor mats will suffice.

## SUGGESTION FOR CONSIDERATION: HOME COOKING OR CANTEEN MEALS

We propose that you have the flexibility to choose between cooking at home or relying on the canteen, based on the majority's preference. However, if practicality dictates otherwise, feel free to disregard either option. Additionally, we allow exceptions for individuals who are sick or elderly and unable to walk to the canteen hall. They may receive parcels.

## CANTEEN MANAGEMENT AND CURRENCY HANDLING

The canteen supervisor or manager should meticulously record purchases made from shops for the canteen, as well as expenses related to member houses. Each house is assigned a specific currency, which can be used both in the canteen and other shops within the unit. Staff members must become adept at recognizing this currency instantly based on their assigned numbers, simplifying accounting procedures.

## SERIAL-NUMBERED CURRENCY FOR MEMBER HOMES

Currency issued to member homes will be serialized. When distributing currency, the assigned numbers should be disclosed in the range of 000001 to 000100, and then from 000100 to 000200, and so forth. Each member will have a separate number, ensuring efficient currency management.

## CANTEEN USAGE AND IDENTIFICATION

Members can use the currency issued to their homes in the canteen. To verify authenticity, a member or their representative can sign with the bearer's name. This way, the canteen can provide meals, and other shops can offer groceries, stationery, or any other necessary items.

## IMPROVED VERSION:

When using coupons, ensure you match them with the specific item available in the store or canteen. Your unit's clerk or cashier will record the amount on the coupon. It's essential to maintain accurate billing records, and you can note the currency details behind each product for future reference. To streamline accounting procedures, promptly upload these records to the computer without delay.

Obtain a printed coupon book associated with your membership. Each coupon bears an allotted number and the seal of your unit's department or section. Remarkably, these coupons have no expiry date, allowing you to use them at any time. Treat them as equivalent to the country's real currency within your unit's limits.

Consider an efficient approach: utilize complete currency amounts when redeeming coupons. By doing so, both buyers and suppliers can save valuable time. However, be aware that this method doesn't prevent misuse, as it relies solely on the member number and a signature.

By entrusting your currency to the canteen or shop, you can conveniently obtain the required items. This method streamlines the accounting system for both the shops and the canteen. The canteen maintains an account associated with the serial numbers of the currency notes.

Another approach involves considering your currency as not having a fixed value. Instead, the value you write on the currency represents its worth. Imagine it as a currency account within your unit, akin to a bank overdraft. There's an upper limit set to control maximum spending.

This policy applies uniformly to all members: each currency has a certain maximum value. The unit manager will communicate this policy during member meetings and personal interactions, emphasizing your financial security.:

When submitting a coupon for a parcel or food at the canteen, provide detailed information: date, quantity, and price. Attach the coupon to the currency each time and have the concerned member sign it. Consider adding the date of the day for better record-keeping.

Previously, we relied on government support due to our status below the poverty line. Now, as a collective unit, we embark on a venture from our current zero financial position, aiming for maximum growth based on our skills and abilities.

**Introduction Clause:** "At the outset, it is emphasized that families and their members are free to hold political beliefs. However, these beliefs should never disrupt the smooth functioning of our unit. All members, including those in responsible positions, have the right to cast their votes. However, they are prohibited from assuming any responsibilities within a political party. If such a situation arises, they may choose to resign from unit activities."

**Comparison with Politicians:** "While politicians serve the entire nation, our unit also contributes to the well-being of a part of the nation, including our families. If any member desires independence from the unit's constraints, they are welcome to permanently resign along with their family."

**Balancing Limitations and Control:** "The unit operates with necessary limitations and controls. Handling public funds entrusted by our members requires vigilance. Without these safeguards, the unit could be vulnerable to misuse."

**Flexibility and Resignation:** "Individuals need not hesitate to leave the unit for any reason, no matter how trivial. Such decisions extend to their entire family. Whether due to religious or caste considerations, anyone seeking a position within their faith can do so after resigning, similar to political scenarios."

**Unit's Purpose and Politics:** "Our unit was established for the welfare of its members, aiming to address their problems. While we remain apolitical, members are free to hold their political beliefs. However, we discourage the formation of factions within the unit, promoting a harmonious environment akin to a family."

1. **Prioritizing Family Welfare Over Politics**: We've grown weary of following various political parties, hoping for their assistance and support. Instead of focusing on our well-being, these parties prioritize their own interests. We've formed a cohesive unit dedicated to our family's welfare. The unit's decisions regarding limitations and boundaries directly impact our freedom.

2. **Learning from the Eagle and the Crow**: Among birds, only the crow dares to peck at an eagle. It perches on the eagle's back and nips at its neck. Remarkably, the eagle doesn't retaliate or engage in battle with the crow. It wisely conserves its time and energy, refusing to be drawn into futile conflicts. This lesson holds true for rural communities: avoid unnecessary fights and invest your time in personal growth.

# CHAPTER X

# THE UNIT

## "OUR UNIT BOLSTERS THE COOPERATIVE MOVEMENT FOSTERING GENUINE SOCIALISM."

The governance of our unit is refreshingly straightforward when every member cooperates and adheres to its bylaws. After the unit's formation, the following guidelines must be strictly followed. Each point has been crafted with your safety in mind, ensuring that neither fellow members nor outsiders can harm you.

**Remember:** *you are the architect of your own destiny in the days to come.*

While we warmly welcome many of you to join us, contribute to our economy, and experience a moderate lifestyle, it requires a collective effort and sacrifice during the unit's infancy. Embrace these rules with the mindset that readiness to sacrifice is expected from each of you. This commitment will pave the way for a peaceful future.

Avoid harboring ill feelings from the locals. As the saying goes, living solely for one is a "selfish word." Let us break free from rigid thinking and embrace a different perspective within our unit. Our motto is simple: "Live for each other." In a world where everyone seeks personal gain, this attitude sets us apart.

We must adapt our mindset according to the situation—it's our only path forward. The lives of those in old rural areas varied from region to region, often comprising tribal communities. Their existence was characterized by simplicity, cleanliness, and contentment. They didn't yearn for grand houses, fancy vehicles, or excessive wealth. Instead, they found fulfillment in what they had, leading lives of quiet happiness.

1. **Empowering Tribal Livelihoods**: The upliftment of tribal communities is achievable through concerted efforts within their own ranks. By adhering to government rules and regulations, they can establish functional units that address their needs. By embracing a cooperative system, they can overcome scarcity and eradicate backwardness and illiteracy from their region. _Unit for them separately will help them to safeguard their culture or mingling with others they can come forward with many new cultures_

2. The abundant resources scattered across their land can be harnessed for their benefit. This collective unity will not only mitigate their fear of wild animals but also pave the way for a modern and up-to-date lifestyle—a dream project that the government aims to fulfill.

3. **Self-Reliance over Easy Gains**: Rather than relying on external sources, the path to prosperity lies in hard work and collaboration. Pursuing easy money through illicit means—such as theft, violence, or prostitution—does not elevate us from mere animals to enlightened beings. Childhood adversity shapes us, but we must break free from its grip. Each of us must take the initiative to create self-sufficient conditions, living our lives differently from our ancestors—a brief yet meaningful existence as human beings.

## OUR ENDEAVOR IS TO TRANSFORM THIS SITUATION GLOBALLY

# "CREATING POSITIVE CHANGE FOR YOUR CHILDREN: A CALL TO ACTION"

If you truly love your children, consider making a meaningful impact in their lives. The world has undergone significant transformations, yet only a few find themselves in a mysterious and transformative stage. As parents, it's essential to explore alternative lifestyles that can benefit your kids.

In any collective endeavor, knowledge is power. Each member should fully understand the unit's details and operational procedures. Address any doubts during the initial General Body Meeting. Before signing any papers, emphasize that this effort is a collaborative endeavor for the welfare of all members. Awareness of every aspect of the unit will serve as your shield.

The unit represents a segment of the rural area chosen for a joint venture involving 200 homes. With approximately 1,000 individual members across these homes (averaging five members per household), everyone must willingly embrace their responsibilities. By allocating tasks, each member gains an opportunity to contribute to the unit. Sincere participation allows individuals to showcase their expertise within specific sections.

Equality is our foundation. Initially, we share the workload based on our abilities and skills. As we allocate and shuffle responsibilities among different sections, we collectively train all members. Importantly, the unit does not burden anyone, especially those physically weak. Voluntary participation is encouraged, and experience validates one's ability to hold specific positions.

## OUR ULTIMATE GOAL

**To ensure that every member becomes familiar with the unit's operations, without relying on external assistance this is our unwavering AGENDA."**

**Unit Ownership and Responsibility**: Our unit operates uniquely—we don't elect members or teams to manage it. Instead, each of us is both a **member and** an **owner.** We collectively shoulder responsibilities, running the unit's business and other activities with mutual support.

**Active Participation and Vigilance**: Within our unit, we discourage theft and cheating. Since this unit is our own, we work for our well-being. Everyone should actively engage in all aspects of unit work without waiting for others. This collaborative approach sets us apart.

**Shared Ownership and Rights**: Imagine our unit as a family property. We aim to run it jointly, treating its business, activities, and properties as our own. Every member has equal rights. Let's prevent anyone from taking advantage of our resources.

1.  **Leadership and Trust**: Reject the notion that someone else can safeguard our property better than we can. Selecting leaders is unnecessary; we're all adept at protecting our interests. No need for director positions or agreements—our unity ensures our unit's success.

*"We have already encountered that experience, and it left a sour taste. Entrusting our unit and its belongings to others for safekeeping led to betrayal. After observing numerous such cases, we made a decision: we will manage our unit ourselves. We refuse to hand over our property to anyone else.*

We recognize our own competence in managing and safeguarding our properties. The unit members possess diverse skills and abilities that we can harness for personal and collective growth. Rather than expecting miracles from external management, we believe the best remedy lies within our own resources. To enhance productivity, we must adjust our attitudes and habits within the unit. Each of us must overcome laziness.

If we neglect to protect our property, how can we envision a bright future? Each individual is more than capable of safeguarding their belongings. Remarkably, some members who were once lazy and addicted to drugs have transformed into active, hardworking contributors. They not only acknowledge their past mistakes but also prove valuable assets to the unit and everyone involved.

We no longer depend on external teams or elected representatives to enjoy our unit's benefits. Past experiences of losing money have left us disillusioned. <u>We don't believe that someone else will sacrifice for our welfare."</u>

## COLLECTIVE LEADERSHIP: EMPOWERING OUR UNIT

As members, we take pride in collectively managing our unit. Rather than appointing a select few as bosses to oversee affairs and hold all responsibilities, we've chosen a different path. Our approach is one of shared responsibility, treating our unit as a family property.

In our corporate office, staff and officials are selected from our own ranks. They execute their duties based on both our wishes and their individual capacities. Regular guidance from the unit ensures that each section operates smoothly. During member meetings, we prepare the necessary tasks for unit-level execution.

Written guidance, confidential but shared with section heads, ensures clarity. Staff members who sign these circulars are fully aware of their contents and act accordingly. No skipping—everyone reads and follows.

## TAKING CHARGE OF OUR UNIT: A COLLECTIVE RESPONSIBILITY

Once we made the decision not to entrust anyone else with the responsibility of managing our properties—learning from the mistakes of our ancestors who suffered the consequences—we realized that the onus was on us. Each member of our unit now bears the weight of unit-related responsibilities.

## VIGILANCE AND ACCOUNTABILITY

As members, we must closely monitor one another's activities, scrutinize accounts, and stay informed about communications. If improvements are needed, we should offer constructive suggestions.

**Remember:** *we're all new to this, so discharging our duties faithfully and sincerely will yield positive results.*

**Voluntary Involvement** – Safeguarding the unit is our shared duty. Consider it a platform for your performance. Rather than waiting for someone else to prompt you, embrace your responsibilities willingly. Voluntary involvement is expected.

**Strength in Unity** Our joint venture forms this unit, and it will work for our collective well-being. Your lifestyle will transform significantly. Now, you stand stronger and bolder, knowing that others are also committed to safeguarding your rights and properties.

**Caring for One Another, even those without immediate needs, benefits**. We have a network of support to inquire about their well-being. Unlike an insurance policy that pays out only during specific hardships, our unit covers risks from the outset—regardless of individual payments.

**Remember:** *our unity is our strength, and together, we can create a secure and thriving environment for all.*

## GONE ARE THE DAYS OF SINGULAR BOSSES

Gone are the days of singular bosses. Instead, we collectively shoulder the unit's demands, managing its affairs jointly and severally.

Our freedom remains intact, and our properties thrive under this collaborative leadership.

Your organization offers a fresh start and a distinct lifestyle. Many individuals are eager to contribute to your collective well-being and rights. I encourage you to join promptly. Whether it's in agriculture or other business endeavors, you have the opportunity to implement innovative ideas.

Instead of squandering time, embrace modern possibilities across all aspects. The unique skills that have fueled your unit's growth set it apart from others. Explore the abilities of your members and share their resources and facilities with the broader community.

Your unit not only safeguards you but also actively intervenes in your challenges, resolving them systematically. Consequently, you're mentally unburdened from past consequences. Now, your strength enables you to withstand external threats.

The unit diligently upholds the rights of all members. Its voice represents each of you, and its decisions remain steadfast. While you're free to express your opinions during meetings, remember that it's not merely an individual's viewpoint.

Your thoughtful insights will be warmly received by others. Present them eloquently to ensure clarity for all members. If you object to any unit movement, substantiate your reasons, and the unit will rectify any mistakes and acknowledge your contribution.

## ADVOCATING FOR A GENUINE CAUSE

When voicing opposition within a group, it's crucial to recognize the challenges inherent in managing a unit with over 1,000 members living in unique circumstances. Many struggle to sustain even a small family of 4 or 5 individuals under these conditions. While unit members enjoy considerable freedom and independence to express their opinions, it's essential to foster a strong sense of cohesion to counter any baseless suggestions put forth by fellow members.

"Our primary focus is on achieving the growth of the unit within the limited time available. Let's steer clear of unnecessary disputes and instead strive to comprehend the underlying reasons, acting accordingly."

Avoid engaging with those who consistently view others' opinions negatively. Such interactions not only waste time but also cloud your judgment, especially during the unit's inception when you may lack experience in unit matters.

As part of this collective venture, your responsibility is to ensure the unit operates smoothly without adversely affecting anyone's life. Strive to achieve this goal successfully.

Active participation in unit meetings from the outset is crucial. Major decisions can only be made with the unanimous consent of all members. Your position and rights within the unit are directly tied to this collective decision-making process.

**Remember** *that the strength lies in the collective voice, and the unit does not entertain divergent opinions from its members.*

*During meetings, all suggestions should be resolved through unanimous agreement. Any pending matters must carry over to the next meeting, with priority given to addressing previously deferred agendas. Additionally, personal matters within member households should be taken seriously. Swift rectification is necessary upon learning of any recurring incidents.*

*Lastly, refrain from presenting individual opinions during unit meetings. Instead, express ideas with majority support. Presenters can expect written replies if desired.*

# THE UNIT AS AN INDEPENDENT BODY

We wish to reiterate that our unit maintains complete independence from any governmental, semi-governmental, or private entities. We do not interfere with their affairs, nor are we associated with any other organizations or individuals beyond our own members. Importantly, we are not active politicians.

While we retain the right to cast our votes, we choose not to publicly disclose our political affiliations. Our unit serves as our lifeblood, and we operate based on a self-sustaining plan that reduces the burden on the government. This approach mirrors the way rural populations increasingly rely on government support.

The unit's primary purpose is to assist in eradicating poverty, combating theft, promoting a drug-free environment, and dispelling intangible beliefs and outdated thinking among our members during challenging times. We eagerly seek wholehearted cooperation and support from the government, and in return, we offer numerous benefits that you can expect.

By addressing issues such as law and order within our unit, we provide significant relief. As time progresses, our members will become the unit's owners, effectively turning it into a family business. All internal affairs will be resolved among them, ensuring a self-sufficient and harmonious environment.

From day one, our unit has taken responsibility for its members' well-being. We prioritize their needs, offering facilities and support while managing all matters efficiently.

## ADDRESSING POVERTY ERADICATION AND URGENT CHALLENGES

Efforts to eradicate poverty are of paramount importance. Alongside this goal, we must address other pressing issues, such as water scarcity, food insecurity, and inadequate clothing. Additionally, cases and charges involving law enforcement or the government will be resolved.

## HOUSING PRIORITIES AND FINANCIAL PLANNING

While independent houses are a priority for all members, we should not dwell on this during the unit's early stages. Instead, our current plan focuses on implementing apartments for all members once our financial position improves.

## UNIT INDEPENDENCE AND WELFARE

Our unit operates independently, with a sole focus on the welfare of its associated members. We do not extend beyond these boundaries, which are fixed in rural areas and defined by our properties.

## ADVANTAGES FOR GOVERNMENT, UNIT, AND MEMBERS

By adhering to these principles, our unit can unlock numerous advantages. These benefits are detailed in a separate chapter.

**Remember:** *the following rules are strictly enforced within our unit*

## STRICT GUIDELINES FOR THE UNIT

1. **Political Neutrality**: We do not allow any political involvement in our unit's operations. While some of you may have political affiliations, our primary concern remains the well-being and maintenance of our families, akin to the responsibilities of politicians.

2. **Family Well-Being and Collective Growth**: Whether one is a high-ranking official, a politician, or an individual public figure from any walk of life, one's primary intention often revolves around the well-being of one's family and followers. Your own intention aligns with safeguarding your family, ensuring their protection, and meeting their basic needs.

Rather than functioning as a solitary individual, consider the potential for tremendous growth when operating collectively. Dealing in bulk allows for substantial income, but it also necessitates vigilant management of every transaction to avoid errors. This collective unit provides comprehensive support, allowing you and your family to thrive under its protective wings.

As you contribute to the unit's growth, it reciprocates by enhancing facilities day by day.

**Addressing Urgent Needs and Fighting Poverty**: While we are currently in the early stages (akin to infancy), we must plan ahead. One crucial step is to prioritize medical treatment for all members.

Although this may take 2 or 3 years to fully implement, it remains essential. Our urgent requirement is to combat poverty. To achieve this, we'll establish a fund by allocating a percentage of our total income. By doing so, we can address urgent needs during critical periods. Additionally, exploring group insurance options for all members opens up further possibilities for collective well-being.

3. **Addressing Substance Abuse in Our Rural Homes:** One crucial approach is to tackle the habit of drinking or drug use within our households. If necessary, we should provide treatment to addicted individuals—whether they are drunkards or drug users. By doing so, we can save lives and entire families that depend on these addicts.

4. Furthermore, these individuals, once rehabilitated, can contribute significantly to society. Offering a helping hand to the addict allows them to recognize their mistakes and value, ultimately leading them to support the community. Whether through treatment or, if needed, by involving their female family members, we can effectively address this issue.

It's essential not to allow the addict to revert to their old ways for more than a month, as complacency can set in. Our unit's efforts will continue to safeguard families, even after the loss of a dependent, providing a priority and advantage to our homes.

5. **Accountability and Financial Integrity:** <u>We must never allow a member who has been previously suspended due to financial malpractice involving the unit's money to hold any responsible position again. Especially when handling financial matters, caution is crucial.</u>

6. Ensuring that such individuals do not regain positions of trust is essential for maintaining financial integrity.

7. **Combating Theft and Ensuring Safety:** Poverty often drives theft. As a responsible unit, we should strive for a theft-free environment. Safeguarding each family is our duty, particularly our lady members, who deserve the same freedom as their male counterparts. Let us protect and empower the female members of our families.

## STOP ILLEGAL TRAFFICKING FOREVER

1. **Addressing Illegal Practices:** The rural population often lacks education, making them vulnerable to exploitation. Outsiders, as well as their own families and neighbors, take advantage of their ignorance. <u>As we form this unit, it is crucial to put an immediate stop to these illicit practices. Every member must be aware of legal matters, and we should never tolerate cheating within our ranks.</u> Anyone caught engaging in such behavior should face appropriate consequences without any leniency.

2. **Prohibition on Liquor Production and Sale:** Our unit strictly prohibits the production and sale of liquor among its members. While it may seem like an easy way to make money, the legal formalities and potential consequences far outweigh any gains.

3. Remember, money earned through illegal activities carries accountability and punishment. Additionally, maintaining private accounts is not allowed. Violating these rules could result in expulsion from the unit, jeopardizing your family's safety and well-being. Let's adhere to these guidelines as part of our agenda.

## EMPOWERING YOUR EFFORTS FOR THE COLLECTIVE WELL-BEING

Now, harness your efforts for the betterment of our community. Remember, this isn't just about safeguarding yourself; it's about protecting all of us. Refrain from associating with anyone involved in illegal activities, even if they dangle tempting offers or share familial ties. Uphold the integrity of our unit.

Reflect on the hardships you've endured alongside your family—the struggles fueled by liquor and drugs. But now, you're on the cusp of a brighter future. Together with your family and neighbors, you're taking small steps toward progress. However, tread carefully; engaging in illegal activities can lead to imprisonment and undesirable consequences. Sacrificing the harmonious family life you cherish within our unit isn't worth it.

## A COMPASSIONATE APPROACH TO PROSTITUTION

Let's address the issue of prostitution. Poverty often drives individuals into this profession. Extend a helping hand to those ensnared by its clutches. By doing so, you offer them a chance to escape and rebuild their lives. The gratitude they'll feel is immeasurable.

**Remember:** *a simple act of kindness can break the cycle—they won't turn back.*

However, be cautious. While assisting them, avoid entangling yourself romantically. Such entanglements can lead to heartache.

Entrust this responsibility to our senior lady members—they'll handle it with care.

## SHARING POSITIVE EXPERIENCES WITH OTHERS

Taking the time to share your positive life experiences is essential. Whether it's a daily, weekly, or monthly practice, sharing these moments with others, including children, can be beneficial. By doing so, you contribute to their awareness and caution in similar situations. While it's impossible to narrate all experiences in a single day, spreading them out over time allows for meaningful sharing.

Participants can proactively register their names in the relevant section of the unit office. They can then prepare speeches that serve the purpose of entertainment. Depending on the intervals, consider involving more members in this campaign.

During these sharing sessions, speakers should refrain from criticizing unit members, discussing politics, or making contradictory comments that confuse the audience. Life, in its essence, is simple, yet we often complicate it needlessly.

**Remember:** *that you have the freedom to recount your genuine life experiences. By doing so, you help others avoid similar situations, especially young individuals. Many of the challenges we face stem from social and economic imbalances, a legacy of the apartheid system introduced years ago. Despite progress, a significant portion of the population remains trapped in below-average circumstances, created cleverly by external factors.*

## PROMOTING UNITY AND EQUALITY WITHIN OUR COMMUNITY

The purpose of our unit is to disseminate essential knowledge that benefits all its members during their stay. However, we must also address the glaring disparities in income distribution and living standards within our community. Let us strive to eliminate bias and partiality, recognizing that our unit functions as a family for all its residents.

As we adapt to our new environment, we must undergo a significant mindset shift. Our past perspectives, once clouded and limiting, no longer define us. Instead, we now understand that true peace transcends the mere absence of trouble; it resides in the presence of a greater force.

## SHARE YOUR POSITIVE EXPERIENCES WITH OTHERS

Take time—whether daily, weekly, or monthly—to share your life's positive experiences with fellow members, including the children. These stories serve as cautionary tales, guiding them through various situations. While you cannot narrate all your experiences in a single day, spread them across multiple interactions.

Participants can register their names with the unit office in advance. Prepare speeches that entertain and uplift, aligning with the campaign's purpose. Depending on the intervals, more members may be involved in this endeavor.

**Remember:** *speakers should refrain from criticizing fellow unit members, engaging in political discussions, or making contradictory remarks that confuse others. Life is inherently simple; we complicate it unnecessarily.*

**Lastly,** *share your genuine life experiences to prevent similar situations from arising in the lives of others, especially the younger generation. Many of our challenges stem from historical social and economic imbalances, which we must actively address.*

## IMPACT ON A VULNERABLE POPULATION

The repercussions of a particular method have been felt far and wide, affecting a significant portion of the global population. Unfortunately, this method continues to be employed universally. Many individuals find themselves trapped below the average standard of living, unable to break free from circumstances cleverly orchestrated by others.

## UNITING FOR CHANGE

Within our collective unit, there lies an opportunity to disseminate essential knowledge. As members of this unit, we share a familial bond. However, we must address the extreme disparities in income distribution and living conditions without bias. Our unit should be a sanctuary for all its inhabitants, fostering equality and compassion.

## A SHIFT IN MINDSET

Embracing a new environment demands a transformation of our mindset. Our past beliefs, once entrenched, no longer serve us. Instead, we recognize that true peace isn't merely the absence of trouble; it resides in the presence of inner strength and resilience.

## UNVEILING HARSH REALITIES

Some haunting images emerge from the shadows—the brothels, where sex workers toil under the oppressive grip of powerful criminal syndicates. These common people, caught in the web of exploitation, suffer silently. Who bears the blame for this ongoing tragedy?

## THE GLOBAL SCOURGE OF HUMAN TRAFFICKING

Human trafficking remains a grave menace worldwide. Those living below the poverty line are particularly vulnerable, targeted by ruthless criminal networks. Regrettably, state and national governments often fall short of providing adequate assistance to these victims.

**Remember:** *these words are a call to action—a plea for awareness and change. Let us strive for a world where compassion triumphs over cruelty and justice prevails for all.*

## SOCIETAL INEQUITIES AND OUR CHANGING MINDSET

The impact of societal inequities affects a significant portion of the population, often with adverse consequences. Unfortunately, these disparities persist globally, as the same methods continue to be followed everywhere. Many individuals remain trapped below the average standard of living, unable to escape situations cleverly created by others.

As a collective unit, we must prioritize knowledge dissemination among all members. However, we should also address extreme income inequalities and living standards within our own community. Our unit functions as a family for all its inhabitants, and impartiality is crucial in bridging these gaps.

1. **Shifting Mindsets and Recognizing True Peace** Our mindset must evolve to align with the new environment we've chosen for the next phase of our lives. Yes, it's true that our past mindset was flawed—a hub of outdated beliefs. But we've undergone a transformation. We now understand that peace isn't merely the absence of trouble; it's the presence of a greater power that transcends challenges.

2. **The Dark Reality of Human Trafficking** Some haunting images emerge from brothel areas—scenes where sex workers toil under the oppressive grip of powerful criminal syndicates. These individuals are forced into labor and victims of human trafficking. Sadly, those living below the poverty line are often the prime targets. Despite this crisis, state and national governments have not provided adequate assistance to combat this heinous crime.

1. **Social Security and Our Perception**: Many individuals lack social security because they still believe they are bound to live in such conditions. Animals, too, fall into two categories: those beneficial to humans and those harmful to society. A truly enlightened

civilization treats both types of animals with equal compassion, embodying the best qualities of humanity.

2. **Preserving Our Culture and Compassion for Animals**: Across cultures, there exists a shared commitment to saving animals, even if it means personal sacrifice. Sadly, our cultural heritage is gradually slipping away. We must actively pass down this legacy to our children, emphasizing selflessness over selfishness.

3. **Empowering Rural Communities through Media**: For those who struggle with illiteracy or laziness, multimedia platforms—such as videos, books, and newspapers—can bridge the gap. By disseminating knowledge, we empower rural communities to become self-sufficient. Unity remains their shield against life's challenges, especially in remote areas.

4. **Balancing Online Learning and Traditional Reading**: While online classes benefit students, excessive reliance on them can hinder essential skills like reading and critical thinking. Content, proofreading, and book references are invaluable. The cost of acquiring knowledge is insignificant when its value is immeasurable.

## ACCOUNTABILITY

*From the inaugural general meeting, it becomes your responsibility to communicate to all members their duties and the boundaries within which they can operate within the unit. The unit aims to introduce a novel way of life—one that you may not have previously encountered—characterized by discipline, self-control, and an absence of deception.*

As part of this community, your collective effort contributes to maintaining an exemplary and trustworthy neighborhood—a place you call home. Accountability serves as a tool for those who struggle to relinquish old habits. It fosters loyalty and nobility in your interactions with others.

Each member must adhere to accountability, whether for their individual tasks within the unit or on behalf of the entire group. By consistently practicing accountability, even minor oversights yield high-quality results. We anticipate the emergence of honorable and authentic members who contribute positively to both the unit and the nation.

Should any member engage in purposeful misconduct, resolution lies not in external legal remedies but rather through the unit's customary disciplinary measures, which extend to their entire family.

**Transforming Care: A New Unit System** The implementation of this innovative unit system aims to eliminate the need for existing children's homes and old-age facilities. Within this unit, both elders and children receive comprehensive care, and none of the members or their relatives bears any financial burden. Even when living with their own families, individuals no longer perceive themselves as dependent or troublesome.

**Equal Rights for All** In this unit, children and seniors enjoy the same rights as other members. Previously, there existed a mindset that financial resources should be allocated specifically for the elderly and children, often at the expense of their own offspring. **However, the unit now covers all necessary expenses related to their well-being.**

**Financial Accountability** All expenses associated with the elderly and children are meticulously recorded and submitted annually to the government. This includes medical costs. In many cases, the government provides reimbursement for these expenses, ensuring sustainable support for the unit's members.

**Retirement Considerations** The initial generation of unit members may choose to retire earlier due to improved health and well-being after joining. While there is no fixed retirement age or specific benefits, those who wish to continue contributing or who consider their health conditions may retire at their discretion. Remaining actively engaged in unit affairs is encouraged to maintain overall health and well-being.

**Empowering Individual Lifestyles:** We believe that individuals should be allowed to lead the remaining part of their lives in a way that aligns with their preferences without adversely affecting others. Whether it's enjoying a typical lifestyle or forming their own unique groups, everyone deserves the freedom to choose. As a community, we can support one another by providing preferred food, allowing rest, and ensuring well-being. However, we strictly prohibit the consumption of drugs or alcohol, maintaining a pragmatic approach.

**Environmental Stewardship:** Our commitment extends to creating a healthy environment within our community. To prevent diseases, especially during pandemics, we prioritize access to clean water. Abundant water sources serve both immediate needs and future sustainability. Used water can be repurposed for agriculture and gardening, either through filtration or direct use.

**Industrial Responsibility:** As an interior countryside community, we refrain from hosting polluting industries within our boundaries. Such industries not only harm our residents but also impact neighboring areas and the global environment. Our focus is not on easy money but on combating hunger and promoting overall health. Let us collectively strive for positive change everywhere.

## MEMBERS SHOULD BE WELL-INFORMED ABOUT THEIR UNIT

Within a span of 6 months, all members should acquire a thorough understanding of their unit and its bylaws. To achieve this, encourage active participation and ensure that members are well-versed in the unit's functions through classes and practical experiences. For illiterate members, explanations should be provided in the local language to ensure full awareness. Any attempts to mislead them must be met with appropriate consequences.

Out of a total of 200 members, it is essential that at least **80% actively participate in all meetings**. Meetings should be scheduled at times convenient for all members, and any resolutions passed require an 80% attendance to be valid. Additionally, monitor continuous absenteeism and take necessary actions. Our unit's administration involves both officials and staff, collectively responsible for managing the unit's affairs.

The unit manager plays a crucial role in ensuring that all members find suitable positions within the unit. Utilize the full manpower available from the unit's inception. Decisions of significance should bear the signatures of all members. If anyone consistently misses meetings, the manager should take note and address the situation appropriately. Members cannot be absent from meetings without the manager's knowledge or consent.

In cases of absence, leave, or being away from the unit, specific reasons must be documented in the leave application. A prescribed form should be designed for this purpose, along with remedies to address absence. Absences without prior notice from superiors should not be tolerated, and appropriate warnings should be issued.

For non-urgent matters, advance notice of at least 48 hours ensures maximum participation. Attending meetings is crucial—it keeps you informed about unit activities. Remember, even a single vote holds significant value during the voting process.

## EFFECTIVE PARTICIPATION AND ATTENDANCE IN UNIT MEETINGS

As dedicated members of our unit, it is essential that we remain actively engaged. To facilitate this, we encourage all team members to be present on the unit premises during working hours. By doing so, they can actively participate in meetings and contribute their valuable suggestions and opinions.

To ensure practicality, we emphasize that meetings should be scheduled at times when most unit members are available. Additionally, we discourage frequent absences from consecutive meetings. Even if a team member is temporarily away from the unit, the manager should closely monitor attendance and allow them to participate in meetings when feasible.

Meeting attendance records are crucial. We request that all participants sign in during meetings. While some meetings, such as those related to awareness classes or financial matters, may not be critical, obtaining attendance records in the meeting book remains important.

For ease of verification, members' signatures or attendance can be recorded against their membership numbers. This practice simplifies tracking attendance at the officer or manager level.

Furthermore, all meetings should be documented in books, noting essential details and decisions. We acknowledge that our unit lacks elected representatives, but we operate efficiently through the manager and staff selected from our own ranks. Remember that lapses in attendance or failure to sign in can impact your responsibilities. Let us prioritize active participation and accountability for the benefit of our unit's success.

## UNIT DECISION-MAKING PROCESS: SIMPLIFIED AND EFFICIENT

In our unit, which comprises 200 members representing individual households, we've streamlined the process to avoid excessive signatures. Instead of requiring every member's signature for every decision, we aim to obtain at least 80% participation (approximately 160 signatures) during major decision-making.

The unit operates under the management of its staff and manager. Day-to-day tasks are carried out by staff and officials appointed by the unit members. Not all members need to be directly involved in running the business; their active participation is essential during key discussions.

As a member, you have the opportunity to contribute your ideas during meetings. You can choose to:

1. **Write and Share**: Draft your suggestion and present it during the meeting. Alternatively, submit it in writing to the meeting organizer, who will acknowledge receipt.
2. **Verbal Input**: Express your suggestion verbally during the meeting, ensuring all members can hear.

**Formalizing Suggestions: The Process When submitting written suggestions, follow these steps:**

1. Write down your proposal.
2. Hand it to the meeting organizer.
3. Obtain an acknowledged copy for your records (prepare in duplicate).
4. This ensures that your suggestion becomes part of the meeting's agenda.

**Signatures and Resolutions** During resolution passages, signatures from participating members are crucial. Each signature should include the date and indicate the meeting's location. However, it's unnecessary to insist that members who missed the meeting sign old documents from previous sessions.

**Meeting Locations and Quorum** Meetings can be held anywhere, but decisions made without the required 80% quorum are considered void. All members are encouraged to actively participate in keeping everyone informed about unit affairs on a daily basis.

As a proud entrepreneur or unit owner, it is essential that you familiarize yourself with every nook and cranny of the property associated with your unit. This includes both movable and immovable assets. Additionally, adherence to unit rules and regulations is crucial.

Regarding office functions, I encourage you and fellow members to engage in discussions. You can also approach the manager to organize informative sessions with experts among your group.

## STAFF SELECTION

Running a successful business requires a competent staff. To achieve this, consider the following steps:

1. **Planning**: Begin by listing the specific initiatives you intend to launch within the unit. Based on these plans, create a comprehensive list of staff requirements for each section.
2. **Skillful Accommodation**: Given the diverse membership within the unit, allocate roles wisely according to individual skills and abilities. We must utilize our manpower efficiently, avoiding any wastage.
3. **Decision-Making**: During the initial general meeting, make informed decisions regarding plans, estimates, and official responsibilities. Assign roles to staff and laborers accordingly.
4. **Computerization**: Upload member details into the computer system. This facilitates easy access to information such as education, age categories, and other relevant data. Embracing technology streamlines administrative tasks and ensures efficient management from the outset.

Remember, with computerized records, you'll have essential information at your fingertips, allowing for smoother operations and better decision-making.

1.  **Unit Management and Honesty**:

The principal officer, responsible for overseeing the unit, relies on recruits to assist in various aspects of unit development. Honesty toward the unit and fellow members stands as the primary qualification.

No specialized skills are necessary—honesty suffices. Past histories of individual members are irrelevant; what matters is their commitment to the unit's well-being.

2. **Trust Registration and Financial Considerations**:

After registering the trust, convene a meeting and pass a resolution. Prepare duplicate copies—one for the bank and the other for the unit's records.

When seeking financial support, consider utilizing an overdraft facility. It aligns well with the unit's nature and allows for the preparation of project reports and estimates before engaging with the bank.

If there are lawyers within the unit, involve them in compliance procedures and documentation related to bank advances.

3. **Legal Matters and Land Rights**: Lawyers can handle trust registration and document preparation systematically.

Address legal matters, including documents submitted to government and semi-government offices, as well as land rights.

Excess government land within the unit's limit should be accounted for and brought to the government's attention. Seeking regularization and remedies for legal issues is essential.

Unused government land or excess land can serve various purposes. For instance:

Mini-Forests and Parks: These areas can be transformed into mini-forests or recreational parks, providing green spaces for the community to enjoy.

**Playgrounds**: The land can be repurposed as playgrounds, offering children a safe and fun place to play.

## GYMNASIUM

In our unit, we now enjoy an abundance of nutritious food and a healthy environment. However, despite these advantages, many individuals remain inactive. It's essential to establish a system for maintaining good health.

To address this, we propose the creation of a gymnasium with basic facilities. This facility will cater to both genders, allowing those who wish to prioritize their health to engage in physical activities. The demand, especially among young people, necessitates such provisions.

Regularly updated equipment will be available on a provisioning basis—every 3 months, six months, or yearly. If you believe that your current efforts suffice for maintaining your body, there's no need to exert additional effort at the gym.

By participating in gym workouts, you can develop and maintain specific muscle groups, contributing to overall health. Not only will your body benefit, but you'll also reduce the risk of diseases and illnesses.

Additionally, we plan to allocate space for walking grounds. These areas will cater to seniors and other individuals with varying physical abilities. Located on the outer boundaries of the mini forest and rest area, they provide a serene environment for exercise. Furthermore, we propose creating a children's play area nearby, which will undoubtedly capture the attention of our elders.

## WATER STORAGE TANKS:

By excavating large tanks, we can collect water for bathing and simultaneously use it to irrigate agricultural plants.

**Natural Water Purification**: The stored water can undergo natural purification processes, benefiting both the environment and agriculture.

In summary, utilizing such land creatively can enhance recreational spaces, promote physical activity, and contribute to sustainable water management.

The excess land or government land can be used for entertainment areas like mini-forests and park Playground – A big tank can be used for baths and the water for watering the agricultural plants – So that the water will purify.

4. **Equal Rights for All Members**: Your property remains in your name with same identity. Besides, regardless of position, all members enjoy equal rights within the unit. <u>No differentiation exists, emphasizing fairness and unity</u>

**Assistant Manager Position** The role of an assistant manager within the unit is crucial for its smooth functioning. While this position may not be initially required, it becomes essential when the manager needs additional support. The assistant manager should possess a strong educational background and be capable of efficiently managing staff, handling day-to-day operations, and maintaining accurate accounts in the books. Additionally, they should ensure that daily data is promptly uploaded into the computer system.

- **Qualifications and Responsibilities**

  The assistant manager must be equally qualified and competent as the manager. Their responsibilities include overseeing the unit's operations, directly engaging with staff members, and maintaining professional interactions with business clients and customers. Maturity and politeness are essential attributes for this role.

- **Promotion and Efficiency**

  Promotion to the assistant manager position can be considered for the most eligible existing inspectors. Rather than waiting for an extended period, this transition can occur promptly. The experience gained from working closely with the unit will enhance its efficiency in managing its affairs.

- **Problem-solving and Dedication**

  The assistant manager's close relationship with every unit member allows them to address most issues independently. If necessary, they seek ratification from the manager. Their dedication lies in leveraging their skills—especially in fields such as crops, industrial production, material procurement, and sales—to propel the unit forward.

## EFFECTIVE LEADERSHIP AND SUPERVISION

While there are dedicated sections and officials responsible for oversight, your active involvement is crucial. As a manager, your daily success hinges on supervising each section's final outcomes and engaging in discussions with your subordinates. Take time to appreciate staff members whose actions contribute to the unit's success, surpassing previous achievements. Simultaneously, address any shortcomings or lapses in service that impact the overall unit.

Your presence in the production area and interactions with third parties—especially staff members and other employees—will foster enthusiasm. By encouraging them indirectly, you create a positive work environment. Cultivate qualities of genuineness and patience when dealing with unit members; these traits are equally essential.

## ROLE OF INSPECTORS

Regardless of gender, all unit members have the authority to review day-to-day accounts. Whether directly qualified or through other members or inspectors, their vigilance matters. The unit manager compiles a list of inspectors based on qualifications and experience, subject to approval by the members' meeting.

Inspectors play a critical role: if they identify errors or malpractices, they promptly report them to the unit manager. Remember, the unit is your responsibility—never shield anyone or conceal secrets that could jeopardize your career or harm your family.

**Revised** Furthermore, you are eligible for promotions to higher grades, increments, and other benefits. However, if anyone misuses their authority to authenticate an account for personal gain or causes financial loss to the unit, they must rectify the mistake and recover the involved funds. Failure to do so will result in the suspension of not only their membership but also that of their entire family, as authorized by the inspector.

Only after resolving the issue and recovering the funds can the suspended membership be reinstated. As members of this unit, your commitment to honesty and integrity is paramount. Whether you are staff or officials, practicing honesty with your co-members is our primary expectation. Your dedicated service to the unit will propel you to heights you never anticipated.

**"In cases where a unit member's actions result in financial loss, we propose the following approach:**

**First Offense:** If a member's involvement leads to a loss, they should be pardoned after fully reimbursing the amount. Forgiveness is extended for the initial mistake.

**Second Offense:** However, if the same member repeats the offense, a more severe consequence is warranted. In this scenario, the entire family of the member should be expelled from the unit."

Remember, *these guidelines aim to strike a balance between accountability and compassion within the unit. You are all part of the same family within this organization.*

Our Agenda: *Honesty remains the core qualification expected from every member of this unit.*

# CHAPTER XI

# THE CHILDREN'S EDUCATION

We recognize that education is a powerful tool that opens our eyes to new possibilities. Our unit was established with the goal of alleviating the hardships faced by our members and enabling them to lead prosperous lives. However, we made a deliberate choice: initially, we did not prioritize higher education for our members' children due to our limited funds, which are also allocated for emergencies.

We recognize that education opens our eyes to new possibilities. Our purpose in forming this unit is to alleviate the sorrows faced by our members and enable them to live more abundantly. We stand unwavering in this commitment.

Initially, none of our members envisioned providing higher education for their children through this unit. Our limited funds are allocated to address various emergencies, ensuring your survival.

**Success lies in talent, not merely in graduation.** Throughout their lives, many have demonstrated this truth. The unit's primary focus is the welfare of our member inmates and the eradication of poverty in rural areas. Rather than emphasizing higher education, we prioritize enhancing the inherent skills of each member.

While we can offer basic education to all young individuals, our immediate goal is to combat poverty effectively. Simultaneously pushing for both education and poverty eradication would dilute our efforts.

Your experience, rather than formal education, equips you to overcome the challenges of scarcity. Most of us aspire to secure jobs worldwide. The unit supports you in continuing with your family, emphasizing the essential minimum education required.

**Unit Limitations and Education**: Despite facing financial constraints, the unit remains committed to educating its members. This education extends beyond the conventional school syllabus, equipping them with the necessary knowledge to effectively manage the unit. The ultimate goal is to foster prosperous lives for all unit members.

**Simplifying Academic Syllabus**: Rather than burdening members with complex lessons, the unit encourages simplicity. Genius minds within the unit collaborate to identify a suitable academic syllabus—one that aligns with the unit's unique needs. Clear communication ensures that timely updates and necessary adjustments are shared with all members.

## REGULATIONS AND AWARENESS:

Regular unit meetings serve as a platform to discuss amendments and prevent oversights. It is every member's responsibility to stay informed about unit regulations. Avoid the easy escape of saying, "I don't know." Familiarize yourself with the practical and legal aspects of running the unit effectively.

*Your oversight could lead to losses for the unit. To prevent this, it's crucial to strictly adhere to established procedures. This disciplined approach ensures the unit's best interests are safeguarded. We actively educate our members both in classrooms and through practical field experiences. By doing so, we equip them to meet the unit's requirements, fostering the development of their innate abilities and skills.*

*Every individual has the opportunity to address their doubts during classroom sessions or other occasions, such as meetings. It's essential to recognize that true education extends beyond traditional schooling. Self-education plays a vital role.*

*While students can clarify doubts within the unit, children can also attend local schools for primary education and language learning. If feasible, establishing a school within the unit or combining resources across units could benefit the government's efforts to support education.*

*Special education examinations for unit members conducted either at the school-level or by class are determined by the units – schools. Those who fail to achieve the required scores may face disqualification, with an opportunity to qualify within the specified time frame.*

*Our educational focus aims to equip students with proficiency in multiple languages and mathematical skills for bookkeeping. After completing primary education, students can continue to high school. Practical education within the unit, spanning 90 to 180 days in each section/department, allows us to assess skills and plan for future promotions.*

## MOVING FORWARD, INVESTMENT AND EDUCATION IN THE UNIT

In the future, our unit's investments will be guided by a commitment to guaranteeing useful education for our members. **Currently, we assure employment opportunities to all members, regardless of high qualifications.** Our primary aim is to provide education that equips individuals and their families with the skills needed to secure a livelihood.

Your personal skills and abilities play a crucial role in growing our unit's business and other ventures. By leveraging your talents, you can create financial prosperity and elevate your position within the organization. It's essential for all members to acquire practical business skills through hands-on experience and learning from others.

While we recognize the value of higher education, we recommend focusing on it for the second generation once we achieve sufficient financial stability. As a family business, everyone can actively participate in unit activities. However, it's important to remain open-minded about job opportunities—accept what is available and, based on your skills, strive for upward mobility.

Avoid over-qualifying yourself for current roles; doing so might limit your mindset and willingness to accept any job within the unit. Until nationwide changes occur, refrain from unnecessary spending on education. Encourage your children to utilize their skills to contribute to the unit's growth, which will benefit their education and future employment prospects.

**Enhancing Skills and Confidence**: The unit will organize specialized classes covering languages, accounts, computer skills, banking, net banking, and public speaking. Active participation in these classes is essential for all students. By facing these challenges, you'll gain confidence and learn to assert yourself, even when saying "No" is necessary in life. Embrace this as an opportunity to practice regularly.

**Empowering Employment Opportunities**: Additionally, occasional meetings conducted by specialists can offer various classes. Legal education, for instance, helps you understand how to differentiate between legal and illegal activities, as well as your rights as a citizen. Attend these sessions and take notes to stay informed.

**Global Communication and Education**: Coordinating across units, we can collect e-mail IDs and phone numbers from around the world. This facilitates communication and promotes progressive standards in developmental education. To maintain effective communication skills, acquire essential knowledge through study and practice.

**Balancing Existence and Improvement**: Recognizing that both affordability and existence matter, let's explore skill-related industries. After high school, children can join these diverse industries for further studies, ensuring a practical approach to their future endeavors.

**Gaining Practical Experience in the Industrial Unit**: Providing an opportunity for individuals to work within the same industrial unit can significantly enhance their experience. The study or training should align with their interests, skills, and the availability of job openings within the unit. Additionally, suitable industries can collaborate with the unit to offer practical experience to those who have studied outside the field.

**Education and Poverty Eradication**: While basic education for rural children is essential, our commitment extends beyond that. We have pledged to eradicate poverty for all our members. Fulfilling this commitment remains our top priority before considering additional facilities.

**Employment Opportunities for Educated Youth**: Our unit stands out by providing employment opportunities regardless of whether your children have pursued formal education. Unlike government programs, we do not guarantee jobs solely based on education. Our focus is on addressing unemployment, poverty, and hunger for your children on an ongoing basis.

**Balancing Education and Immediate Needs**: Given the circumstances of poverty and hunger, we recommend limiting your children's education until these challenges are overcome. Our unit assesses your youngsters based on their skills and abilities rather than formal education. Our ultimate goal is to generate income and uplift thousands of our members.

**Shared Responsibility in the Joint Venture**: Your hard work and innovative ideas drive our joint venture forward. The unit entrusts this responsibility to both parents and their young ones.

**Remember**, *the unit is your collective property, and its value belongs to each of you equally.*

**Education, Skill, and Safeguarding Property**: The unit's governance rests with the educated and skilled members tasked with safeguarding your shared property. It is your fundamental duty to vigilantly observe every movement within the unit.

**Balancing Education and Financial Realities**: While some of our children may be brilliant, financial constraints can hinder their education. Families and children alike must recognize this reality and collaborate with the unit. Employment within the unit can be their path to success; education remains essential for livelihood, as we all understand.

**Guaranteed Employment Opportunities**: *Whether they pursued formal education or not, the unit guarantees 100% placements for all. Employment opportunities await each member, ensuring a secure future within the unit.*

## NURTURING PEACE OF MIND IN YOUTH THROUGH EDUCATION REFORM

In the current education system, many young individuals find themselves studying without a clear purpose. Uncertainty looms over their employment prospects based on their academic pursuits. To address this, we propose a shift toward compulsory basic education that prioritizes peace of mind for the youth.

Our approach involves ensuring free education for all children. The unit manager, during general body meetings, will assess the number of children to be educated and consider the unit's financial position. For those unwilling to pursue traditional studies, an alternative path awaits within the unit's industrial programs. Technical training and skill development can occur here.

Furthermore, if students remain uninterested in technical studies, they can explore civil works labor. This includes roles such as item shifting, tractor driving, vehicle loading and unloading, and work in paddy fields and other agricultural lands. The unit must emphasize the long-term consequences of not pursuing education. Without a minimum level of education, individuals may struggle to communicate effectively, participate in meetings, or face gatherings confidently.

*By completing compulsory education, young minds gain a deeper understanding of life, paving the way for a more secure and fulfilling future.*

## BALANCING EDUCATION AND EMPLOYMENT OPPORTUNITIES WITHIN THE UNIT

When an individual decides to discontinue formal education, an employment offer from the unit awaits. However, there's a crucial condition: they cannot join the unit until they attain a legal majority. During this transition, it is essential that they invest in their future and contribute to the unit's growth.

To achieve this balance, the student must complete their basics through the unit's school. This foundational knowledge is a prerequisite for working within the unit. Afterward, a free training period of at least six months awaits them. Only upon successful completion of this training can they officially join the unit-based on their educational qualifications. The unit will then appoint them to an appropriate position.

Until the individual reaches legal adulthood, they should continue attending school. Working during their minority period is not permissible. The unit takes responsibility for their education, closely monitoring their progress each month by collecting progress reports from the relevant classes.

To maintain integrity, malpractices related to marks or other educational reports are strictly prohibited. The unit emphasizes this to all governing members. Vigilance from all sides is expected, and severe consequences await those who violate these guidelines.

**Revised Paragraph 1:** Instead of relying solely on parents, unit officials should actively monitor children's education at least once every alternate week. They should collect detailed reports on each student's progress, including subject-specific performance, marks, behavior, and attitude. These reports should then be submitted to the manager along with any relevant comments. Additionally, a copy of the evaluation report should be shared with the student's family.

**Revised Paragraph 2:** Our current education system offers a multitude of courses, often with the hope that students will find their niche. However, there are no guarantees. The unit provides education and insists that the children of its members meet minimum educational requirements. If a child is uncooperative, there's no need for coercion or punishment. Instead, consider channeling their skills and abilities within the unit. In cases where their interests diverge, offer alternative paths or consider them for basic roles.

**Revised Paragraph 3:** Our primary requirement is that education equips individuals with the capacity and knowledge to manage a unit like ours. Effective communication, behavioral correction, and a positive attitude toward others are essential. Only after meeting these educational standards does the unit extend job opportunities to all its members.

The unit offers employment opportunities to all of you and provides basic study provisions for your children. However, it may not be sufficiently capable of supporting higher education. From childhood, earning for your family gradually accumulates wealth in each household. Importantly, no child labor is allowed; these periods of study are facilitated through offers from national schools and the unit's own schools.

The primary purpose of education should be to secure jobs for you and your family rather than merely gain the ability to manage the unit. In the current situation, many individuals pursue various courses, often facing significant struggles, without any guarantee of employment aligned with their education.

Unfortunately, this pursuit can sometimes harm their careers, as they refuse to work below a certain standard or dignity—preferring white-collar jobs. This ego-driven mindset can lead both them and their families into financial hardship.

The unit recommends a bachelor's degree for children's education, considering our current financial limitations. Beyond that, nothing more is necessary to operate this unit.

**Balancing Education and Sacrifice**: Instead of spending exorbitant amounts on education without any guarantee for the future, consider making sacrifices that align with your educational goals. Tailoring your career and securing your future within this unit can be achieved through thoughtful choices.

**Employment within the Unit**: Rather than sending educated individuals outside for employment, the unit should encourage highly educated members to contribute their skills within the organization. Since external job opportunities are scarce, internal vacancies remain open.

**Education in the Outskirts**: Those who wish to pursue education can do so in the outskirts of our unit. Initially, the unit need not establish a college for higher studies due to financial constraints.

**Remember,** *our association's primary purpose is to uplift members from poverty and related hardships.*

**Addressing Poverty and Education**: Our current focus is to alleviate poverty and hunger among rural unit members. Collaborating with other rural units, we can establish schools to provide education up to the school-level if the government does not take the initiative.

**Considering Higher Education: Balancing Financial Position and Unit Goals** Our approach to higher education is pragmatic. We believe that pursuing advanced studies should align with an individual's financial stability or their role within the unit. Initially, we prioritize providing basic education for all members. However, as time progresses, we encourage further studies for those interested.

**Candidate Intent and Unit Support:** Should any member wish to pursue additional education, they must present their case to the unit management. This includes details such as the chosen institution, estimated costs, and how the acquired knowledge will benefit the unit. If successful, the unit supports their educational journey.

**Accountability and Refunds** In the event of academic failure or unmet course expectations, the candidate is responsible for reimbursing the unit for the entire amount spent on their education, along with other charges and levies. However, if success is achieved, there is no financial obligation.

**Expanding Educational Opportunities** Beyond individual pursuits, we explore opportunities to enhance education. This includes collaborating with management schools to establish schools in rural areas, ensuring quality basic education for children. While this may initially impact our core agenda, it contributes to a stronger, more informed community.

We must strive to uplift every member without exacerbating poverty and hunger. It has become evident that investing significant time and resources in traditional education does not guarantee success. Rather than squandering money and time, consider joining our unit.

However, for exceptionally bright and talented individuals, pursuing higher studies outside our unit is an option. Upon completing their education, if they choose to remain with us, they can explore business ventures, manufacturing units, or self-employment.

For those who work as a team, our unit offers comprehensive financial support either through bank assistance or direct funding. To access this support, they must present a well-prepared project report, demonstrating feasibility to the unit management and members.

We are committed to assisting with all projects. If the project reports demonstrate viability, individuals can embark on various business endeavors. In today's rapidly evolving world, technology plays a pivotal role in societal transformation. Let us break away from the mold of uniform education and foster innovation.

**"Without Considering Job Opportunities for Graduates:** Unfortunately, the transition from university to the workforce often lacks adequate consideration for job vacancies. As students graduate, the availability of suitable positions is not given due attention. This oversight can lead to a situation where many postgraduates find themselves working as casual laborers on daily wages. It's a common sight, and it highlights the need for a more thoughtful approach.

**Investing in Education and Its Meaning:** Investing in education is crucial, and it must be extended beyond mere academic pursuits. While we allocate resources to educate our children, we should also focus on providing them with relevant job opportunities. Merely obtaining a degree without corresponding employment prospects renders the investment in education somewhat meaningless.

Parents, too, often invest their entire assets in their children's education, hoping for a brighter family future. However, this investment should align with practical outcomes.

**Choosing Courses Wisely:** Colleges offer a plethora of courses, but not all are equally beneficial for a job in the unit.. Some students unwittingly join undesired courses, completing their studies merely for the sake of it. Fortunately, today's youth are more discerning. They carefully consider their future paths, avoiding courses that won't contribute significantly to their career goals.

**Education for Progress:** Our goal should be to educate our children not solely for wealth accumulation but to equip them with the necessary skills for personal and societal progress. Financial stability for families and nations hinges on practical knowledge and skill utilization. If we pour all our resources into boosting their studies, we must ensure that these investments lead to tangible outcomes—outcomes that can safeguard our families even in uncertain times.

**Navigating Life's Precious Moments:** Sometimes, accumulating wealth doesn't necessarily benefit an individual or allow them the luxury of contemplating their family or personal priorities. However, there comes a point when life's final chapter approaches—a moment when everything dear to them slips away, and they realize it might be time to bid farewell.

**The Catalyst of Earning Money:** When you impart the knowledge of earning money to your child, they often venture out into the world and never return. Instead, that knowledge acts as a catalyst, propelling them into servitude within affluent households. They dream of lives akin to those of the wealthy, comparing their own indelible experiences of poverty to the opulence they witness.

**The Illusion of Riches:** Amidst the harsh reality of poverty, the desire for wealth takes root. Driven by this longing, some seek to marry into affluence, only to discover that their pursuit is a trap. The struggle to thrive in opulence proves more challenging than enduring a modest existence, leaving them feeling like mere jesters in a grand play.

**The Transformation of Youth**: For the younger generation, their collective endeavors—whether in business or money-making—are akin to joint ventures or factories. From childhood, they practice a different way of life, one that provides for their needs without fostering a desire to return to their humble origins.

*"Many of us recognize that investing in a child's education is akin to playing the lottery. Without a well-defined system to guide educated youth toward careers aligned with their qualifications, we risk leaving them adrift. Despite this awareness, some parents continue to invest in their children's education, hoping that their offspring will eventually care for them.

However, it's time to shift our mindset. Let's encourage parents to candidly discuss the realities and challenges of finding a job that matches their child's qualifications. Rather than harboring unrealistic dreams, young individuals can kick-start their careers with practical steps.

Comparing our lives to others is futile. Each person faces unique circumstances. While some may pursue higher education, there are also opportunities within the workforce. Let's empower students and parents, especially those from economically disadvantaged backgrounds, to recognize that basic education often suffices. Higher education, in turn, benefits society as a whole."

**Utilizing Hard-Earned Money for Family Welfare**: Why don't individuals use their hard-earned money to benefit their families? At the very least, some members of our community recognize that pursuing higher education can prevent them from accepting jobs that they feel are not suitable for their educational qualifications.

**Facing the Truth about Job Vacancies**: Let's acknowledge the reality: job vacancies are scarce worldwide, and many positions are already filled. It's time to accept this truth and reset our mindsets. Doing so will empower us to achieve success in life.

**Investing in Education and Career Prospects**: Parents and students hesitate to invest in education unless they are confident that it will lead to a job aligned with their qualifications. However, we must recognize that even highly educated professionals, including doctors and engineers, sometimes find themselves struggling and performing basic tasks. They set aside their ambitions to make a living.

**Taking Charge of Your Destiny**: Remember, the BONANZA project involves each one of us. There's no external boss; you are self-employed. As paymasters, you hold the reins. Your families are counting on you during this critical time. Take an oath to persevere and emerge victorious in your endeavors.

**Unemployment as a Strategic Creation**: It can be demonstrated that unemployment was intentionally engineered. The notion of idyllic imagination, lost in the annals of time, sometimes squanders one's life. However, harboring dreams without exerting genuine effort is sheer folly—a pitfall that has ensnared previous generations.

**Family-Centric Business Opportunities**: Presently, numerous vacancies exist that are meticulously crafted for your families. This family-oriented enterprise aligns with your education and abilities, enabling you to amass wealth—an ultimate goal of education. While I don't discourage young aspirants, it's essential to ponder: if education lacks prospects, why endure immense struggle, potentially jeopardizing your family's financial stability? Some may wield influence and secure fitting employment.

**Parents, Education, and Responsibility**: Your parents, despite their financial constraints, prioritize your family's well-being. Even after investing their hard-earned resources in your education, you remain a vital concern to them. Henceforth, self-reliance is paramount; your past need not haunt you. This unit—the family legacy—is your own. Joint ventures offer a path to prosperity devoid of deceit or corruption, as you all share a common lineage.

**Eliminating Unemployment**: the unit being family-oriented business house their active participation eliminates unemployment among them.. Such businesses operate with family members collectively managing the unit's assets, much like a joint family tradition. When everyone contributes, there's no room for unemployment.

**Leveraging Skills and Ideas**: Whenever possible, tap into your skills and ideas—whether gained from experiences outside the business or interactions with others. Express your unique perspective to contribute to the unit's growth. Remember, the unit serves as a platform for sharing ideas, and there are no limits. Everyone rallies behind you when you showcase your skills, turning them into advantages. Utilize the collective potential of all members.

**Maximizing Manpower**: Achieve 100% manpower utilization within the unit is anticipated.. Whether skilled or unskilled, every individual plays a crucial role. Additionally, prioritize nutritious food, including organic options. A healthy environment benefits all, especially those who have overcome addiction and returned to life. Together, we can create a pleasant and thriving ecosystem within the unit.

**Education: A Double-Edged Sword:** Education, often regarded as a powerful tool, can be wielded in two distinct ways. While it has the potential to uplift society, nation, and the world, there exists a darker side. Neglected or misused, education becomes a weapon, perpetuating harm and discord. Unity becomes essential for survival, as this negative trend threatens to perpetually harm others.

Consider the following example: within the confines of a tightly secured camp, emotions find expression through clandestine notes. Even today, similar methods are employed to inflict harm on others. In light of this, one might question the emphasis on high education for all. Perhaps, instead, we should prioritize fostering a pleasant and peaceful life for everyone. Let those who desire advanced education pursue it, but let us not forget that even a countryside dweller requires basic education to navigate life, recognize deception, and defend against attacks.

Interestingly, after World War II, a poignant letter emerged from a Nazi concentration camp. Addressing teachers serves as a stark reminder of the impact education can have, both positive and negative.

## DEAR TEACHER,

As a survivor of a concentration camp, my eyes witnessed horrors that no person should ever see:

1. **Gas chambers** constructed by learned engineers.
2. **Children** poisoned by educated physicians.
3. **Infants** killed by trained nurses.
4. **Women and babies** were shot and burned by high school and college graduates.

Given these experiences, I harbor suspicion toward education.

**My plea to you:** Help your students become truly human. Your efforts should never yield learned monsters, skilled psychopaths, or educated illiterates.

Remember that **reading, writing, and arithmetic** matter only if they contribute to making our children more compassionate and humane.

Additionally, let's address the educational unit:

This educational unit functions as a family, and our collective goal is to promote the unit's syllabus. It's essential that the unit's aim aligns with practical life skills. After secondary education, students should be well-versed in family management—knowing how to run a household, handle essentials, and create a nurturing home environment.

Furthermore, consider making informed decisions, such as producing **chemical-free, organic food** for personal use and sale. Proper kitchen maintenance, cooking skills, expense control, housekeeping, and waste management are crucial.

Utilizing earthworms to compost waste and convert it into valuable manure can be an eco-friendly solution.

Let us empower our students not only with knowledge but also with the ability to lead meaningful lives.

1. **Optimizing Water and Electricity Usage**: Instead of allowing unrestricted consumption, we should collectively manage water and electricity resources. Upgrading our systems to harness energy from sustainable sources is crucial. By reducing wastage, we can mitigate scarcity. The unit's management and individual members must collaboratively address existing challenges.

2. **Addressing Shortfalls and Implementing Solutions**: Vigilance is essential in identifying shortcomings within the unit. Whether individually or collectively, we must find remedies promptly. Immediate implementation of these solutions is vital. When funding becomes available, we can execute innovative ideas to enhance unit operations and foster financial growth.

3. **Our Vision: A Journey to Wonderland**: Our unit's agenda transcends mundane concerns. It aims to enrich our lives, leading us to uncharted territories—a wonderland of possibilities.

# CHAPTER XII

# THE POWER OF PARTNERSHIP BUSINESS

In this chapter, we explore the concept of partnership business as an innovative approach that transcends traditional boundaries. While our focus extends beyond rural areas, the principles apply universally.

**Why Partnership Business?**

The prevailing mindset often pits businesses against each other, leading to legal complexities and mutual distrust. However, a more promising path exists in partnership business. It stands out as the ideal choice for enterprises worldwide, regardless of their economic status—is it poor or middle-class?

## UNLOCKING POTENTIAL

Partnerships thrive not only among the affluent but also within the middle-income bracket. By pooling resources and expertise, joint ventures can unlock new possibilities. Even in non-rural settings where challenges persist, partnerships offer a beacon of hope.

## SAFETY AND GROWTH

When partnerships demonstrate their safety and reliability, investors gain confidence. Whether in bustling cities or quite countryside, these collaborative efforts can ignite a wave of entrepreneurial ventures—both large and small.

**Remember**, *thinking differently isn't just a choice; it's a catalyst for progress. Let us embrace the power of partnerships and transform the business landscape together.*

1.  **The Power of Partnership**: We must recognize that **partnership** stands as the most favorable business model for individuals with both small and large investments, regardless of their location. By safeguarding investors' rights through legal mechanisms, the partnership ensures reliability and safety.

However, to truly thrive, we need **government support** in these endeavors. Such backing can address unemployment significantly and contribute to the financial well-being of families. The positive ripple effect extends beyond specific regions, fostering the growth of numerous small and large businesses.

2. **Challenges in Current Partnership Rules**: While the concept of partnership holds promise, the existing rules fail to adequately protect the common person. Many have experienced frustration due to dishonest practices in partnership deals. Consequently, these rules are deemed unacceptable.

To rectify this, the government should consider **amending partnership laws**. Such changes would empower the neglected segments of the population, ensuring they no longer remain dependent on uncertain circumstances.

1.  **Addressing Financial Cheating Worldwide**: Financial cheating is a pervasive issue worldwide, necessitating government intervention. By legally supporting the weaker sectors, we can empower young individuals to establish employment opportunities. These efforts should extend across geographical boundaries, allowing for widespread economic growth.

2. **Recognizing Varied Intelligence and Challenges**: It's essential to recognize that <u>not everyone possesses equal intelligence or the ability to overcome challenges</u>. Relying solely on individual wit to combat cheating is unrealistic. Instead, governments should establish new rules and systems that uplift neglected sectors. By doing so, we create a fairer playing field for all.

3. **Encouraging Progress and Hard Work**: When individuals experience even modest progress and profit from their investments, they become more willing to embrace hard work. Laziness is not the issue; rather, <u>it's the lack of opportunities</u>. Government support through legal frameworks can bridge this gap and empower those who have been left behind.

4. **The Reality of Partnership Businesses**: Even in small partnership businesses, trust is crucial. A guilty conscience on the part of any partner can undermine growth and lead to business closures. It's essential to foster an environment of integrity and fairness, where partners collaborate honestly rather than resorting to deceit for personal gain.

## SECURED INVESTMENTS: EMPOWERING SMALL BUSINESSES FOR NATIONAL GROWTH

Encouraging partnership businesses and ensuring the well-being of their members can alleviate various financial challenges. By directing resources toward rural development and supporting underprivileged communities in urban and other areas, we can generate substantial tax revenue and additional income. Both small and large business enterprises play a crucial role in this endeavor.

## WHY SMALL INVESTORS THRIVE IN PARTNERSHIP BUSINESSES

1. **Shared Responsibility**: Small investors thrive in partnership businesses because they actively contribute to the growth of the

enterprise. With three or four owners managing the business, decisions are made collectively, fostering a sense of shared responsibility.

2. **Traps Unveiled**: Historically, talented and educated young individuals hesitated to pursue entrepreneurship due to perceived risks. However, we aim to dispel these misconceptions and create an environment where aspiring entrepreneurs can confidently explore their potential.

3. **Parental Support**: Parents play a pivotal role in guiding their children toward viable solutions for unemployment. When young minds come together to establish businesses aligned with their interests, they not only address their own needs but also contribute to the overall economic landscape.

## BREAKING FREE FROM DEPENDENCY ON GOVERNMENT:

The prevailing trend of relying solely on government support and waiting for opportunities must shift. By empowering individuals, we enable them to actively participate in our nation's growth. Our agenda is clear: prioritize individual necessities, foster self-reliance, and protect the collective well-being. Together, we can build a stronger, more resilient future.

**From Small Unit to Expansive Business Group**: Today's small unit has evolved into a substantial business group with numerous branches. This growth is attributed to the skill and ability of its partners, coupled with the support of government policies. As they continue to expand, their potential knows no bounds.

**Government Support against Cheating**: Rather than relying solely on financial aid or rural development programs, introducing laws against cheating can significantly benefit self-sufficient populations. These laws would safeguard rural communities from deceptive practices and confusing advertisements. A sincere push from the government, along with the assurance that they have backing, can empower these individuals to thrive. Their resilience enables them to face any adversity with confidence.

**Creating Opportunities for Livelihood::** Instead of sporadic financial assistance, the government has to focus on establishing secure investment facilities. This approach encourages active participation and self-reliance. By doing so, individuals can proactively seek out livelihood opportunities and overcome challenges. Underestimating their capabilities would be a mistake—they are more than capable of achieving great things.

## THE "BEGGING."

The beggar population has ingeniously transformed their art of begging into a thriving enterprise, capitalizing on human sympathy and weaving an intricate illusion of need. Their meticulously rehearsed performances, complete with costumes and pitiful body language, evoke compassion from passersby. However, beneath this facade lies a complex network.

In addition to beggars, many old-age homes and children's shelters operate in a typical manner, presenting their residents with a sympathetic light to collect funds. These institutions issue tax benefit receipts, leading some individuals to choose this path instead of paying taxes directly. Some believe that supporting such homes is a way to attain heavenly rewards. Notably, several companies also contribute to these institutions to gain income tax benefits.

To permanently eradicate this practice from our nation, implementing a well-structured system could be the solution. By providing comprehensive support through dedicated units, individuals facing critical situations could find relief. If such a system exists, why would anyone persist in the begging profession?

**The Tactics and Victims** One disturbing tactic employed by this enterprise is the kidnapping of children—often younger than ten years old—as a means to sustain its business.

## FOSTERING ENTREPRENEURSHIP: A ROLE FOR GOVERNMENT

In a world where entrepreneurship thrives, governments play a pivotal role in safeguarding and nurturing business ventures. By shielding partnership businesses from threats and risks, they pave the way for a multitude of small and large enterprises to flourish. These ventures, fueled by the financial capacity of unemployed youth, transform local landscapes and contribute to the fabric of modern living.

Rather than relentlessly seeking traditional employment, many young individuals discover their entrepreneurial spirit. These budding entrepreneurs establish small-scale units that not only sustain their livelihoods but also invigorate their communities. As these enterprises grow, they bring remote or overlooked areas into the limelight, elevating them to prominence.

The bonds forged through friendship become even stronger when shared entrepreneurial pursuits are at play. Families, too, find common ground as they collectively invest in these ventures. In this symbiotic ecosystem, everyone benefits—the entrepreneurs, their families, and the community at large.

Ultimately, the success of these small and large business units reverberates on a national scale. They contribute significantly to the growth of the economy, and the government's role in safeguarding investors becomes paramount. By fostering an environment conducive to entrepreneurship, governments empower the nation's economic engine to thrive and prosper.

The current state of civil cases, where individuals wait for **a minimum of 20 years or even more** for resolution, is a glaring issue. This outdated system requires **urgent reform** by the government to align with the demands of the modern era. Let's delve into the key aspects:

## SYSTEMIC INTERFERENCE

The government has to systematically intervene to eliminate unnecessary delays that plague the existing legal framework. These delays hinder justice and frustrate those seeking remedies.

Purposeful amendments are essential to streamline the process, ensuring timely resolution of civil cases. The focus should be on safeguarding the rights of common citizens.

## PARTNERSHIP BUSINESS MODEL

Instead of perpetuating a system where the clever can exploit others, consider promoting partnership-based approaches.

Encouraging partnerships in business could alleviate the burden on the legal system. When disputes arise, partners can resolve them more efficiently, reducing the strain on courts.

## QUALITY OF LIFE

A person's life is fleeting, and spending a lion's share of it in courtyards is disheartening. The toll extends to their family as well.

**Suicide, though tragic**, often remains unnoticed. Public discourse on this matter lasts only a day or two, failing to address the underlying issues.

**Legal Inefficiencies:** Many suffer throughout their lives due to the inadequacies of the legal system. Cunning individuals exploit these gaps, while efficient lawyers perpetuate the cycle.

**Relying solely on the skill of advocates**: Perpetuates an outdated method of contesting cases we must seek more equitable and efficient solutions, in summary, the government's proactive role say has to innovative legal reforms, and a shift toward collaborative approaches can transform the landscape of civil justice, benefiting society as a whole with money and time can be convert into productive.

1. **Rehabilitating Offenders**: An individual with a criminal history often associates with fellow criminals, preventing them from breaking free from their past. *However, the purpose of a rehabilitation program is to reintegrate such individuals into society.* By addressing their circumstances and providing remedies, these programs can transform former offenders into productive members of the community. This is very well possible through this unit system as there are many to watch them.

2. **Unit-Based Approach**: *Rather than relying solely on government systems for silly matters, specialized units can play a crucial role. Within these units, members have a unique advantage—they can closely assess the qualities of those under their supervision. Whether through guidance or more assertive measures, these units can revive individuals who possess the potential to contribute positively.*

3. **Protection and Support**: Many ex-criminals face threats from their previous affiliations. It becomes essential for the unit to safeguard not only the individual but also their entire family, ensuring a fresh start from their grassroots-level of existence most of them turn to much productive and useful to the unit and the society.

## LEGAL CASES AND DISPUTES

Legal proceedings can be incredibly time-consuming, and beyond mere financial losses, they often strain relationships among families.

*Historically, court cases were meant to impart lessons rather than focusing solely on winning or losing. Remarkably, this same approach continues to be prevalent today.*

Despite significant global development, certain traditional methods persist, particularly in rural areas. Consequently, numerous cases remain pending in courts. Prioritizing these cases and finding resolutions is crucial.

It's essential to recognize that each case involves multiple lives. Whether civil disputes or business-related matters, the impact extends beyond the immediate parties. Unfortunately, due to the limitations of democratic governance, not everything can be rectified during a single term. The pressure of time constraints affects decision-making, making it challenging to address the needs of the present situation and expedite the resolution of long-standing cases mired in its processes.

## ADDRESSING LONG-PENDING CASES: A CALL FOR ACTION

In our legal system, long-pending cases pose a significant challenge. These cases, languishing for years, impact the lives of those involved. It's time to prioritize their resolution and find an alternative. Which suits the present situation to save money and time?

The unit system will save society from legal complications as they have no time or chance to fight.

## ECONOMIC IMPLICATIONS

**Youth Unemployment**: Earlier wandering in search of jobs harms our economy.

**Alternative**: Channel their energy into productive endeavors.

**Collective Responsibility**: Let's create opportunities for our youth through the units.

**Remember,** *addressing long-pending cases isn't just about legal reform; it's about shaping a brighter future for our nation and its productive youth.*

We must establish an alternative system to resolve business-related cases and disputes. This separate system should operate swiftly, avoiding delays that could harm the aspirations and endeavors of young entrepreneurs and their families directly and our nation indirectly.

The cases through the emergency settlement process using an innovative fast-track method are to be introduced. Closely monitoring for timely execution by the court is essential as these are mainly involved documents an authority can oversee and enforce measures to prevent unnecessary delays.

"Introducing such a system would safeguard businesses against legal challenges from competitors or influential personalities. By nurturing collaborations and championing self-employment initiatives, we empower young individuals to tackle unemployment head-on.

Even struggling small-scale industries (SSIs) can find their footing again, creating livelihood opportunities for the less educated—without relying on government assistance or external agencies. This self-sufficiency becomes a distinct advantage, allowing these industries to thrive."

Being fully engrossed in one's work, rather than wasting time on arguments or interfering in others' lives, signifies progress. It benefits not only individuals and their families but also contributes to the nation's development.

Ironically, existing laws meant to protect victims often place an undue burden on them. Victims must deposit a percentage of the disputed amount, along with court fees, to proceed. For many, this financial hurdle is insurmountable. They face a dilemma: prioritize recovering lost funds or meeting day-to-day family needs.

In cases involving substantial amounts, victims encounter a catch-in situation. To pursue recovery, they must find additional funds to deposit in court. While there may be a few genuine cases, the majority suffer due to this requirement. Perhaps exemptions could be granted to priority if the government wishes to choose to address this issue.

**Streamlining Evidence Verification**: In civil cases, substantial reliance is placed on evidence from books and documents. Rather than navigating cumbersome alternative arrangements, a direct verification process for documents, receipts, and other evidence should be established. This streamlined approach can significantly enhance efficiency.

1. **Direct Access to Certificates**: Courts can go for a system of directly obtain certificates from relevant authorities such as revenue offices, tax departments, and banks or other financial institutions.. By doing so, cases can be settled promptly. The public expects the government to prioritize time-saving measures and safeguard the well-being of those involved in legal proceedings.

2. **Embrace Digital Solutions**: <u>Continuing with outdated, time-consuming systems is counterproductive.</u> Computerized offices offer efficient solutions that can expedite processes. It's high time we modernized our legal infrastructure, thereby saving lives and ensuring a better quality of life for dependents.

3. **Accountability and Verification**: To ensure authenticity, officials issuing certificates and necessary documents for court proceedings should be held accountable. Implementing a cross-verification mechanism can further enhance the purity and reliability of submitted documents.

1.  **Streamlining Legal Procedures for Efficiency**: In many instances, a streamlined procedure is followed to avoid the need for physically bringing books and records to court. This not only saves valuable time for court officials but also expedites the process. Swift resolution is particularly feasible for many cases.

## ACCOUNTABILITY TO BE IMPOSED ON OFFICIALS

"The individual responsible for issuing the certificate bears a significant duty. Their accountability for their actions could significantly streamline processes, benefiting both the court system and other stakeholders."

2. **Accelerating Civil Case Settlements**: Rather than languishing for two decades or more, numerous civil cases can be resolved within a few months. Other than a few complicated cases, this efficiency is possible when accurate certificates issued by responsible department officials support the case. Since civil case outcomes hinge on documents and evidence, many disputes can be settled promptly.

3. **Government Intervention for Change**: The government holds the key to legal remedies, and it can only alter this trend. Currently, the system involves filing a case and waiting for an extended period before it reaches the court. In the past, cases were seen as opportunities to impart lessons to wrongdoers, and time was abundant. It is still part of this system, which is a pity.

4. **Modern Imperatives: Time and Productivity**: However, times have changed. Modern life revolves around time, and as a nation, we must optimize our manpower resources that can play a big role in our economy.. The goal should be to convert time into productivity.

5. **Anticipating Progress with Government Involvement**: The nation eagerly awaits a swifter legal process facilitated by government participation. Reducing bureaucratic delays benefits both parties involved in court cases. It saves time, preserves health, and prevents

unnecessary financial losses. The possibility of a fresh start after a case hinges on this efficiency.

Though there are many openings for youngsters according to their skill, ability, and financial support through partnership, very few actually step forward to consider the consequences and legal formalities involved.

Any partner has the potential to cause a business to fail. When a partner passes away or becomes permanently disabled, ensuring their rights pass to their heirs becomes a significant challenge and delay under current laws.

If the government prioritizes protecting investors' rights in business, especially in partnerships and similar small enterprises, it could lead to substantial growth aligned with government expectations. This would contribute to reducing unemployment among the younger generation.

Numerous business opportunities exist, including small and large-scale industries, agriculture, and allied activities. The government can monitor youth development, and self-help teams are emerging in remote areas, fostering comprehensive progress. Families benefit from improved business outcomes.

The high economy will lead the entire remote area to rich and affluent by a systematic way of disciplined lives of the unit mates. It is the proud of the nation it move to the highest position in the world wide.

## REVISED PARAGRAPHS

Despite numerous opportunities for young people based on their skills and abilities, very few take the leap to consider the consequences and navigate the legal requirements associated with partnerships.

The government only can actively safeguards investors' rights in business, particularly in partnerships and other small enterprises; it could lead to significant growth, addressing youth unemployment.

Various business avenues, spanning small and large-scale industries, agriculture, and allied fields, await those with the right skills and interests. Monitoring youth progress and fostering self-help teams in remote areas through the units can contribute to holistic development, benefiting entire families.

## THE PRECIOUSNESS OF TIME IN LEGAL CASES

When legal cases drag on for an extended period—say, 15 to 20 years—a significant chunk of the lives of those involved, as well as their dependents, is knowingly squandered. The time that could have been utilized for personal and familial progress or even national development is instead wasted.

*The cases in-between the inmates of the units can be withdrawn or compromised by the unit so that most of the legal remedies are possible to settle.*

Consider the plight of the litigant: not only is their own future compromised, but their family's prospects are also marred. In some cases, the struggle becomes so dire that the family finds itself among the most destitute. Had the legal remedy been swift—resolved within a year or even less—it would not have significantly impacted the family's trajectory. However, the reality often unfolds differently, leading to irreversible consequences for everyone connected to the case.

Moreover, waiting years for a court decree can prove futile. Sometimes, a technicality may turn the tide against the very person seeking justice. The cheated party may unexpectedly find themselves on the losing side due to a legal loophole. Regardless of the case's outcome—whether positive or negative—the delay exacts a toll beyond mere financial losses. It affects health, well-being, and emotional resilience.

In the end, expediting legal proceedings benefits both parties. They preserve their precious time, which can be considered their stroke of luck. Whether victory or defeat, the swiftness of justice ensures their life continues, unencumbered by prolonged legal battles.

As the decree is handed down, the plaintiff's recovery prospects—whether financial, physical, or otherwise—remain a critical concern, influenced by factors such as muscle power and other parameters.

Remember, *time lost in legal limbo cannot be reclaimed, and the impact reverberates far beyond the courtyards.*

1. **Simplifying Legal Decrees**: When the court issues a decree to pay an amount or vacate a position, it can prevent further disputes through execution. By directing relevant departments, such as the police, to intervene and settle the matter, the case can be resolved promptly.
2. **Challenges After the Decree**: However, even after obtaining a decree, seeking legal remedies involves navigating various parameters beyond the directives. In some cases, the recovery process becomes arduous after years of struggle in court.
3. **The Need for Efficiency**: A streamlined system could address this. With efficient counters, execution processes, and recovery mechanisms, causes related to recovery and property rights could be resolved more effectively.
4. **The Value of a Decree**: Despite spending significant resources—money, time, and health—possessing a decree often feels like holding a mere piece of paper. Unfortunately, actions against this situation have been lacking, leaving complainants without resolution.
5. **A Proposal for Timely Closure**: To improve this, consider adding a line to decrees that sets a time limit for case resolution. If not

settled by that date, the court would take action. <u>Such a provision could save time and prevent prolonged legal battles</u>

1. **Legal Efficiency and Human Impact**: The court promptly examines the submitted records, identifying any necessary additions to make an informed decision. Swift case processing has a profound impact on the lives involved, allowing them to move forward. Unfortunately, some cases lead to tragic situations and unproductive outcomes. While cases serve as lessons, they can also disrupt families' chances at a better life.

2. **Civil Cases and Timely Discharge**: Beyond serious criminals, the nation must prioritize civil cases for early resolution. Currently, such cases often face unnecessary delays. By addressing this, we can prevent prolonged suffering for those affected.

3. **Partnerships and Hidden Struggles**: Small business partnerships sometimes collapse due to deceit by one partner. These situations, akin to unspoken experiences in rape cases, remain hidden. Let's recognize that these struggles impact both parties and provide an advantage to those who exploit vulnerability.

1. **Challenges in Partnership Business**: Ordinary individuals often hesitate to engage in partnership businesses due to their fear of unexpected events. Their mindset tends to be cautious, and they may perceive partnerships as risky endeavors.

2. **Entrepreneurs and Insufficient Investments**: Entrepreneurs face their own set of challenges. Some lack sufficient capital to run businesses or undertake projects effectively. Poverty forces them to withdraw from their investments, leading to project failures and perpetuating their financial struggles.

3. **Joint Ventures and Progress**: In certain cases, individuals may not possess the necessary skills to run a business successfully. In such situations, joint ventures or partnership businesses can be beneficial. Collaborating with others allows them to pool

resources, share expertise, and collectively lead a business toward progress and success.

4. **Insufficient Funds and Proprietary Businesses**: Proprietary businesses, relying solely on individual funds, often struggle if capital is inadequate. However, partnerships have the potential to thrive when legal protections safeguard investments and promote stability.

**Remember** *that effective collaboration and legal safeguards play crucial roles in the success of any business venture.*

**Partnerships**: While some individuals shy away from risk, partnerships offer an alternative path. By pooling efforts and sharing risks, businesses can experience tremendous growth. The alignment of views, ideas, and mutual confidence propels them to new heights.

1. **Ideal for Idea Sharing**: Partnerships are an ideal platform for sharing ideas, coordinating, and executing them within a business. Particularly suited for ventures with modest investments from a few partners, legal protection becomes crucial. Without it, ambitious endeavors can inadvertently make the weakest partner a scapegoat.

2. **Challenges of Legal Proceedings**: Unfortunately, the current system of closing a business through court proceedings affects all partners. The prolonged legal battle, lasting 15-20 years, not only drains their resources but also impacts the nation. Spending a significant portion of their lives in courtrooms, partners rarely explore positive resolutions. Instead, the case becomes a wearying pursuit, leading to losses on both sides.

3. **Embracing a Different Approach**: Perhaps it's time to shift focus. Rather than pursuing court battles, consider alternative solutions. The absence of civil or criminal cases in our AGENDA underscores the value of cooperative units.

**Remember**, collaboration and innovation can transform challenges into opportunities.

## ENHANCING EFFICIENCY AND PROSPERITY IN LEGAL DISPUTES

In various legal cases involving products, sheds, tools, machinery, and even steel, there is an inevitable timeline: **15 to 20 years**. Over this period, these assets deteriorate, and the financial stakes are significant. Nationally, these cases impact not only the lives of plaintiffs and defendants but also the overall well-being of our country.

To address these losses, we propose innovative solutions. By establishing specialized units, we can swiftly reinstate lost properties and manpower, thereby capitalizing on their inherent advantages. Imagine a parallel system—a **speedy decree mechanism**—initiated by the government. This system would operate independently of ongoing business activities, saving substantial resources: money, time, and human effort otherwise spent in courtrooms.

Consider the potential transformation: machinery and inventories, currently tied up in legal battles, could be reactivated within **24 hours**. These units would promptly withdraw cases, facilitating swift settlements. As a result, businesses would thrive, partnerships would flourish, and a diverse array of products and services would find global markets. Lives would bloom, and the economy would receive a much-needed boost.

Moreover, the sheer number of business units—large and small—holds promise. By streamlining legal processes, we could eradicate poverty more effectively. No longer would big business houses be swallowed by smaller, ancillary suppliers. Instead, they would coexist harmoniously, contributing to a vibrant economic landscape.

1. One fine morning, these ancillary units are shutting down their operations because their fraudulent practices remain hidden from public awareness. They lack the ability to confront their powerful superiors, fearing threats to their lives or harm to their families.
2. Cheating small businesses has become routine, with false promises and enticing offers for new projects and bulk business opportunities. Unfortunately, these small units are unable to react due to various constraints, including the high cost of legal remedies.
3. Family responsibilities and other circumstances force them to think twice, and pursuing legal action through the court system is often time-consuming. Many wise individuals choose not to follow this lengthy process.
4. Establishing a new legal body could be a solution to protect small units. By verifying genuine documents and records maintained by both parties, cases could be resolved swiftly instead of dragging on for years.

## STREAMLINING LEGAL PROCESSES FOR EFFICIENT CASE RESOLUTION

In our legal system, an overwhelming number of cases with diverse complexities often lead to backlog. Unfortunately, this backlog prevents timely decisions based on authentic records. Additionally, courts grapple with competing priorities, especially when entrenched in outdated procedures.

To address this, we propose a pragmatic approach. Rather than allowing cases to languish indefinitely, we can expedite resolution. How? We request that both parties present relevant documents, categorized using a checklist provided by government-authorized officials. These officials would oversee verification, ensuring accuracy and efficiency.

The benefits are manifold. First, substantial time savings would allow courts to focus on other critical matters. Second, leveraging invoices, delivery notes, and bank transactions as evidence streamlines proceedings. Finally, empowering officials of equal rank to swiftly settle cases during a single or minimal sitting could revolutionize our legal system.

Consider implementing a specialized court for business-related cases. Such a move would not only save manpower and financial resources but also foster national growth. Let's prioritize efficiency and justice, ensuring a brighter future for all.

The early resolution of legal cases or court decrees not only provides financial and mental relief to the parties involved but also benefits their dependents, families, and employees. By avoiding prolonged legal battles, individuals can escape the burden of mental anguish, poverty, and other hardships. Moreover, the nation as a whole benefits when dormant resources become active after the resolution of a decree. Additionally, this discourages malicious individuals from creating baseless cases out of enmity, serving as a lesson to others.

However, the current system has its challenges. For instance, a certain percentage of the disputed amount must be deposited in court, and related expenses can be prohibitive for smaller entities fighting against more powerful opponents. Furthermore, cases related to cheating often fail to reach or impact the wrongdoer, who may cleverly manipulate the situation to hinder the growth of small and marginal units. Consequently, families connected to such cases often face dire circumstances, resorting to begging or even contemplating suicide.

An alternative approach could involve accepting an affidavit from the affected party, allowing the case to proceed while collecting the owed amount later upon decree. This streamlined process could alleviate financial strain and provide a more efficient resolution for those involved.

1. **Court Directives and Speedy Remedies**: When a court issues a directive, it carries significant weight, and compliance is generally expected. Such directives can be beneficial for complainants seeking justice. However, there's a common issue: large corporations often create delays when cases are brought before the court. These delays can stretch for years, causing frustration for litigants. To address this, we need effective remedies that protect small businesses. Perhaps a new law could provide a swift resolution mechanism, ensuring justice without unnecessary delays.

2. **Preserving Small Business Units**: Unfortunately, when a small business shuts down, it often goes unnoticed. Yet, these enterprises are essential economic contributors. Governments should prioritize their protection rather than allowing them to vanish forever. Perhaps senior officials, supported by a small team, could handle document-related cases efficiently. Verifying financial records promptly could benefit both businesses and their employees. This approach avoids overwhelming the court system while safeguarding economic growth.

3. **Confidence in Investments**: Encouraging small investments among friends and relatives can be a powerful tool for family stability and national progress. However, people often worry about the safety of their money. <u>To change mindsets, the government has to take the initiative to instill confidence through well-crafted laws and regulations</u>

The cheating practices are spreading on a large-scale, and legal protection against them seems impossible for an ordinary person. The government should take steps to instill self-confidence among the public, which is crucial for the nation's economic growth.

In cases beyond the control of existing legal provisions, individuals should be allowed to approach higher authorities. However, these higher-ups must operate within the boundaries set by law and its clauses.

Court decrees should carry significant weight, and related records should prevent further appeals to the apex court. Clear guidelines on whether a case can be appealed or not would help avoid unnecessary litigation at the lower court level.

Additionally, we must consider the loss of manpower to the nation at various levels.

## REVISED PARAGRAPHS:

Rampant cheating practices pose a significant challenge, and legal remedies often elude the average citizen. To bolster economic growth, the government must foster public confidence.

When existing constitutional provisions fall short, individuals should have recourse to higher authorities. However, these channels must operate within the bounds of established laws and regulations.

Court decrees should carry substantial weight, and relevant records should discourage further appeals to higher courts. Clear guidelines on appeal possibilities would streamline the legal process and reduce unnecessary cases.

Beyond legal matters, we must also address the loss of human resources across different sectors, a critical consideration for our nation's progress. **Ensuring Justice**: At this level, the correctness of both parties is safeguarded. All decrees are grounded in recorded evidence and established causes. Given this, why should a second chance be granted if the decision remains stable and correct, verified through official records?

**Efficiency and Well-Being**: Consider the time spent in courtrooms and the associated financial costs. By optimizing these resources, significant savings can be achieved. When individuals have the means, ample time, and good health, innovative ideas emerge. Collaborative efforts, such as joint ventures, can lead to the cultivation and marketing of organic food grains. This, in turn, has the potential to reduce hospitalization rates and other medical interventions.

# CHAPTER XIII

# UNCONVENTIONAL PUNISHMENT: A DIFFERENT APPROACH

"This approach aims to streamline processes and save time. Minor or trivial cases can be handled by the unit manager. Additionally, other team members can observe the disciplinary steps. It's important to note that these punishment systems are not meant to permanently exclude individuals from the community but rather to encourage a positive change in their attitude toward life."

In this unique form of punishment, the accused need not endure questioning or physical torment. No police or authorities are involved; instead, they remain within the unit, keeping the matter confidential. Compared to the nation's existing methods, this punishment may seem trivial.

Rather than opting for a conventional approach, this modern style of punishment focuses on mental impact. It provides ample time for reflection, discouraging repetition of the offense. The primary goal is to prompt introspection—to make the wrongdoer contemplate their actions. It's akin to disciplining a family member, where the objective is not to sever family ties permanently.

The initial punishment lasts only 12 months, while subsequent offenses extend it to 24 months. Importantly, this system denies a third chance to the household, effectively barring them from continued membership. After all, if they resist change, why should we concern ourselves with their rehabilitation?

## EMPOWERING SELF-RESPONSIBILITY: RISING FROM ADVERSITY

We recognize that none of us are inherently criminals; our actions are shaped by the environment we inhabit. Within this unit, our mission is to cultivate moral citizens who contribute to society, not only for our nation but also for the global community. Despite your challenging background, you possess the potential to elevate yourself to a world-class level.

Let us acknowledge a fundamental truth: no one else will champion our cause. Our lives are our own responsibility, and waiting for external validation or assistance is futile. We must grasp that our destiny lies solely in our hands. Anticipating rescue or expecting others to pave our path is unrealistic.

Consider this: achieving greatness from adversity is commendable. Unlike a privileged child, whose ascent is facilitated by parental care and resources, your journey from a neglected sector to a position of prominence is extraordinary. Embrace your uniqueness and appreciate the resilience that brought you here.

"You have been chosen from a special category because your value extends beyond society, our nation, and even the world. Your worth must be demonstrated through unwavering dedication and sacrifices for the greater cause. As you continue your journey, rest assured that recognition and commendation await you.

Respectfully, your life has been transformed from its previous state. Each facility and improvement has been meticulously provided, considering financial constraints. Your daily experiences reflect this positive change.

Despite our efforts to persuade and enlighten you, your unwavering attitude toward the unit and your neighbors remains unyielding.

**This steadfastness sets you apart, proving your uniqueness twice over** *We are a busy unit, each of us engrossed in our respective duties. We cannot afford to allocate time to monitor typical members like you, nor can we continue to pardon your repeated mistakes. Your actions have the potential to adversely affect other members, and as a result, the unit has made the difficult decision to evict you and your family.*

When faced with challenges, a weak mind falters, but a strong one transforms adversity into opportunity. In this case, the unit has chosen to prioritize the security of the other 199 families by granting your wish for relief.

Your property and belongings can be sold to the unit or purchased by willing members. The home you once occupied is no longer associated with the unit. All financial transactions will be settled through the bank account in full."

*Without causing any dispute, the unit manager and the legal adviser must handle the situation. The unit should not decide the fate of the member; it is up to them to suffer or enjoy. If they request a certificate related to their unit membership, we can provide one with the necessary details, without hiding anything.*

*Why is such a typical punishment imposed when mistakes are made? If a member acts against the unit and it financially impacts the unit, we should first recover the money and then suspend the member's household (including all family members) for 12 months. During this suspension period, they won't be allowed to avail of benefits from the unit, but they can continue their association with the unit.*

*We should forgive members for their minor mistakes, but financial harm to the unit cannot be considered trivial. Whether intentional or not, they must recognize the error. Therefore, every member should thoroughly understand the bylaws, and a copy should be provided to each of them.*

*While 12 months may not seem long, it is necessary for members to realize their mistakes. Despite being a straightforward punishment, all other family members suffer as well. They are once again forced to return to their previous lifestyle due to the guilty conscience of one family member, even after receiving guidance and assistance from the unit and other members.*

*To address this matter without conflict, the unit manager and legal adviser should take charge. The unit itself should refrain from determining the fate of any member; that responsibility lies with the individuals involved. Whether they suffer or find joy, it is their prerogative.*

*When a member seeks a certificate related to their unit affiliation, we can provide one, transparently stating the relevant details. Concealing information is not our practice.*

*As for the seemingly harsh punishments for mistakes, consider this: if a member's actions negatively impact the unit financially, we must prioritize recovery. In such cases, suspending the entire household (including all family members) for 12 months becomes necessary. During this suspension, they forfeit benefits from the unit, but their association continues.*

*While leniency is appropriate for minor errors, financial repercussions cannot be dismissed lightly. Whether intentional or not, members must acknowledge their missteps. To ensure clarity, every member should be well-versed in the unit's bylaws, and each should receive a copy.*

*Although 12 months may appear brief, it serves as a crucial period for self-reflection. This seemingly straightforward punishment has broader implications: other family members share the consequences. Despite the unit's guidance and support, they find themselves once again navigating their previous lifestyle due to the guilty conscience of a single-family member.*

*From the very next day onward, individuals within the unit sever their connections with one another until their punishment period concludes. If any member harbors revenge against fellow unit members or the unit management, or if they trespass on unit properties—even if those properties are technically theirs according to bylaws—they face double the original penalty. This extended period amounts to 24 months away from the unit, during which they must remain apart.*

*The unit takes a compassionate approach, refusing to view its members as inherently criminal. Instead, they treat them as family, choosing to forget their past transgressions. The unit acknowledges the difficult circumstances these individuals have faced. Their vision is to foster a culture where members support one another, compensating for the years of love and assistance they may have lost.*

*Rather than solely punishing wrongdoers, the unit aims to help them recognize their mistakes. Even after extensive persuasion and education, some members persist in their selfish habits. In such cases, the consequences extend beyond the individual—impacting the entire unit like a closely-knit family.*

**Why does punishing one member affect the entire family?** When a family member faces consequences for their actions, it places immense pressure on them. Their actions may have caused suffering for everyone in the family, leading to a dreary and unfulfilling life. By suspending their membership, they forfeit certain privileges, including discounted prices on purchases within the unit and other helpful facilities they previously enjoyed.

<u>Going forward, the unit will treat this member (referred to as "Home") as an outsider for either twelve or twenty-four months, depending on the circumstances.</u>

Even after the suspension period ends, they won't regain the right to participate in financial matters or unit management, potentially impacting their career growth within the unit. During this time, other members are strictly prohibited from interacting with them or providing any assistance, as such actions are punishable.

**Remember:** Punishment significantly impacts your career growth. *Once a member leaves the unit, they won't be eligible for any leadership positions. However, they can continue as an ordinary member. They'll be exempt from political, caste-related, and religious promotion activities. While they remain free to practice their religion, their involvement in unit functions will be limited. In politics, they can cast their vote but are restricted from other related activities.*

**Avoid Politics, Embrace Unity**: In this unit, politics is strictly prohibited. While the unit comprises 200 members, refrain from forming any political factions. Instead, focus on your civic duty by casting your vote. Political maneuvering won't save you; prioritize a life of abundance and well-being.

1. **Building Bonds, Achieving Goals**: Our unit's agenda centers on fostering relationships among members and creating a sense of family. This camaraderie is essential for achieving our collective objectives. Let go of criminal tendencies and recognize that hard work is the path to overcoming poverty.

2. **Financial Progress and Lifestyle Shifts**: As the unit progresses financially, adapt your lifestyle and learn from past mistakes. Remember, you have only one life—live it fully. Avoid animosity among members; forgiveness is key to our success.

3. **You Are Capable**: Many underestimate the abilities of rural folks, but you possess the power to manage your affairs. Through this unit, prove your capabilities. Rather than blaming the government, let's transform our mindset and uplift ourselves.

"We are confident that our unit will thrive, encompassing every corner of the countryside. It will illuminate the lives of our members beyond their wildest expectations. Within a mere few months, rural life will transform, elevating its inhabitants to above-average citizens. The population will awaken to the realization of past mistakes—years squandered in vain.

Never underestimate the countryside folk; they are bright and skilled contributors to our unit. Their hard work serves as the cornerstone for our growth. Through unwavering dedication, they will ascend to prosperity, leveraging their abilities and strength. These achievements unfold daily, accessible to all who care to listen. Your progress as a collective force is remarkable—a lifelong strength that transcends individual membership.

Take a moment to compare your past and present lifestyles when you find yourself free. The joint efforts of our members, multiplying income and prosperity day by day, constitute the very essence of our unit's success. Remember, you are the masters of all unit properties; there's no need for guilt. Each co-member's earnings are on par, a truth inherent to our shared membership."

# CHAPTER XIV

# UNIT MUST BE BUSINESS ORIENTED

When we transform our units into paradises that attract members from outside, a natural flow will begin toward these units. It's essential to avoid direct competition with other units by offering unique products and maintaining positive relationships.

During the formation of a unit, whether in business or agriculture, we should consolidate existing businesses under its umbrella. Expert evaluation of these businesses is crucial. By providing high-quality industrial products and machinery, we can meet the demands of our members.

However, we must be mindful of our impact on the environment. Factories should not disrupt the lives of residents or harm the local ecosystem through pollution. Consider supporting small-scale industries that coexist harmoniously with human beings and animals. Our goal isn't merely financial gain; it's to create a peaceful living environment for all members within each unit.

1. **Acing Initiative in Product Marketing**: To attract orders and customers, your unit must proactively market its products. Focus on offering **selective and high-quality** items, even if the range is limited. Sometimes, a **single standout product** can alter the course of your entire business history.
2. **Becoming a Hub for Visitors**: As your reputation grows, visitors will flock to your unit. Your **masterpiece products**—perhaps just

one or two—will make you famous. These visitors will entrust you with their ideas and drawings, recognizing your ability to meet their needs. This influx of creativity will transform your unit into a bustling hub.

3. **Balancing Urban and Rural Influence**: While the distinction between city and rural areas may not be stark, reaching a certain equilibrium is crucial. Once your unit attains this level, there's no need to look back.

4. **Prioritizing Growth**: Acknowledge that we are behind in terms of progress. However, it's not a mistake; it's an opportunity. Let's focus on our growth. As our financial position improves, we can contribute to our nation in meaningful ways, and the government will likely support our endeavors.

## EMPOWERING RURAL COMMUNITIES FOR POSITIVE CHANGE

The government faces challenges in implementing rules and regulations within rural populations, particularly due to high illiteracy rates and the stubborn nature of many individuals. However, there are several advantages that can significantly transform lifestyles in a short period. Let's explore these benefits:

1. **Corporate Unit Formation**: A corporate business model has been established, with plans to operate through its employees. This unit aims to enhance rural livelihoods and economic prospects.

2. **Ownership and Membership**: The unit is akin to family property, and its ownership vests in 200 carefully selected homes. Each member holds equal rights, contributing to a sense of collective ownership.

3. **Skills Enhancement**: To thrive in this dynamic environment, individuals must invest in education, gain practical experience, and seek knowledge from diverse sources. This will equip them

to manage large-scale businesses, agriculture, allied activities, and industries effectively.

4. **Learn From Failures**: It's Essential To Assess Failures Objectively And Learn From Them. By Doing So, Rural Entrepreneurs Can Adapt And Improve Their Strategies.

5. **Vigilance and Trust**: While collaborating with fellow members, remain vigilant. Be cautious of any deceptive behavior. Trust should be earned through genuine actions, not mere pretense.

**Remember:** *empowering rural communities requires collective effort and a commitment to growth.*

1 **Leverage Your Studies and Experience**: Your education and practical experience hold immense value for the growth of our unit. Each time you apply your knowledge, it contributes to our collective progress.

Beyond the syllabus, explore life's lessons and find ways to implement that wisdom within our unit. Unite with others to enhance our overall performance.

2. **Embrace Your Bright Ideas**: Each one of you possesses unique brilliance and a wealth of ideas. Now, you have the opportunity to showcase these ideas to your peers, who can then put them into action within our unit.

Remember, our unit serves as a platform for your performance. Unlike your ancestors, who lacked this chance, you can freely share your seemingly small or unconventional ideas. Discuss their positive aspects and outline how you envision implementing them.

3. **Skills That Transform**: Cultivate various skills; they will propel our unit toward becoming a proud business entity swiftly.

Recognize that this gift—unavailable to your ancestors—allows you to draw from their experiences and the struggles they endured merely to survive. Your understanding of their stories adds depth to your journey.

1. **Leverage Experience for Unit Growth**: Utilize your experiences to contribute to the unit's development. Avoid repeating the mistakes of your ancestors within the unit. Discuss your ideas openly with others, ensuring clear communication and shared visions.

2. **Overcoming Ancestral Struggles**: Break free from the struggles and hardships that plagued your ancestors in their countryside lives. Abandon the habit of relying solely on government support. Instead, work diligently to make the unit self-sufficient and prosperous. By doing so, you'll not only benefit personally but also enhance your family's lifestyle.

3. **Aiming for Excellence**: Aspire to create a world-class lifestyle through collective effort. Every member must closely monitor each stage of the unit's growth. Be vigilant about negative influences within the unit. Detecting and addressing these issues early on is crucial to maintaining steady progress.

4. **Remember** that the unit's success hinges on your ability to confront any negative behavior among fellow members. It may take time, but eventually, you'll realize how the unit positively impacts everyone involved.

Never allow any member to undermine your unit, even through words. By establishing similar units across the nation in rural areas, you can foster developmental activities and collaborate with other units. Seize control of their growth, and soon, you'll witness substantial progress in your family business.

## CENSUS DETAILS – LANDS

The unit's responsibility is to furnish the government with comprehensive information about land. This includes details such as total area, land type (wet or dry), and its current use. Additionally, the unit must differentiate between government-owned properties and private or individual rights to ensure an accurate understanding of the land within its jurisdiction.

By accessing data from multiple units, the government can promptly identify land details and any unauthorized encroachments. If the government compensates the units for services rendered—such as providing land information, collecting revenue, and granting concessions on outstanding taxes—it can significantly bolster the unit's financial stability.

1. **Land Classification Based on Ownership**: The total area of land can be categorized into two distinct ownership types: private land and community land. Private land is individually owned, including plots and private farming areas. In contrast, community land is collectively owned by the local community for common purposes such as gathering fodder, fruits, nuts, or medicinal herbs.

2. These **Community Lands** Are Also Referred To As Common Property Resources. Examples Of Community Land Include Public Gardens And Community Forests.

3. **Data Collection through Census**: The government gathers essential information through various units, including birth and death records. Additionally, data on individuals—such as men, women, and children—along with their age groups, dates of birth, educational backgrounds, and current assets and liabilities are collected. This comprehensive data helps inform policy decisions and resource allocation.

4. Assessing Area Growth: By analyzing the available data, the government can assess the growth and development of a specific area. These details are stored in their system, allowing for periodic evaluations. Furthermore, the unit responsible for data

collection can also provide insights into its activities, including investment details, income sources, and expenditure patterns.

**Remember::** *that this information serves as a general overview, and specific procedures may vary based on local regulations and administrative practices.*

## THE IMPACT OF THE UNIT ON MEMBERS' LIVES

From its inception, the unit has significantly transformed the lifestyle of its members. Operating as a cohesive group, these individuals leverage their inborn skills and abilities to contribute effectively. As a result, they have become more resilient in facing life's challenges.

The unit's association with a large community has gradually infused its members with enthusiasm. They now confront difficult situations head-on, drawing strength from their collective bond. Whether it's government offices, semi-government institutions, schools, hospitals, or even residential spaces, the unit maintains detailed records of all its particulars, including access to light and water sources.

While infrastructure development, such as roads and public transport, lies beyond the unit's purview due to cost constraints, essential amenities like gas and electricity connections are accessible to all members. Moreover, the government efficiently collects revenue from unit members, streamlining the process by consolidating payments into a single lot.

1. **Reducing Charges for Rural Houses**: The unit has the option to request the government to waive charges imposed on rural houses for a duration of 5 to 10 years. This waiver would apply until the unit becomes financially self-sufficient. If your unit is conveniently located near main roads or highway bypasses, consider exploring the possibility of establishing a petrol pump as an additional business venture.

2. **Apartments for All Members**: Instead of constructing new individual houses or repairing existing ones (which can be costly), the unit could consider developing a complex of multiple apartments within its boundaries. Placing these apartments strategically in corners of the unit would allow members to oversee their properties effectively.

3. Prioritizing this apartment project and allocating units to those in need can be facilitated through bank financing. The goal is to complete 200 apartments within 3-4 years. By adopting this approach, we create an apartment system that offers safety and essential amenities for all members, while minimizing unnecessary expenses related to maintaining and repairing old houses.

1. The families can watch over their properties if they settle in the corners of the unit limit. Apartments for all are situated in the four corners of the properties, with a total of 200 apartments (50 per corner). These apartments feature spacious rooms and facilities suitable for joint families. By ensuring uniformity among the apartments, we can prevent unnecessary arguments and differences among the members.

2. Within the unit, each family's income and rights are well-defined. All members have permanent employment, and their needs are collectively supported by the unit. In this context, there is no inclination toward separating nuclear families or breaking away from the main stem family. The unity among the houses and members becomes a strong bond.

3. The unit can share information about its members through the census with the government. In return, if the government provides a service charge to the unit and credits it to their bank loan, it would serve as additional financial assistance for the unit and its members.

4. The government's allocation of funds helps in constructing apartments for the members. Although the funding is

repayable, the unit can manage it effectively. Additionally, the government's financial aid temporarily supports their essential projects.

## UNIT-LEVEL EXECUTION BEYOND INFRASTRUCTURE DEVELOPMENT

Apart from large-scale infrastructure projects, essential tasks fall under the purview of individual units. However, even for these tasks, we must seek approval from government authorities. Our current financial situation restricts us from investing in infrastructure beyond basic necessities like food and daily routines.

Additionally, the funds allocated to our unit can be treated as a refundable loan, which will facilitate regular repayments.

## GOVERNMENT RURAL FUNDS: A PATH TO TRANSPARENCY

The government has an opportunity to distribute rural funds transparently, avoiding corruption and malpractices. By channeling these funds through local units, we can ensure they reach genuine beneficiaries. This shift not only saves money and effort but also optimizes staff resources that were previously dedicated to remote area development. Similarly, redirecting rural funds from their former use benefits the countryside.

"The census system was an organized method of accounting where each unit meticulously recorded and reported data to the government. These records were based on actual collections or events, making them more reliable and accurate. With computerized backups, statements or copies can be accessed on any given date, providing an immediate advantage for government use.

The establishment of such units would significantly alleviate financial burdens for the poor, as it directly benefits the beneficiaries.

Furthermore, the government can efficiently allocate rural funds without third-party interference or lapses. Payments and financial support can be routed through loan accounts or other debts held by the unit, thereby reducing their liability. These funds are essential for running the unit, including activities like land cultivation, converting wasteland, and utilizing government lands with proper permissions.

Additionally, if permits are granted, the unit could purchase government land or have it allotted in the names of unprivileged members, bringing this matter to the government's attention."

## OVERDRAFT LIMIT IN BANKS

An overdraft limit, subject to periodic review, can be extended indefinitely. Given the frequent daily transactions, the bank closely monitors each entry. The manager may delegate this responsibility to one or more subordinates, who meticulously comment on every entry in a diary or similar record.

Authentication by the designated officer on special duty is not a prerequisite for passing an entry. However, entries lacking comments from the officer or team head are not approved. These comments can be either brief or detailed.

Banks furnish comprehensive information to account holders regarding each transaction in their accounts.

Rather than relying solely on overdrafts, banks can structure loans with repayment schedules spanning 240 months, commencing after an initial 60-month period. Remarkably, no interest is levied during this grace period. Such an arrangement significantly benefits operational units.

While interest-free loans from banks remain unlikely, gradual accumulation over several years is a viable approach. Additionally, if the government extends support to the unit, outstanding bank interest can be settled using rural fund allocations. The overdraft facility of the unit may also receive credits from rural funds or similar government assistance to cover interest payments on financing.

1.  **Government Assistance and Loan Management**: When government payments, including service charges and other encouraging funds, are allocated to the unit, it is essential to maintain a proper account of these transactions within the loan or overdraft (OD) limits. By doing so, the unit can efficiently track government assistance. Additionally, the unit has the flexibility to close its financial obligations earlier than the bank's fixed repayment schedule.

2.  **Direct Crediting of Government Assistance**: Given that the unit oversees the affairs of all its members, the financial aid received from the government can be directly credited to the unit's loan account. These details should be meticulously recorded in the unit's records. While the settlement can occur at a later stage, it is crucial to inform the relevant authorities about the received amount.

3.  **Asset Creation and Equitable Distribution**: The funds received through government channels can be strategically utilized to create assets for members who are significantly less well-off than others. This approach aims to equalize the overall assets held by unit members. **Meeting Unexpected Needs**: The unit ensures that the needs of all members are met. In cases of unforeseen requirements, members can submit written requests to the manager for approval, whether in cash or in kind.

## LAND LIMIT ADJUSTMENTS FOR MEMBERS

The land limits among members vary, leading to potential disparities. To address this, we propose an adjustment based on leasing assets for official purposes.

1.  **Minimum Land Limit**: Each member should possess a minimum of one acre of land. This standard ensures fairness, especially for those with significant differences in land holdings.

When there's a substantial gap between members' land sizes, the manager can establish a lease amount for excess land. This payment should be ongoing, acknowledging that it exceeds the existing fund vested in the unit.

2. **Implementation and Record-Keeping**: The unit should maintain a record of this arrangement.

   After 36 months, the process begins one member at a time, clearing excess land based on the unit's financial position.

3. **Documented Agreement**: The member and the unit can execute a formal document or agreement.

   The excess amount can be deposited with the unit for a minimum of five years, with interest applicable (Bank rate + 2%).

4. **Withdrawal Process**: Members can withdraw the amount gradually without disrupting the unit's smooth functioning.

   This approach ensures equitable treatment while maintaining operational efficiency.

"All unit members are well-informed about the fund status, including the bank balance and the reasons behind fund fluctuations. In non-emergency situations, it is advisable to refrain from withdrawing funds from your deposits. These adjustments and payments aim to equalize property holdings among member homes.

To address excess land ownership, convene a meeting with landlords. Obtain a lease agreement in the unit's name from eligible owners who possess more land than the unit's minimum requirement of land is fixed. The agreement should allow owners to release their property by paying the due amount to the unit at any time.

By releasing the property from the unit that member is not gaining anything other than no liability is exist on it. But, until the regularization or equalization of land is completed among all members either you can sell that property to other members or to the unit to meet any extra ordinary requirements.

According to the nature of the land and properties the rate will be vary, you can very well depend the government rates declared in that area/ locality..

Even if a home releases or pays the lease amount, the unit will retain custody of the property. Using the cumulative fund associated with member houses, the unit can allocate land to individual members to balance property distribution.

Any surplus funds can be deposited within the unit to help reduce the overdraft limit. Additionally, the manager can issue deposit receipts to concerned members, payable after 60 months, along with the specified interest.

## FOR LAND LEASING, A FIXED ACREAGE DETERMINES THE PAYABLE AMOUNT FOR EACH MEMBER."

1. **Land Agreement and Deposit Receipts**: Suppose an owner possesses 2.5 acres of land, but the required limit for the unit is only one acre. In this scenario, the unit must pay the landlord for the excess of 1.5 acres. To formalize this arrangement, an agreement should be executed between the unit and its members. Additionally, deposit receipts should be issued to all parties involved. Any remaining surplus land should be allocated among other members based on their proportional ownership.

2. **Deposit Receipts and Withdrawal**: The Deposit Receipt serves as a commitment by the unit to repay the specified amount within 60 months, along with accrued interest. If any member urgently needs to withdraw their deposit before maturity, they can do so on a priority basis, subject to the manager's decision.

3. **Profit Distribution and Debt Adjustment**: Profit sharing among the 200 homes should occur equally through their respective accounts after 36 months or once the profit reaches a 33% threshold from the fourth year onward. If any member has outstanding debt related to their house or land, the unit can use their share of the profit to offset that liability.

4. However, the total profit distribution should not exceed 50% of the net profit. Any remaining liabilities should be adjusted by the respective member from their share of the profit.

The outside debts of our members on their property, if it affects the unit, only the unit manager has to interfere in such cases of loans or other types of debts, and the matter gets amicably settled. If it is a small amount and able to be borne by the unit financially, it can be settled through the unit obtaining proper documents from the debtor and creditor.

A lien of a certain amount has to be created on the document, and it has to be cleared from the amount that is paid from the unit to the particular home. The document to that effect has to be prepared by the unit's legal adviser and registered, and kept under the unit's custody until the debt is cleared.

For this purpose, the unit can fix a lease on the land and make a note of it in the unit's records to calculate among the members. The unit cannot undertake the huge liabilities of the members but can help to the maximum extent if the financial stability of the unit allows it to do so.

Rather than clearing the outside liability of a few members, the unit has to safeguard the majority of the members so that the financial position can be kept stable to meet any emergency in the future.

When our members incur external debts related to their property, the responsibility for intervention lies with the unit manager. In cases involving loans or other types of debts, the matter is resolved amicably. If the debt is relatively small and within the unit's financial capacity, it can be settled by obtaining proper documentation from both the debtor and the creditor.

To address outstanding debts, a lien is placed on the relevant document. The unit must ensure that the amount owed is deducted from payments made to the specific home. Our legal adviser prepares and registers this document, which remains under the unit's custody until the debt is fully cleared.

As part of this process, the unit may establish a land lease and record it in our official records for member calculations. While the unit cannot assume substantial liabilities on behalf of its members, it strives to assist with its financial stability.

Rather than prioritizing the clearance of external liabilities for a few members, the unit's primary duty is to protect the majority. Maintaining a stable financial position ensures readiness to address any future emergencies.

"The members with much liability can join in the venture. The entire family has to work for the unit. Since the unit meets the day-to-day requirements, the salary will be set aside to meet your liabilities. Whether it is related to payments made by the unit toward loans or other financial matters, you can collect the statement of account from the unit.

A lease agreement must be executed with the unit, specifying all particulars of the property. Additionally, compile a list of nominee names, including their details such as name, date of birth, relationship, and other legally required information as advised by our legal adviser."

## REVISED VERSION

"Individuals with significant responsibilities can participate in the venture. The entire family is expected to contribute to the unit's operations. As the unit fulfills day-to-day needs, a portion of the salary will be reserved to address your liabilities. Whether it pertains to loan repayments or other financial transactions, you can obtain account statements from the unit.

To formalize this arrangement, a lease agreement should be drafted with the unit, outlining specific property details. Additionally, compile a list of nominee names, including relevant information such as their names, dates of birth, relationships, and other legally necessary details, as advised by our legal expert."

1. **Membership and Payment Collection**: The unit is responsible for collecting membership fees and other necessary payments. New members are eligible for a proportionate share of the annual payment previously received by existing members. To join, individuals must sign a copy of our bylaws, complete an application form, and maintain a file as required.

2. **Emergency Fund and Disbursement**: In case of emergencies such as accidents, the unit establishes a fund. This fund is intended to provide assistance to affected families. The fund's limit is ten times the last drawn annual income of the family or is determined based on a parameter set by the manager. Repayment occurs over 36 months in equal installments, interest-free.

3. **Funeral Expenses**: Certain expenses, such as those related to funerals, do not require reimbursement. As the unit grows, we

plan to introduce additional welfare schemes, adjusting the amount allocated for expenses accordingly.

4.  **Membership Across Units**: Members of a home or unit can also be part of other units. It's advisable to inform both units if necessary, even if you don't currently reside in either of them.

5.  **Farming and Fencing** While financial stability is often our primary focus, safeguarding our crops, products, and valuables is equally crucial. Consider starting with temporary fencing. Instead of constructing multiple buildings, sheds, or storage spaces, opt for fencing as a practical alternative.

Despite the cost, fencing becomes a necessity. Transform your entire land into a gated property to protect your loved ones, properties, and crops. Rather than fencing each property separately, a single fence can serve all your needs.

Growing anything is a challenge, but the key lies in safeguarding it and converting it into value. As a landowner, vigilance is essential—protects your crops and valuables from theft and other threats. We all know that production costs can be steep.

Initially, adopt indigenous methods to safeguard your assets for the first 3-4 years. Later, consider investing in robust fencing or compound walls. Whether it's small or large crops, exercise care. Never allow unauthorized access to your property without your consent and knowledge.

*With a limited number of members, we can enhance our safety by restricting access to outsiders.* Since all 200 family members know each other, identifying an unfamiliar person becomes easier. *Never allow entry to a third-party onto your property without permission through the unit office.*

*To manage third-party access effectively, Consider the following steps.*

1. **Register Entries:** Maintain a register at the unit office to record details of visitors. If anything seems suspicious, closely monitor the individual.
2. **CCTV Records:** In the current scenario, surveillance footage from office CCTV cameras can provide crucial information and potentially save lives.

## ADDITIONAL BENEFITS OF LIMITED MEMBERSHIP

1. **Swift Issue Resolution:** With fewer members, addressing issues becomes more efficient. Problems can be resolved promptly.
2. **Security and Peace:** Outsiders attempting illegal activities can disrupt the peaceful lives of community members. Vigilance is essential.

## EMPOWERING MEMBERS

1. **Education and Awareness:** Regular study sessions and awareness classes will boost members' knowledge and alertness.
2. **Police Collaboration:** Coordinate with police officials to conduct educational sessions for residents under their jurisdiction.

**Remember:** *safeguarding our lives and maintaining a harmonious community requires collective effort.*

## FENCING AND PROPERTY PROTECTION

Securing your property is essential, even though fencing can be costly. Instead of fencing each individual land or crop, consider enclosing the entire property under one unit. Additionally, explore other security measures such as **CCTV surveillance**. While expenses may seem daunting, remember that they can often be recovered from the yields of forthcoming crops.

## FISH FARMING

When your farm and the surrounding area are fully covered or fenced, it becomes feasible to focus solely on farming. Although fish farming requires significant investment, it offers potential rewards. Theft is a concern, especially in certain areas.

To maximize efficiency, break down the farm into smaller units based on water availability. Utilize the workforce effectively—every member should contribute to the unit's tasks. The unit manager plays a crucial role, overseeing operations from the very beginning.

**Remember:** this is your business, and success depends on everyone's active participation and vigilance.

**Fish Farming Simplified**: Fish farming has gained immense popularity, with both local and export opportunities opening up. The production process is straightforward and easy to follow. To set up a successful fish farm, consider the following key points:

**Fenced Area**: Establish the farm within a fenced area.

**Individual Tank Fencing**: Each tank should have its own fencing.

**Night Security**: Implement security measures to prevent theft, especially during nighttime.

1. **Choosing the Right Fish Variety**: Instead of dealing with multiple fish varieties, opt for a single species with a simple rearing method. This approach saves time and makes maintenance more manageable, especially when operating on a large-scale. By avoiding competition between different units, you can enhance overall efficiency. Remember to feed the fish timely and maintain water quality.
2. **Adapting to Climate and Maintenance**: Some fish species thrive in adverse climates. Consider these hardy varieties to reduce maintenance efforts. Additionally, members can rear tasty fish in two tanks or exchange fish with neighboring units
3. **Scaling Up and Fund Viability**: Start with a straightforward method and later expand based on available funds and crop viability. Prioritize the welfare of unit members by choosing an approach that facilitates easy fundraising and ensures their well-being.

**Remember**: *successful fish farming requires thoughtful planning and adherence to best practices.*

**Attention, every one:** Let's keep a close eye on our resources within the unit. There are lucrative opportunities awaiting us through activities like fish farming, poultry rearing (chickens and ducks), goat husbandry, and even cow farming. These ventures promise quick returns. To kick-start this, consider adopting straightforward methods that suit your circumstances..

**Remember**, *no plot of land within our unit should remain unutilized or idle.*

For those who may not be keen on direct farming, there are alternative ways to contribute. You can actively participate in other unit activities or propose financial support. Our agricultural pursuits encompass a variety of options: cultivating paddy, growing vegetables, nurturing fruit orchards, and tending to flowers. Assess the available land and choose crops wisely. Cash crops like coconut, rubber, pepper, and medicinal plants can yield substantial profits. Additionally, if our terrain allows, consider hilly plantations such as tea, coffee, or oranges.

Beyond crops, let's explore animal husbandry. Raising livestock for meat and milk—whether it's fish, chickens, ducks, or rabbits—can be a rewarding endeavor. Even our homes can become centers for egg and meat production. Experienced individuals with knowledge of cow or goat rearing can contribute alongside those focusing on poultry and fish.

**Remember:** *all investments will be made collectively by the unit."*

## ORGANIC FOOD CULTIVATION

When it comes to cultivating organic food, those who adulterate or poison food items pose a greater threat than a mere killer. To ensure a nutritious diet, consider growing food items directly within your unit. However, rearing animals may not be suitable for all units. If you lack the means to raise goats or cows, you can conveniently purchase milk from the nearest dairy.

Investing in milk need not be a significant expense if your environment isn't conducive to animal husbandry. Your nearby dairy unit can supply you with ample milk. Similarly, if you have sufficient water facilities, you can venture into fish farming and chicken rearing. Keep the involvement of manpower minimal to streamline operations.

Now, let's address the issue of doors in chicken farms. Constructing a shed in a canopy style can mitigate this problem. Erect a sturdy pipe as a central pillar punctuated with large holes. These holes should be positioned just above the height of the shed. Additionally, consider installing an exhaust fan. When the fan operates, it will expel the noxious air from the shed, ensuring a more pleasant environment. However, always be mindful of how the lingering smell might affect your neighbors.

1.  **Ventilation System for the Shed**:

Position a pipe vertically in the center of the shed at a height of 20 to 30 feet.

Seal the top of the pipe with a sheet, leaving about one foot of clearance. This allows air to escape.

This system effectively removes bad smells from the shed, ensuring a more pleasant environment.

2.  **Choosing the Right Pipes**:

Use broad-diameter plastic pipes for the bottom and narrower ones for the top.

Instead of repairing exhaust fans, consider replacing them entirely.

Ensure the pipe accommodates three full-time fans, which can be used alternately.

3.  **Efficient Farm Management**:

Alternate fan usage prolongs their lifespan.

Run the fans for one hour, four to five times a day, maintaining a fresh atmosphere.

These decisions can be discussed in a general meeting with experts and experienced members. Our focus is on generating quick revenue to meet urgent needs rather than prioritizing convenience at this time.

## HARVESTING AND MARKETING OF PRODUCTS

From a marketing perspective, we can initially promote all our products within our unit through the unit office. To facilitate this, we need a suitable area or building where we can store the entire crop, which will be managed by the unit office. From there, members can purchase the products.

Given that our unit represents around one thousand members, we have significant bargaining power when it comes to purchasing agricultural equipment and household necessities. However, we acknowledge that this approach doesn't provide a long-lasting solution to the challenges faced by rural communities.

Our primary goal is to find resources that allow us to live independently without relying solely on the government. While we continue to earn money and establish the flow of funds, we can explore more permanent solutions. Perhaps, with time and collective brainstorming, we'll discover innovative ways to address the rural population's needs.

When making bulk purchases, buyers will come directly to our unit. This presents an opportunity for us to negotiate extensively, ensuring favorable terms. Additionally, we can occasionally sell surplus products through these buyers without incurring additional discounts or commissions.

1. **Marketing and Development**: We have the opportunity to market our crops and other produce locally, leveraging the available resources. The growth and progress of our unit depend on our collective efforts. To ensure transparency, all income and expenditure should flow through our unit office. This way, every individual member can stay informed through regular updates from the office.

2. **Visible Growth and Data Collection**: The unit's growth is evident through the cash flow that reaches all families. It's a unique experience for each member. As part of our responsibilities, we must gather data to identify suitable markets for selling our products. Utilize your contacts and other sources to explore potential avenues.

3. **Planning for Further Development**: This information will guide us in determining the necessary steps for future development and increasing yield and income. Importantly, agricultural income is often not taxable in many countries, especially for units like ours. So, there's no need to worry about tax implications.

4. **Transparency and Reporting**: Be forthright in documenting the unit's income. Transparent records will facilitate access to bank finance when needed. Additionally, avoid concealing accounts from fellow members. Regularly share progress updates through statements posted on the office notice board for everyone's awareness and verification.

"Until the unit has financial stability, we must control our expenses. We need to understand that the unit was formed for our well-being, but without income, we cannot sustain it for at least the first three months. Our efforts should focus on generating income during this initial period. Both income and expenses must be diligently recorded by the unit office."

"The unit will initially manage our needs, including purchasing products, until a specified timeframe. Let's cooperate and support the unit during its financial challenges in the early stages. Our collective effort aims to exceed expectations, and we are committed to achieving our goals."

"Now that the unit is established, we can breathe a little easier and enjoy a more peaceful life. However, we still need to be patient and persevere until the unit grows enough to provide daily financial support."

"**Remember**: *All your needs are met by the unit. While others may spend extravagantly, the manager will set targets for non-essential purchases.*"

1. **Financial Stability and Income Generation**:

Until the unit achieves financial stability, it is crucial that we exercise strict control over our expenses. We must recognize that the unit was established for our collective well-being.

2. However, without a steady income, sustaining the unit during its initial three months becomes challenging. Our primary focus should be on generating revenue during this critical period. Both income and expenses must be meticulously recorded by the unit office.

3. **Early Support and Collective Effort**: In its initial stages, the unit will manage our essential needs, including product purchases. Let us collaborate and wholeheartedly support the unit during its financial challenges. Our combined efforts aim to surpass expectations, and we remain committed to achieving our shared goals.

4. **A More Peaceful Life**: Now that the unit is firmly established, we can breathe a sigh of relief and enjoy a more tranquil existence.

However, patience and perseverance remain essential until the unit grows sufficiently to provide daily financial support.

5. **Prudent Spending and Managerial Targets**: Remember that all our necessities are fulfilled by the unit. While some may indulge in extravagant spending, the manager will set specific targets for non-essential purchases.

## UNLOCKING SUCCESS: FROM GRASSROOTS TO PROSPERITY

Imagine a vibrant life for all members of your unit, where dreams take flight and aspirations soar. Your unwavering positivity propels you forward, transforming grassroots beginnings into the realm of above-average citizens within a mere 36 months.

Hard work becomes your ally, yielding positive outcomes. Collaborating with fellow members enriches your journey, infusing it with joy and fulfillment. As you embrace organic practices, your products become a beacon of health, attracting robust demand in the market. Strategically pricing these goods for bulk sales in distant cities promises increased profits.

Quality matters in the organic realm, and rightfully so; you can confidently command higher prices, knowing that your efforts contribute to the welfare of the organization and ultimately benefit even the most economically challenged members.

Navigating the market landscape, you encounter eager buyers—malls, supermarkets, wholesalers, hostels, hotels, and sprawling apartments—all seeking your offerings. While price negotiations may be necessary, the consistency of regular business remains your greatest advantage.

1. **Market Strategy for Subsequent Crops**: As you venture into subsequent crop cycles, consider exploring new avenues to

reach potential buyers. Diversify your marketing methods and adopt more effective approaches. Engage with the market daily, seeking opportunities to showcase your products.

To enhance brand recognition, package your goods with distinctive unit identities and emblems. These eye-catching packages serve as additional advertisements, reinforcing your product's appeal.

**Remember:** maintaining product quality is crucial. Avoid any adulteration or substandard practices. Upholding high standards will build goodwill in the market, ensuring your products remain sought-after.

2. **Balancing Product Growth and Marketing**: Growing products is often simpler than effective marketing. Recognize that selective product choices can streamline your efforts. Align your crop selection with market demand and seasonal trends.

By doing so, you'll find it easier to promote your offerings. Additionally, when dealing with bulk sales, optimize management processes. Consider direct supply to buyers through an engaged vehicle. This approach minimizes manpower requirements while ensuring efficient payment collection. With strategic planning, your products can establish a lasting foothold in the market.

1. **Wholesale Strategy**: Instead of dealing with retail sales, focus on direct wholesale buyers. Bundle your products and supply them directly to these buyers. This approach is more viable for the unit, even though the margins might be lower.
2. **Harvesting Approach**: When harvesting vegetables, fruits, or any other crops, start from one side and work your way to the other end. This method allows the unit to assess the harvested area accurately. The specific method (whether it's a chicken, fish, or goat strategy) is up to you.

3. **Care and Vigilance**: Every member of the unit should take responsibility for the crops and products. Avoid any chance of losses by being vigilant and proactive.

4. **Buyer Considerations**: Aim for bulk buyers and cultivate regular customers who will purchase the entire product when it's ready. However, ensure that the unit has a good understanding of the market and sets prices strategically rather than accepting whatever the buyer bargains for. Also, avoid growing crops that are already prevalent in neighboring units to prevent unhealthy competition.

5. **Payment and Harvest Confirmation**: Don't harvest the product until both the rate and quantities are confirmed. Collect advance or full payment before proceeding. Once the full payment is received through the bank, the unit office should inform the relevant official in writing, providing details about the product, where to start harvesting, and the expected quantity.

**Efficient Crop Handling:** We have a sufficient workforce to manage the unit's operations. When selling crops, we adhere to rigorous standards—weighing, counting, and assessing quality. Our commitment is to provide fresh produce without taking unnecessary risks.

**Evergreen Tiny Forest:** Within our unit, we're creating an entertainment area for kids and families. This mini forest, conveniently located, will also serve as a welcoming space for guests. Maintenance is crucial, and we encourage walking within this area. Instead of cement, we've opted for sand and thoughtful landscaping to enhance the ambiance. Walking barefoot or connecting with the earth directly can significantly impact your well-being.

**Addressing Climate Challenges:** The consistent rise in temperatures across rural areas poses a threat to lives. Recognizing this man-made hazard, our solution lies in the tiny forest. By providing sprinklers for tree watering, we maintain this green oasis—a natural remedy against environmental challenges.

1.  **Maintaining a Healthy Environment**:

Ensuring your unit's well-being involves more than just regulating temperature. Adequate water supply sparks creativity and provides insights into maintenance. Remember, health is wealth. Cultivate a clean and wholesome atmosphere for your family, instilling awareness about cleanliness.

2. **Community Gathering Spaces**:

Dedicate an hour—whether daily or weekly—for family gatherings. Amid busy schedules, this time fosters connections. Urbanization and climate change have replaced scenic landscapes with concrete jungles, leading to rising temperatures.

3. **Green Initiatives**:

Drawing from your farming backgrounds, consider creating evergreen mini-forests within your community. Compete to beautify these spaces. Involve ladies and children—they can nurture these green havens. Arrange indigenous seating for communal meetings.

4. **Beautiful Landscapes**:

Imagine a fenced garden visible to all, protecting against kids and animals. Adorn it attractively. Install indigenous and modern play equipment, fostering a sense of unity. As your financial stability improves, prioritize timely renovation, repair, and replacement.

# CHAPTER XV

# MANY TRAPS IN RURAL

In rural areas, certain financial practices can ensnare unsuspecting individuals, hindering their progress. Let's delve into some of these traps:

**Chit Funds**: These rotating savings and credit associations are prevalent in India, Bangladesh, Sri Lanka, Pakistan, and other Asian countries. Chit funds can be organized by financial institutions or informally among friends, relatives, or neighbors. Participants pool money, and each month, one member receives the total sum. However, there are risks associated with unregulated chit funds. Some key points include:

**History**: Chit funds have ancient origins and have evolved over time. In the 20th century, they underwent formalization, with various entities participating, including partnerships, co-operatives, and joint-stock banks. The Kerala State Financial Enterprises, established in 1969, aimed to provide an alternative to unscrupulous private-sector chit-fund organizers. But they don't have branch operations in rural. Hereafter, the unit can safeguard them.

**Geographic Distribution**: In urban areas of Tamil Nadu, Karnataka, Andhra Pradesh, and Kerala, 5 to 10% of households participate in registered chit funds. However, they are less popular in North India, except in Delhi, Gujarat, Maharashtra, and Haryana.

**<u>Financial Inclusion</u>**<u>: For rural populations lacking access to formal banking infrastructure, chit funds serve as a sound savings instrument and a dependable source for raising emergency funds.</u>

**Unscrupulous Practices**: Unfortunately, rural residents often fall prey to deceptive practices:

**False Promises**: Some organizations promise substantial returns or deliver the initially promised amount to gain trust. However, once they accumulate the targeted sum, they vanish, leaving investors empty-handed.

**Lack of Education**: Unprivileged and uneducated rural individuals lack financial literacy. They entrust their hard-earned money to neighbors or unauthorized lenders, often resulting in losses.

**Gold Loans and Sellers**: Unauthorized gold lenders and sellers exploit vulnerable rural populations, spreading false advertisements and trapping them in debt.

**Cautionary Tale**: Rural communities must be cautious, seek financial education, and choose legitimate avenues for investment. Let's empower them to make informed decisions and break free from these traps through units.

In rural areas, a peculiar situation prevails—a plight akin to that of prey ensnared by cunning eagles. These individuals lack secure spaces to protect themselves, and their vulnerability is heart-wrenching. Without safe havens to safeguard their hard-earned money, they often resort to entrusting it to neighbors—a practice that has led many to fall victim to deceit.

In response to these challenges, a collective of such individuals, drawing from their shared adversities, has formed a venture: **"By them, for them."** This unit will be managed by their own staff and officials, who will henceforth serve as paymasters. The essence of life lies not only in personal happiness but also in spreading joy to others. Let us respect and love one another.

While the government can provide financial support to some of these units, their financial conditions may still be precarious. Regardless, the unit members can work together to nurture and sustain the venture. However, the road ahead will be arduous due to the scarcity of funds for essential functions. As we all know, insufficient resources hinder the growth of any business concern, and this unit is no exception.

Nevertheless, the unit can assert its claims through official channels, striving toward the goal of lifting its members above the poverty line. Together, they can forge a path toward brighter prospects and improved livelihoods.

**Dowry system:** The **dowry system**, which was once confined to a few communities, has now proliferated like a relentless plague, affecting various other social groups. Even after the dowry is paid, the demands persist without any regard for the financial strain on families. This unyielding cycle perpetuates itself, leaving many lives in ruin due to relentless harassment. Sadly, such stories of suffering have become a daily occurrence in our society.

## BREAKING THE CYCLE: EMPOWERING VULNERABLE COMMUNITIES

For years, a pervasive issue has silently plagued impoverished communities, leaving an indelible mark on countless lives. The cycle begins innocuously, but its impact is far-reaching and irreversible. After one or two marriages, families find themselves trapped in a perpetual struggle. Life becomes a mere existence, overshadowed by mounting debts and insurmountable challenges.

The government bears the responsibility of safeguarding these vulnerable families. However, mere legislation falls short; enforcement is the key. By implementing a stringent unit-based system, the government can dismantle archaic practices like the "SATHI" system forever. With unwavering support, unit can break free from this cycle and empower those who need it most.

**Collective Well-Being**: Instead of focusing solely on individual households, the government now considers the entire community as a unit. Any funding allocated to this unit is utilized for the well-being of the entire population within it benefiting the real beneficiaries.

1. **Empowering the Vote Bank**: By coordinating 200 homes in a village area into a single unit, we address the needs of a low-income population concentrated in a specific locality. However, these 200 homes alone may not form a financially robust unit. In such cases, government support becomes essential.

2. **Balancing Membership Selection**: When forming these units, it's crucial to ensure that the selection of members doesn't exceed 10-20% of the very poor. Additionally, neighboring units should share similar economic conditions to promote balanced growth.

3. **Skillful Inclusion**: While selecting members, consider including skilled workers. Their expertise can contribute significantly to the unit's development.

4. **Financial Efficiency**: Redirecting Government Funds Through These Units Can Lead To Better Results. It Allows For More Effective Utilization Of Resources, Avoiding Wastage That Previously Occurred In Rural Areas Without Reaching The Intended Beneficiaries.

## ENSURING TRANSPARENCY: REPORTING RURAL FUND UTILIZATION

The unit responsible for managing the rural fund is committed to transparency. Not only will it present the final results, but it will also submit a comprehensive account with detailed statements to the government. This ensures that an official record exists, and the government can cross-verify the utilization through its staff.

## THE RURAL DEVELOPMENT FUND (RURAL FUND)

The government now has the opportunity to witness 100% genuine utilization of the rural fund in these areas, surpassing previous experiences. By meticulously tracking the real beneficiaries and documenting their benefits, the government can fulfill its responsibilities using accurate records and receipts.

Upon receiving payments, the unit will promptly acknowledge them. A utilization report, outlining the expected benefits for members through fund utilization, will be submitted to the government. Additionally, a detailed statement of account will facilitate government officials in inspecting the unit's progress and verifying its growth. Remarkably, all these services are provided free of cost.

In neglected regions, forming units should consider including landowners or grassroots-level individuals as members. Even if they possess smaller plots of land, their skills and contributions can make them valuable regular members of the unit.

1. **Empowering Neglected Units**: The unit has the potential to thrive even with those who have been overlooked. By accounting for and informing local government bodies about government lands within the unit's limit, we can facilitate access for landless members. If these lands are allotted to the landless or other marginalized sector members, they can maintain their standing

alongside others who possess more land and properties, thus benefiting from their rightful share within the unit.

2.  **Political Support for Rural Communities**: The political parties that have supported rural communities during their struggles remain steadfast allies. Their commitment is unwavering, and you can trust that they will stand by you indefinitely—unless, of course, they encounter an opposing reaction or a different experience from you.

By helping morally in the beginning, supporting the unit in overcoming the red tape of government and semi-government offices, and advising the unit management on how to proceed to achieve their aim of implementing the unit system in the countryside.

Politicians can easily influence the management and members, and in return, the units can offer a lot of votes that assure success in their area. The give-and-take policy will benefit both the unit and the political party mutually. However, the unit refrains from engaging in any political activities; instead, they contribute by casting votes.

Politicians can create "vote banks" with each unit, fostering mutual understanding and becoming a valuable asset for the political party.

## REVISED VERSION

Initially, by providing moral support, we assist the unit in navigating bureaucratic hurdles within government and semi-government offices. Our guidance helps unit management strategize and achieve its goal of implementing the unit system in rural areas.

Politicians wield significant influence over management and members. In return, the units contribute substantial votes, ensuring success in their respective regions. This symbiotic approach benefits both the unit and the political party. Notably, the unit abstains from direct political involvement, focusing solely on casting votes.

Politicians can cultivate "vote banks" through collaboration with each unit, fostering mutual understanding and enriching the political party's resources.

# CHAPTER XVI

# REVIVING INDIGENOUS BUSINESSES

In the realm of business, units have the power to invigorate various enterprises, including small-scale industries (SSIs) and local micro-businesses. Unfortunately, many traditional small businesses have faded away due to disinterest from the younger generation. However, there's hope in revitalizing these ventures through cultural programs and strategic initiatives.

**Ayurveda** and **medicinal plants** hold immense potential. By collecting recipes passed down from previous generations in rural areas, we can reintroduce indigenous and flavorful food products. These offerings not only evoke nostalgia but also possess practical benefits, such as extended shelf life.

Imagine resurrecting forgotten delicacies—products that the new generation hasn't even heard of. These treasures are not limited to just a handful; they span a multitude of possibilities waiting to be explored.

Moreover, let's not overlook the culinary heritage of our villages. **Vegetarian and non-vegetarian food preparations**, known for their delectable taste, can be remained. Each countryside and village can contribute to this revival by embracing unique business tactics.

In summary, thinking differently and tapping into our rich cultural heritage can breathe new life into indigenous businesses. Let's honor tradition while embracing innovation!

1. **Embrace Rural Flavors for Popularity**: Introducing the unique tastes of the countryside and rural foods can significantly enhance the popularity of your unit. By reviving traditional flavors, you not only reap monetary benefits but also revive an old culture that remains unfamiliar to the new generation. Let this cultural revival be your path to fame.

**Remember:** *there's no need to compete with other units.*

**Create a Distinctive Product**: Develop a special product that sets your unit apart. Whether it's a culinary delight or a practical solution, ensure it serves others effectively. Such a product can propel your unit to the pinnacle of recognition. In fact, your unit might even become synonymous with this remarkable creation.

**Urban Markets and Preservation**: Your products have a place in both cities and faraway locales. The key lies in preserving their unique flavors. Urban dwellers appreciate rare sweets and other exceptional offerings. Capitalize on this by promoting your products during gatherings, festivals, ceremonies, and functions, especially when selling in bulk.

2. **Mindset Shift and Collective Support**: The future of your unit hinges not only on business acumen but also on a bold change of mindset. Encourage unity and support among your members. Beyond business, explore diverse avenues like agriculture, plantations, cultivations, cattle rearing, fish farming, and poultry. These possibilities can lead to success on a grand scale.

1. **Empowering Self-Reliance**: You have access to all necessary resources, ample funds, and a capable workforce to manage and protect your assets and production. Consequently, you can explore various possibilities daily and pursue your aspirations.

Engage in discussions with fellow members and even consult the manager to finalize decisions.

2. **Breaking Dependency**: Just as you resolved not to rely on your parents as you grew up, we follow a similar principle here. We do not depend on the government for our basic needs; instead, we earn directly through our endeavors. By doing so, you can set an example for your co-members and their families, encouraging them to embrace self-sufficiency

3. **Self-Help Business Units**: Each one of you should strive to be self-reliant, avoiding reliance on external entities like the government. The proliferation of self-help business units across the nation will contribute significantly to our economy. Let us challenge the prevailing mindset that encourages deceit and extravagant living.

4. **Taking an Oath**: Going forward, each member must pledge to cease any activities that involve cheating.

**Remember**, *dishonesty only shifts the pain from one leg to the other. Let us collectively avoid such practices and work toward a more ethical and prosperous future.*

# CHAPTER XVII

# MISCELLANEOUS INCOME SOURCES – WIND TURBINES

If the local environment permits, consider installing wind turbines within your unit area. Seek permission from the government or local authorities to proceed. While the initial installation cost may be high, the returns are significant, and the process requires minimal manpower.

## HOW WIND TURBINES WORK:

1. **Blades**: Wind turbines use blades to capture the kinetic energy from the wind. As the wind flows over the blades, it creates lift, causing them to rotate.

2. **Drive Shaft and Generator**: The blades are connected to a drive shaft, which, in turn, drives an electric generator. This generator produces electricity.

By strategically placing wind turbines in areas with consistent wind patterns, you can tap into a reliable and abundant energy source. The generated electricity can serve your own consumption needs and even be sold back to the grid. While the initial investment is substantial, the long-term benefits make it a worthwhile endeavor.

**Solar Energy:** Solar energy, particularly in rural areas, is an excellent solution to meet power requirements within specific limits. Unlike regular electricity supply, which can be costly, solar energy offers a more cost-effective alternative. However, it's essential to understand the rules and regulations governing electricity generation through solar means. Additionally, seeking necessary permissions and understanding any associated charges from the government is crucial.

**Electricity Challenges:** Many remote areas suffer from inadequate power access, significantly impacting rural development. To address this, units can take control by managing connections and bulk requirements. These payments, consolidated into a single transaction, allow the unit to demand electricity effectively. While dependence on electricity is widespread, interruptions or delays can severely affect unit operations. <u>To mitigate this, consider exploring solar and wind turbines alongside traditional electricity sources.</u>

## SOLAR CONNECTIONS AND QUALITY MACHINERY

Implementing solar connections for complexes, homes, motors, shops, street lights, and other necessary locations is essential. However, it's crucial to prioritize the use of **high-quality machinery** to minimize the risk of malfunction or fire.

## PREPAREDNESS FOR NATURAL DISASTERS

Members should undergo pre-training to face natural disasters effectively. The unit must prioritize awareness and preparedness to handle such situations. When constructing dwelling houses or apartments, it's essential to consider the **potential impact of natural calamities**.

If an area is prone to frequent disasters, it's advisable to avoid it for residential purposes. Instead, utilize such land for agriculture, ensuring it doesn't adversely affect the unit financially. Balancing both sides of the equation is crucial for long-term benefits. As a developing business concern, thoughtful investment decisions are vital for our future success.

## GOVERNMENT-LED CIVIL WORKS: A COLLECTIVE ENDEAVOR

When it comes to civil works, the government has the option to either entrust them to individuals or contract companies or to undertake them directly through its own units. Let's explore why the latter approach can be advantageous.

1. **Guaranteed Accountability**: When government units handle civil works, there's a higher level of accountability. Unlike external contractors, these units are directly responsible to the government. Their commitment to completing the work to the satisfaction of both the unit and government officials is more assured.

2. **Keen Oversight**: Within these units, a watchful eye is cast on every task. With a substantial number of responsible members— often numbering in the thousands—there's little room for typical oversights. As the ultimate beneficiaries of the work, they take meticulous care to ensure quality and adherence to standards.

3. **Collective Growth**: Imagine if everyone within the unit collaborates and takes ownership of its growth. This positive

mindset can work wonders. By actively participating in all aspects of unit development, you wield the power to create magic in your area. Your hard work, skills, and capabilities become the driving force behind progress.

**Remember**: it's not just about individual effort; it's about collective determination and shared responsibility. Together, we can achieve remarkable results.

"Its reverse effect is also almost just the opposite – If you are willing to work for the unit, you can grow along with your family and neighbors. If you fail to find a source through the unit, it is not the mistake of the unit or other members. Hence, no doubt, you, the individual member of the unit, have to decide unanimously."

"The countryside people have already learned a lesson: there is nobody to uplift you in life without your effort. Still, you continue with your adamant nature and laziness. One of the others can lift you; it is your fate – that is the only word, the last word."

## REVISED VERSION:

"The reverse effect is equally true: if you are willing to work within the unit, you can thrive alongside your family and neighbors. Failure to find a source through the unit is not the unit's or other members' fault. Therefore, the decision rests with you, the individual member of the unit."

"Rural communities have learned a valuable lesson: personal effort is essential for progress. Persisting with stubbornness and laziness won't lead to upliftment. Ultimately, fate plays its role, but it's up to you to seize opportunities."

# CHAPTER XVIII

# CENCUS

THE DRASTIC CHANGE IN LIFE AND IT'S BENEFITS TO ALL WILL REVEAL THROUGH CENSUS UNITS MADE COUNTRYSIDE CENSUS EASY.

**"The rural countryside, which constitutes two-thirds of the entire world, has remained relatively dormant for many years without significant progress or growth.** Gathering accurate information about the people living in these areas has been challenging. However, the introduction of a unit-based system has made this task easier compared to relying solely on town or city-data.

By leveraging these units from the countryside, the government can obtain detailed and precise figures without the need for manual census efforts. The census details so collected from each unit will reveal the financial status of that unit and their standard of living can be assessed.

"The environments and situations faced by different units vary significantly. These units encounter numerous challenges, including access to water facilities, variations in landscape, soil quality, and climate conditions. These factors can impact growth both positively and negatively, and they must be carefully considered.

In cases where individuals are dealing with adverse circumstances, the government can play a crucial role in improving their lives. By providing short or long-term financial support, the government can observe the impact of these interventions and monitor the responses of those affected."

Unlike traditional census methods conducted once every ten years, the unit system provides ongoing data collection. Instead of relying on periodic large-scale efforts, the government can now access census figures from these units whenever needed.

This approach not only reduces inconvenience but also ensures more accurate data collection. Considering the high costs associated with conducting a complete census, this unit-based system offers a more efficient and effective solution.

The last official census took place in 2011, and the subsequent one was originally scheduled for 2021. However, due to the COVID-19 pandemic in India, it was postponed. <u>As of now, the next census is planned to occur after the 2024 general election</u>.

**Earlier challenges in assessment have now become accessible at our fingertips, thanks to the advantages offered by units and their functioning systems.** These units provide comprehensive information related to rural populations. Members who actively participate in these units contribute to their own well-being, and the government can take pride in their efforts.

**A shift in perspective leads individuals from lives filled with sorrow to a more heavenly existence.** Unity has proven to be a powerful force, achieving outcomes that often elude individual efforts. People now meticulously account for their life events, providing valuable data for politicians to analyze and express during various stages.

The government benefits significantly from these units, which offer detailed insights into specific areas, individual households, and the overall population. The accuracy and authenticity of this information are crucial. In fact, census teams can swiftly collect such data, thanks to their efficient computerized systems that track unit-related details.

*Previously, the government relied on the costly and labor-intensive census process for data collection. However, the emergence of units has revolutionized this approach, offering a more accurate alternative for forecasting.*

The indigenous census method, whiles the only viable option for many years, incurred significant expenses and consumed valuable manpower and time. Despite these investments, it fell short of perfection. Now, with the advent of computerization, the countryside's accounts and details can be efficiently collected. This shift allows the government to redirect resources toward other developmental initiatives.

In return, the nation can implement numerous schemes within rural areas through these units. Former government officials attest that outsiders were responsible for executing developmental projects within these units.

"The unit has the capability to execute the proposed projects to the satisfaction of its members and the government. Rather than acting as a mere mediator, the unit itself stands to benefit significantly. This is because the rural population is an integral part of the unit. The necessary supporting documents and expense statements will be shared with the government, and the unit will maintain an accessible account.

Regarding census data, the unit already maintains readily recorded details. Instead of the current practice of conducting a census once every three years or even less frequently, the unit could provide this data more frequently—perhaps annually. This would enable faster decision-making for rural development initiatives. The data collected could include precise information on population demographics, education levels, skilled and unskilled workers, marital status, age groups, health conditions, and disabilities. Additionally, the unit could provide insights into land classifications, existing infrastructure, and essential development needs."

"These details are invaluable to the government for effectively implementing developmental programs in rural areas. By providing accurate and genuine figures, the unit ensures that the government can make informed decisions.

The unit supplies comprehensive information about government-owned lands, including details about dry, wet, and barren areas. Suggestions for developing these lands, water facilities, and estimated expenses to convert barren land into usable resources are all shared with the government. Additionally, if there is a surplus of land, the unit explores ways to generate income from it.

Unpredictable income from each unit contributes to gradual growth, elevating the unit's overall performance. Even if a unit possesses barren land, it can repurpose the area for storage purposes—such as warehouses or other facilities—that operate efficiently without excessive water usage.

Once implemented, this unit has the potential to address immediate challenges faced by the rural population, including poverty, food scarcity, and access to clean drinking water. Former anti-social activists are now unit members, actively contributing to positive change. Moreover, the resolution of civil and criminal cases has improved, as these individuals now prioritize their work within the unit."

## ENHANCING COMMUNITY PROSPERITY THROUGH PROPERTY UTILIZATION

In the realm of law enforcement, both government and private properties often fall under the influence of notorious criminals. However, with strategic collaboration, these properties can be reclaimed and put to good use. Regularizing property ownership yields dual benefits: first, it empowers law enforcement units to control criminal activities effectively; second, it allows precious assets to be seized for noble causes.

By securing government consent, nearby properties—originally owned by the government—can be harnessed for the unit's activities. This transformation of idle land into productive spaces is not only a point of pride but also an economically sound move. Moreover, it reinvigorates the dormant rural population, benefiting numerous individuals. Even barren lands, once idle, find purpose in this endeavor.

Furthermore, the untapped potential of wastelands and idle manpower can be fully utilized to combat laziness and promote hard work. As a result, the local economy will soar, earning the government authorities well-deserved accolades. Supporting these units during challenging times ensures their continued success and resilience.

**1 Positive Transformation**: Many of these changes, which create an entirely different environment, are inherently positive. Instead of feeling insecurity, individuals now experience a surge of positive energy. This newfound vitality, previously unknown to them, becomes the unit's triumph and its ultimate mission.

**2 Rural Development and Economic Impact**: Considering that rural areas constitute two-thirds of our nation, their development holds immense potential to transform the economy. By reclaiming vast acres of land and utilizing countless hours of manpower, we cannot only foster growth in these regions but also elevate the quality of life for those who have long endured hardship.

This shift contributes to the nation's economic leap, making it self-sufficient and dedicated to the well-being of all its citizens. As previously unproductive segments of the population become active contributors, these rural areas evolve into high-income hubs, leaving a positive mark in the government's records.

The forthcoming transformation of this system will soon fetch its place in the annals of history. Through its innovative units, the rural population is poised to achieve their long-desired aspirations. As anti-social elements recede from the influential domains, development in these areas becomes a seamless journey for the populace.

The glaring disparity in resources and economic status between the high and low strata fuels the emergence of anti-social behavior. The lower class grapples with limited opportunities for upward mobility, and education, though scarce, offers little respite. For those who have endured immense struggles throughout their educational journey, employment prospects remain elusive. Enter the unit system—a refuge for these marginalized populations, providing guidance on finding solutions.

But the unit's impact extends beyond mere guidance. It not only infuses positive energy into the community but also transforms negative influences into catalysts for progress. Now, devoid of pessimistic thoughts, the community unites under a singular purpose: advancement in their area—a collective AGENDA.

## FROM ANTI-ACTIVISTS TO COMMITTED WORKERS: THE TRANSFORMATION OF THE UNIT

In a remarkable shift, anti-activists transitioned from opposition to active engagement, aligning themselves with the unit's mission. Guided by its distinctive approach, they found inspiration in the unit's functions, leading to a newfound sense of purpose and recognition among their peers.

The once anti-social individuals now form a cohesive bond with the unit members. Their commitment is unwavering as they diligently contribute to the unit's accomplishments. With a resolute focus on **100% manpower utilization**, they strive to maximize efficiency and impact.

Furthermore, the unit has taken charge of civil and criminal cases in the area. As a result, police and court resources are no longer burdened by handling matters related to unit members. This shift not only saves valuable time and manpower but also significantly reduces costs that were previously incurred in legal proceedings.

1.  **Unity Beyond Enmity: A Transformation Toward Humanity**

In a remarkable shift, the absence of enmity among them led to a profound realization about life. Rather than harboring animosity, they embraced gentleness, cultivating positive habits and attitudes. Gradually, they transitioned toward a more humane existence, akin to animals ceasing their fights. Unity prevailed.

2.  **Collective Responsibility: The Unit's Tax and Dues Contribution**

Since the unit's formation, the landscape has changed. Now, instead of individual struggles, the unit shoulders the burden of non-payment and substantial government dues. Their collective effort ensures that taxes and other financial obligations are met promptly, streamlining the process.

3.  **Rising Above Challenges: Turning Adversity into Motivation**

Some people relish seeing others stumble and fall. However, these moments can serve as catalysts for personal growth. When faced with obstacles, seize the opportunity to work harder, break barriers, and move forward with renewed enthusiasm. Initiative becomes the key to overcoming hurdles.

4. **Veiled Struggles: The Unspoken Challenges**

Each person's situation is unique and fraught with difficulties that remain undisclosed even among peers. Despite the silence, they persevere, navigating their individual paths through adversity.

1. **Embracing Alternatives to Hard Work**: Instead of dismissing the idea outright, consider that there are numerous shortcuts available beyond sheer hard work. These shortcuts can lead us to our goals more efficiently. Let's explore how these approaches contribute to the growth of various units and benefit our nation.

2. **Unit-Based Solutions**: Many long-standing issues that previously lacked effective remedies can now be addressed through unit-based efforts. With over two-thirds of the world's population potentially participating, dormant units can spring into action. Their collective work contributes significantly to progress.

3. **Empowering Rural Communities**: Solving problems faced by rural communities, often overlooked by others, represents a significant achievement. As these communities evolve, they gain a deeper understanding of life and ways to improve. Their newfound engagement replaces past indifference, fostering active participation in unit activities.

**Remember**: *progress doesn't always require relentless toil; sometimes, strategic approaches yield remarkable results.*

1. **Leveraging Periodical Census for Data and Clarity**: The periodic census plays a crucial role in gathering accurate data, particularly concerning rural areas. These units serve as valuable tools for the government, providing essential information. They act as ancillary units, aiding in efficient governance.

2. **Empowering Rural Lives through Innovation**: By implementing innovative ideas, these units contribute to the nation's progress. Previously unnoticed regions inhabited by people in remote

areas now receive attention and awareness. Their lives are being uplifted.

3. **Economic Impact and Global Recognition**: The unit's growth—from ground zero to commendable levels—generates substantial revenue through taxes and other income sources. This financial contribution benefits the government. Moreover, the unit's progress reflects the nation's overall advancement, not only within its borders but also on the global stage. Achieving this within a five-year plan is a source of immense pride.

1. **Supporting Community Units: A Kind Gesture** supporting these community units reflects kindness toward both the residents and their fellow community members. If the government extends sympathetic consideration and actively works to alleviate their long-standing struggles, these residents will hold deep gratitude and appreciation.

2. **Political Influence and Expectations:** While the unit members themselves may not directly engage in political activities or endorse specific parties, they collectively form a crucial vote bank. Political parties that have assisted them during times of need are held in high regard, creating a psychological expectation of continued support.

3. **Safe and Regulated Living Spaces** The unit's territory is meticulously safeguarded, ensuring it remains completely free from anti-social activities. Former activists, now loyal members, adhere to the unit's bylaws, living comfortably within its boundaries.

4. **A New Way of Life** The unit introduces a fresh culture and lifestyle. Residents embrace this change wholeheartedly, enjoying the abundant offerings provided by the unit. Their experience is distinct, marked by a sense of safety and contentment. As proud members, they strive to leave their past behind.

**Moving Forward**: Our focus lies in the present and the future as we construct homes for our families and neighbors. We've left behind the bleak, cultureless past that someone once shaped for their own benefit. Those memories no longer haunt us.

**A Rare Attitude**: Among the people, a distinct attitude prevails—one of proactive care for our community. Not merely voicing intentions but actively following through. This commendable approach extends even to those who struggle alone, seeking results.

**Family Bonds**: Families diligently tend to their homes and neighboring units, a practice that, though uncommon, draws attention globally. A secure, pleasant environment satisfies most human beings, regardless of their station in life.

**Reclaiming Lives**: As drug and alcohol addicts find redemption, rural areas become a wellspring of untapped manpower. This transformation combats poverty and scarcity, fostering tangible development and altering mindsets in favor of progress.

The area that belongs to the unit and its limit is safeguarded and made 100% free from anti-social activities. The earlier activists are now loyal members of this unit, respecting and following the rules and regulations of the bylaws. They are living lavishly within the unit for the unit.

A new culture and line of life are provided by the unit. They are ready to move through as they are getting everything offered by the unit lavishly. It is a different experience for them, and they feel safe. We, the members, are a different proud population; we just wish to forget our past.

We have no time to think about the past because we are busy building mansions for our family and neighbors. We are relieved from such an ugly countryside, cultureless situation. That was molded by somebody for their sake, but it is no longer even in our memories.

Within the unit's boundaries, a secure and anti-social activity-free environment prevails. Former activists have transformed into loyal members, adhering to the unit's rules and bylaws. Their opulent lifestyle thrives within these confines.

The unit introduces a novel culture and way of life. Residents revel in abundant offerings, experiencing safety and security. As proud members, we strive to leave our past behind.

Our focus lies in constructing grand homes for our families and neighbors. The bleak, cultureless countryside of yore, once shaped by others, now fades from memory.

## GOVERNMENT BENEFITS IN VARIOUS WAYS

The concept of the unit, along with its land limit, brings forth several advantages. One of the primary benefits is that it shields members from criminal situations, allowing them to embrace an alternative lifestyle. Within this unit, families and neighbors coexist harmoniously, supported by its unique framework.

All our needs and requirements are fulfilled within the unit. Members actively care for one another, emphasizing mutual support, savings, and protection. In the absence of external guardians, we rely on the unit's guidance. As both our bosses and masters, we find contentment. With only 200 homes, the manager maintains close oversight, fostering familiarity among us. Personal data about each member is well-known, ensuring security after the unit's formation.

Life within this community is serene; past enmities have dissolved. We hold property shares, collectively reaping financial rewards based on individual skills and abilities. Emergency funds, including medical provisions, are readily available. **Life insurance:** Our safety precautions and insurance practices eliminate the need for external reliance. After all, why should insurance companies dictate our fate when the unit serves as our ultimate safeguard against adversity?

The insurance premium serves as an investment in our unit's business. We possess the capability to operate our business with substantial profits from our investments. As previously mentioned, each unit must function akin to a corporate office but with a focus on the well-being of its members. These 200 houses constitute our membership base, and their properties define the boundaries of our unit, including any government-owned land.

Despite the scattered nature of resources and possibilities in the countryside, we unite with a common goal and ambition: to leave no inch of land undeveloped. Laziness is not permissible; we strive for progress and growth. This concept is not limited to our local context; it can be experimented with globally, especially in rural areas where unnoticed individuals struggle financially to meet their daily needs. Rather than accepting a pitiful existence, we should explore opportunities for improvement and change.

1. **When Life Throws Challenges:** When faced with individual setbacks despite putting forth your best efforts, consider an alternative approach. Many others have triumphed using this method. Whether it's you or your ancestors who have been deceived, the consequences can be devastating for your entire family, including the children. However, it's never too late to take action. You can uncover the solution and pass it down to the next generation, allowing them to try their luck.

2. **Unlocking Government Lands:** Government-owned lands are scattered across various regions. As a unit, you can create an inventory of these lands, identifying which ones fall within your

jurisdiction. Determine whether they are under the custody of a unit member or an outsider. By sharing relevant information about these lands with the government, you contribute without incurring any expenses.

3. **Addressing Encroachments and Trespasses:** Detecting encroachments and trespasses is crucial. Amicably resolve disputes over land ownership, ensuring that rightful possession is restored to the original owner. Alternatively, advocate for deserving unit members to receive land allotments by bringing such cases to the attention of the authorities.

4. **Exploring Ownership Possibilities:** The third option involves lands within the unit's financial reach. Consider purchasing these lands either in the name of the current possession owner or under the unit's ownership. Seek guidance from government officials to understand the nature of the property and make informed decisions.

**Remember:** each step taken contributes to a better future for all involved.

1. **Land Utilization and Government Permission**: By obtaining permission from government authorities, you can utilize the land effectively. Whether it's for a business unit or any other purpose, the land can be put to productive use. This could involve leasing it temporarily or following any guidelines set by the government. If the government eventually allows, the unit can even purchase the land and develop it according to its needs.

2. **Family Growth and Personal Effort**: The growth of a family hinges on the sincerity, abilities, hard work, and thoughts of its members. Within the unit, it's essential to adhere to this principle. Rather than relying solely on the government, I've realized that I possess untapped potential. With my abilities and skills, I can lead a fulfilling life alongside others. Moreover, I've come to

understand that wealth, like knowledge, multiplies when shared with those in need.

3. **Positive Transformation**: By shifting away from negative thoughts, you can elevate yourself beyond the current situation. Embrace self-effort, tap into your capabilities, and create a brighter future

## EMPOWER YOUR FUTURE: A CALL TO ACTION

Relying solely on the government for basic necessities like drinking water or resorting to strikes against the authorities is an outdated approach. In the past, such actions held little value, but times have changed. Now, you have the opportunity to earn money by the hour. It's time to break away from blind conformity and forge a new path.

**Say No to Begging**: Publicly seeking water from the government should be a thing of the past. Instead, channel your efforts toward transforming your financial status and improving your lives. This unit—your collective strength—can drive meaningful change.

**Equality Prevails**: In this unit, jealousy has no place. Each of you stands on equal ground. Your properties, businesses, and families belong to all. So, why harbor envy? Let's live generously, supporting and loving one another as if we were part of a single-family. This should be our shared AGENDA, and every member should revel in it.

## RETHINKING RURAL DEVELOPMENT FUNDS: A NEW PERSPECTIVE

The allocation of government funds for rural development is a critical endeavor. However, we must evaluate whether these funds are truly effective in fostering growth within local populations. Without proper follow-up, expert guidance, and strategic planning, these assistance funds may fall short of their intended impact.

Rather than merely disbursing funds directly to individual households, we propose a different approach. Let's channel these resources into essential infrastructure projects within each community. By doing so, we can transform the landscape and enhance the quality of life for residents.

The primary goal should be to utilize government funds for general utilities and public welfare. When invested strategically, these funds can work wonders. Imagine the magic that can happen when corruption and intermediaries are eliminated. The targeted amount becomes a powerful tool for completing vital projects through community units.

Moreover, this approach offers significant cost and time savings. By empowering local units to execute projects efficiently, we reduce the need for extensive supervision. Government officials and unit members can collaborate closely, sharing project details and progress updates as needed.

As a result, surplus funds may emerge—resources that can further benefit the community. These surplus funds can be allocated to additional development initiatives catering to both residents and tourists alike.

In summary, let's reimage rural development funds as catalysts for positive change, transforming communities and creating lasting impact

## ANTICIPATING TOMORROW

In rural areas, the population faces a bleak reality. Their hopes have long been extinguished, leaving them to grapple with the harshness of their existence. Each day is a struggle, and they find themselves trapped in a cycle of helplessness, devoid of any clear path forward.

Rather than contemplating the future, their immediate concern revolves around securing today's sustenance for their families. The weight of providing bread for their children and elderly parents weighs heavily on their shoulders, exacerbating the hardships they endure.

Occasional offers of money or gifts provide temporary relief, but these fleeting gestures are insufficient. If only these resources were channeled into meaningful projects, they could make a lasting impact. Unfortunately, the meager amounts they receive merely serve as tokens, failing to address the deeper issues at hand.

The government, too, plays a role in this struggle. Despite well-intentioned efforts, bureaucratic hurdles and limitations hinder effective assistance. The rural populace remains disconnected from the true extent of aid allocated by the government. In remote areas, officials rarely venture, leaving the residents isolated and yearning for genuine support.

## CRIMINAL ACTIVISTS

While the number of criminals remains small, their ability to exert influence over others is significant. Fear often prevents people from confronting them, not due to the criminals' mutual understanding but rather because of their cohesive unity and their possession of up-to-date information about potential targets. Disorganization, coupled with animosity and jealousy among neighbors, further weakens our collective ability to stand up to them. The absence of a shared sense of purpose is evident.

Despite our larger numbers, we rarely harbor resentment toward these criminals, which ultimately works to their advantage. This dynamic is particularly pronounced in remote areas where their tactics thrive. It is crucial to recognize that our strength, unity, and mutual understanding are lacking if we hope to prevail against them.

As a unit manager, assessing the composition of our group becomes essential. Through personal discussions, we must determine whether to engage with families associated with criminal activities or not.

Please note that this rephrasing aims to maintain the original meaning while presenting it in a clearer and more concise manner.

## GOVERNMENT COOPERATION AND UNIT DYNAMICS

The government has the authority to gather updates on any member through the manager, who acts as an intermediary. In cases involving criminal or civil matters within the unit, affected members must withdraw. Amicable compromises can be sought for public nuisances beyond the unit's control. However, if a case is particularly serious, the manager need not invest time in handling it.

## UNIT STRENGTH AND INDIVIDUAL RESILIENCE

As one of the 1000 unit members, you collectively possess significant strength. There's no need to yield to external pressures. You can confidently face challenges either head-on or through peaceful negotiation, ensuring a harmonious life where you currently reside.

## PRESERVING REPUTATION

Being associated with this prestigious unit grants you an esteemed address. Guard its name and reputation diligently, as any tarnish will impact you significantly.

**Remember**: *this is akin to safeguarding your father's legacy.*

## FACING ADVERSITY

While they display force against you, remember that more than 1000 members stand united. Why not join them? Your strength is undeniable. Rise against threats and confront poverty with resilience.

**The Individual Home: A Transformation** In the quiet enclave of our individual homes, we find strength in our small numbers—just five of us. Yet, this very intimacy renders us vulnerable. Without sufficient resolve and mental fortitude, we remain blind to the criminal threats lurking in the shadows.

But there exists another entity—the unit, A formidable force of a thousand strong. With a change in circumstance, we can now confront any adversary head-on. Our fates, though shaped by human hands, need not be dictated by fear. We must ensure that our past troubles do not haunt us further.

Our former allies—drunkards, criminals, and prostitutes—once supported us. Now, with over a thousand members at our disposal, we stand more than equipped to face any danger that comes our way.

**The Oath of Renewal** Our solemn oath is to clear the debris that obstructs our path to the unit. These accumulated wastes, remnants of years gone by, harbor different ideologies and beliefs. Swiftly, we must remove them, leaving no room for hesitation.

**Our vision:** A serene and tranquil environment—havens where threats dissolve like morning mist. The anti-social elements that once plagued us shall trouble us no more. They are now our brethren, transformed into moral sentinels within our unit's boundaries.

## UNLOCKING POTENTIAL: GOVERNMENT LAND WITHIN OUR UNIT

The vast expanse of government land lies within our grasp, waiting to be harnessed. Consider this: all properties owned by our member households, combined with the government's holdings, constitute the boundaries of our unit. These lands must be meticulously documented—a record of our domain, essential for future endeavors.

The government, too, seeks clarity. They wish to discern the contours of land encroached upon by farmers. Now, the decision rests with us: shall we allocate these fertile acres to deserving members or retain them for collective benefit?

## RESOURCE ABUNDANCE AND TRANSFORMATION

Our members—experts in diverse fields—hold the key to unlocking resources. Beyond the vacant, trespassed lands and idle properties lies untapped potential. With ample funds and a robust workforce, we can transform these neglected parcels into thriving assets.

Remarkably, these possibilities have always existed yet remained obscured. Now, as a united front, we can seize them. Our unit's growth knows no bounds, fueled by collective decisions. Bargaining power awaits us—whether in sales or purchases—as we operate on a grand scale.

And there's more: our progress will not go unnoticed. The government stands ready to support our efforts, fostering improvement in our cherished domain.

## UNLOCKING THE POTENTIAL OF BARREN LANDS

In rural areas where barren lands lie untapped, there exists an opportunity to transform them into lucrative assets. Consider the following strategies: The units can identify nearby government properties and work toward acquiring them, ensuring sufficient property for all members."

**Metal Recycling Hub**: These lands can serve as a hub for recycling metals, particularly steel. With steel being widely available worldwide, repurposing it from waste materials can be both environmentally responsible and economically beneficial. By producing hard iron sheets and other materials at a competitive cost, these areas can contribute significantly to local economies. This can start one among 50 units or even more so that they will get the raw materials easily.

**Storage Solutions for Companies**: Many companies seek storage facilities for their materials or products, especially those destined for nearby urban centers. However, city rents can be exorbitant. To address this challenge, constructing sheds with suitable storage conditions on these barren lands can provide an attractive alternative. Companies can store their goods conveniently while minimizing costs.

**Economic Impact**: By leveraging these previously overlooked rural spaces, your unknown countryside can gain recognition. Renowned companies may include your area in their lists, enhancing its reputation. Additionally, agricultural and other products can flow seamlessly through the supply chain, facilitated by drivers and workers associated with these storage facilities. Direct dealings with these units often eliminate the need for bargaining.

In summary, barren lands have the potential to evolve into thriving economic contributors, benefiting both local communities and businesses alike.

The recycling of used steel presents a remarkable opportunity to convert what might otherwise be considered waste into valuable assets. Let's delve into the significance of this process:

**Unlocking Hidden Value**: By repurposing waste materials and discarded iron parts accumulated over the years, we unveil their latent potential. What appears as mere waste can be transformed into currency or contribute to sustaining livelihoods.

**Supply Chain Dynamics**: Large-scale recycling and melting facilities play a pivotal role. Nearby waste collectors become crucial suppliers, bridging the gap between waste and productive materials. This symbiotic relationship ensures a steady flow of recycled material.

**Market for Unique Products**: The recycled steel material finds its place in the market, serving as a resource for crafting distinctive products. Among these, metal-made scrap containers stand out due to their versatility in size and design.

**Essential Containers**: These containers, often used for import and export, assume critical importance. Collaborating with local governments, we can explore innovative possibilities for their utilization. Whether it's shipping goods or storing materials, these containers facilitate global trade.

**From Waste to Iron Materials**: The heaps of waste occupying space for years can be repurposed. Those seemingly insignificant scraps hold the potential to become essential iron materials. Notably, heavy containers, a rarity in many countries, are in high demand.

In summary, recycling used steel isn't just about waste management; it's about transforming discarded resources into a sustainable future. Let's embrace this opportunity and forge a path toward responsible stewardship of our planet's materials.

**Recycling Plant Considerations**: The demand for recycling is global, and local governments play a crucial role in establishing recycling plants. These facilities should be strategically located where scrap materials are consistently available. Before setting up such a plant, assessing the availability of raw materials is essential.

**Environmental Development with Government Support**: With government backing, focus on developing the area by creating broad roads and providing necessary land and assistance. Remember that these developments benefit not only you but also the entire community and the nation.

Plan for long-term sustainability to avoid unnecessary rework during expansion. Infrastructure improvements, including well-constructed roads, are vital for lasting impact. Additionally, consider providing travel facilities to connect with neighboring areas, towns, and cities.

Collaborate with local bodies and offices to enhance educational and healthcare facilities, catalyzing the area's growth.

Unit members are unanimously deciding every decision in their meetings, so the usual delays related to an area can be avoided. The members are thinking more broadly than before, and they definitely consider decisions that benefit more members rather than just individuals.

The unit's fund will gradually increase over time, but until then, some patience is required. You can transform your area into an individual house, decorating it strategically to attract visitors and expand market possibilities.

Overcoming water scarcity can turn your ideas and dreams in your favor. The unit's goal is to achieve self-sufficiency in food production, eliminating the risk of starvation in the countryside.

Instead of focusing on heavy industries, the units can prioritize agriculture and allied activities. This approach not only benefits the local community but also helps keep the countryside free from pollution caused by smoke and factory waste. However, industries in cities have better facilities for managing pollutants.

Within our unit, decisions are made unanimously during meetings, minimizing the typical delays associated with administrative processes. Our members adopt a broader perspective, prioritizing choices that benefit the collective rather than individual interests.

While waiting for the unit's funds to grow steadily over time, consider transforming your area into an inviting individual house. By strategically decorating and attracting visitors, you can tap into market opportunities.

Overcoming water scarcity holds the key to unlocking your ideas and dreams. Our unit's primary objective is achieving self-sufficiency in food production, ensuring that no one in the countryside faces the specter of starvation.

Rather than heavy industries, our focus lies on agriculture and related activities. This approach not only benefits our local community but also preserves the countryside by avoiding pollution from smoke and factory waste. Meanwhile, industries in cities have better pollution management facilities in place.

## SSI UNITS WILL FLOURISH THE AREA

"In rural areas, where small units prevail, managing production with a keen focus on minimizing negative impacts is crucial. Since these units are overseen by their members, it's essential to prevent large companies that contribute to pollution from encroaching on the unit's boundaries. Instead, let such companies operate within cities. By prioritizing a better quality of life over mere financial gains, you can create a pleasant and comfortable environment that doesn't harm lives through pollution. The government will appreciate your efforts in maintaining a pollution-free area.

Emphasize environmental cleanliness, aligning it with renowned tourist destinations. Attracting foreign visitors should be your goal. Beyond this, consider enhancing the area with greenery and flowers—both natural and artificial. As the sole owner of the entire unit, your endeavors will transform it into a place that exudes heavenly charm.

During all seasons, exercise caution with travelers, especially during droughts, floods, or extreme rainy periods. A moderate and inviting climate should be your hallmark.

**Remember:** *that concealing weaknesses from others is more beneficial than revealing them."*

## EMBRACING THE UNIT SYSTEM: A PATH TO PROGRESS

The newly implemented unit system empowers its members and unit management to make crucial decisions regarding the necessity of large, polluting factories within their limits. Rather than being solely driven by financial considerations, they now prioritize safety and well-being. This shift allows them to move toward a socially recognized and better life.

While some may extol the virtues of technology, fast-paced living, and modernity, the truth remains: these factors do not guarantee inner peace. Transforming rural areas into bustling cities may seem tempting, but it's essential to recognize that the decision lies with the local inhabitants.

**Challenges and Alternatives** One significant drawback is the risk of encroachment upon secret areas, potentially disrupting lives. However, an alternative approach emerges, and rather than relying solely on government initiatives, units can play a pivotal role in supporting their communities.

**Unit-Driven Solutions** Units can collaborate with the government in multifaceted ways. By channeling their efforts through the unit, they can efficiently implement plans while ensuring 100% fund utilization. The unit's streamlined feedback and meticulous records replace the costly bureaucracy of the past.

Unlike individual contractors or profit-driven companies, units prioritize lasting construction without imposing additional charges. Their active participation ensures funds are allocated accurately, controlling expenses for the benefit of all members.

In summary, the unit system offers a path toward progress, where collective decisions and purposeful utilization lead to sustainable development.

## UNIT FUNCTIONS AND POSITIVE IMPACT

Despite initial dissatisfaction, the government now benefits significantly from the unit's functions. These functions facilitate the implementation of rules and regulations among unit members. Additionally, the unit effectively manages the area, ensuring peace by keeping anti-social elements at bay. Notably, the unit's efforts have not only shielded the area from anti-social behavior but have also eradicated their influence entirely.

The unit takes on the sorrows of its members, providing unwavering support without differentiation. Every member enjoys equal rights within the unit—a core principle of our agenda. Surprisingly, members experience a transformed life far beyond their expectations. Their commitment to hard work contributes to this newfound quality of life, free from unnecessary hardships.

**Report on Development Projects** The unit diligently provides detailed statements and a final utilization certificate to the government for the entrusted funds. As a result, the government can now execute projects satisfactorily, devoid of corruption and excessive spending. The unit's dedication has left the government content, as it actively works in their favor.

1. **Funds Allocation and Accountability**: When there is a shortage of funds allocated for a specific project, the unit promptly submits this information to the relevant authority. Conversely, if there is an excess of funds, the unit handles it similarly. As a result, government officials are well-acquainted with the unit's work and fund utilization, enabling accurate assessment.

2. **Unit as Beneficiary and Development Executor**: The unit serves as the beneficiary, actively executing developmental projects within their area on behalf of the government. With poverty, water scarcity, and unemployment no longer plaguing their region, their focus has shifted to infrastructural enhancements

across the entire unit. They have abandoned confrontational approaches like agitations and strikes, opting instead to invest their valuable time in contributing to the unit's progress and learning from past mistakes.

3. **Challenges and Responsibilities**: Although essential for the unit's well-being, the members are not directly responsible for infrastructure development such as roads, offices, schools, and hospitals. Instead, the government allocates specialized units capable of undertaking these tasks and ensuring satisfaction among government officials.

4. **Dedicated and Skilled Members**: The unit's members exhibit exceptional dedication and possess a diverse range of skills. Their commitment to the unit's welfare is supported by managers and other concerned individuals who share the same intention.

## TAX AND LEVIES PAID IN LUMP-SUM

The financial health of any organization, as reflected in its accounts, plays a crucial role in determining its eligibility for financial support from banks or other financial institutions in accordance with government regulations. While taxes are an essential part of contributing to the nation's development, there are instances where they need not be paid directly. Instead, these funds can be allocated to various developmental projects that benefit all citizens.

Transparency is key. Concealing financial information or attempting to evade payments is not advisable. The decision of whether to pay taxes can be made during the annual account finalization process. By contributing to the government, we actively influence our nation's financial standing.

Our accounting records should be an open book accessible to relevant officials, auditors, and government inspectors. Additionally, maintaining audited annual financial statements ensures compliance with future requirements.

As our financial stability grows, we can strategically consider tax payments. Fortunately, there are exemptions available for self-help units like ours. Although our initial goal was to form a group of 1000 members, we have decided to limit membership to 200 individuals. This prudent approach ensures effective management and sustainable growth.

"Managing a large unit with numerous members is far more challenging than one might anticipate. Our past experiences hold little relevance once we establish this unit; now, our focus lies on obedience and practicality. We are shaping a refined lifestyle, one that adheres to gentlemanly conduct.

To achieve this, we must adapt everything to suit our current way of life—our mindset, behavior, and attitude. Clean habits and high behavioral standards among members benefit not only themselves but also their families, neighbors, and the nation at large. The unit's responsibility extends to molding its members accordingly.

Our members should be well-versed in interacting with others, both within the unit and when dealing with outsiders. Even during their travels beyond the unit, they should exemplify remarkable behavior without seeking commendation.

Importantly, we must overcome any inherent negative tendencies— such as cheating, corruption, or theft. These traits have no place within our unit. Failure to adhere to these principles will result in expulsion, along with the return of any contributions made upon joining.

# THE SIGNIFICANCE OF BEHAVIORAL DISCIPLINES IN TOURISM

Tourism, both at the national and international levels, thrives on effective advertising. However, beyond mere promotional efforts, maintaining a conducive environment within your premises is crucial. Your attitude and behavior toward tourists play a pivotal role. Right from the outset, practice a gentle and welcoming demeanor among your team.

While your role may involve civil work, remember that you represent more than just a functional unit. You are a prestigious member, and the way the unit introduces you to visitors matters significantly. Unlike other places, we don't allocate separate civil or loading workers; everyone contributes to the unit's functioning.

When it comes to catering to tourists, prioritize their needs. Offer quality dishes prepared by expert cooks in our canteen. Engage with guests to discuss menu preferences. But here's the key: before serving any food, ensure it's tasted by someone with expertise.

The hospitality you extend will reverberate far and wide. Word-of-mouth recommendations can attract the next wave of visitors. It's like a behavioral game—our consistent actions yield 100% results. By following these principles, we can win their hearts without any extra effort or financial strain.

**Remember:** *it's not just about the physical infrastructure; our behavior shapes the entire tourist experience.*

# ANTICIPATED GOVERNMENT SUPPORT BEYOND FINANCIAL AID

Rather than solely relying on financial assistance, there is a strong expectation for the government to provide moral support in implementing this unit scheme across rural areas. This initiative functions as a self-help team comprising capable members who collectively address challenges and safeguard one another comprehensively. Their needs, including daily necessities, are protected as essential rights within the unit.

The well-being, safety, and property of members are prioritized, shielding them from theft, violence, and other threats posed by intoxicated individuals or criminals. This includes safeguarding women, children, the elderly, and those with disabilities or mental health challenges. By fostering positive moral habits and cultural attitudes, the unit members can collectively contribute to a safer and more harmonious community.

Furthermore, the transition from years of untapped manpower in rural areas to increased productivity holds immense value. This transformation represents potential economic gains amounting to millions of dollars, impacting global growth positively.

Despite enduring hardships, individuals in various nations continue to persevere, often sacrificing for their own well-being or the betterment of their country. Their resilience, even in the face of adversity, remains a testament to the human spirit.

## UTILIZING IDLE MANPOWER FOR ECONOMIC PRODUCTIVITY

The government has a crucial role to play in harnessing the potential of underutilized manpower. By taking affirmative steps to support this workforce, it can transform their idle time into a productive resource. One effective approach is to enact new laws or amend existing ones that protect investors in partnership businesses. Partnerships are a versatile form of business that can thrive anywhere in the world.

**Empowering Partnerships:** Partnerships enable entrepreneurs to pool resources, whether among friends, family, or other trusted associates. This collaborative model facilitates the establishment of enterprises, allowing individuals to combine their skills, capital, and networks. However, despite the benefits, challenges persist.

**Dishonest practices** within partnerships, such as fraudulent schemes and deceptive advertising, pose risks to investors.

## THE MENACE OF DECEPTIVE ADVERTISING

Every day, reliable media outlets bombard the public with advertisements. Unfortunately, some of these ads are misleading, targeting unsuspecting individuals who place blind trust in their claims. Reputed newspapers, weekly publications, television channels, and even cinema theaters feature ads endorsed by celebrities and influential figures. These advertisements can sway common people into falling prey to intentional companies or unscrupulous individuals.

## SAFEGUARDING INVESTORS: A CALL FOR GOVERNMENT INTERVENTION

1. **Addressing Misleading Investment Schemes**: The issue of misleading investment schemes demands **urgent attention** from the government. Robust legislation or amendments are necessary to **protect rural investors**. Additionally, media advertising should not exploit legal loopholes to profit from false promises and deceptive offerings. Many people consider advertisements from reputed sources.

2. **Balancing Protection and Advertising**: While safeguarding innocent viewers and listeners is crucial, we must also consider the advertising companies that benefit financially from such misleading ads. Laypeople, who often unwittingly fall victim to fraudulent schemes, require strong legal safeguards. Ultimately, the government can only protect them from deceiving common people and enticing them into risky investments.

3. **Balancing Protection and Advertising:** While it remains essential to protect unsuspecting viewers and listeners, we must also take into account the financial interests of advertising companies that profit from deceptive advertisements. Laypeople, who frequently become unwitting targets of fraudulent schemes, need robust legal safeguards. Ultimately, it is the government that can only shield them from those who exploit their trust and lure them into risky investments.

4. <u>Unit Formation for Safeguarding Members:</u> *Going forward, the newly formed unit will diligently look after and safeguard its members from investing with fraudulent companies.*

**Nurturing Growth in the Unit:** After the formation of the unit, consider it a platform where active participation is essential Avoid assuming that success is guaranteed or that difficult times are behind you Much like an infant, the unit is in its early stages, requiring concerted efforts for growth. Adhering to bylaws and contributing to the unit's development are crucial steps.

**2. Building Reputation and Charging Fairly:** As the unit gains prominence, it will naturally build goodwill. Consequently, the unit can set reasonable prices for its products and services, following standard practices. Those who missed the initial opportunity to join may face higher membership fees, reflecting the unit's progress.

**3. Transforming Anti-Social Elements:** *Efforts to engage anti-social activists from the local area can yield positive results. Encouraging their participation can turn them into productive members. Simultaneously, the government stands to benefit significantly. By avoiding costly criminal and civil cases, streamlining processes, and minimizing expenses related to jails, food, and security, substantial savings can be achieved.*

**4. A New Trend: Prevention Over Incarceration:** This approach not only saves resources but also shifts the focus from punitive measures to prevention. Even the simple act of providing food to someone on the brink of incarceration can alter their trajectory, creating a new trend in addressing social challenges.

**From now on**, the community has decided to put an end to any anti-social activities that disrupt their lives. Outsiders are no longer allowed to interfere in their affairs. The community members, well-versed in handling such situations, take responsibility for maintaining safety within their area. The result? A cleaner, safer environment.

**Everyone desires peace and a stress-free existence**, even those who were once considered anti-social. However, they struggled to find a path leading to such a life. Now, the community provides them with all necessary amenities without demanding hard work until financial stability is achieved.

**Life within the community is now unpredictable, peaceful, and pleasant**—a stark contrast to their previous experiences. The unit effectively addresses anti-social behavior, bad habits among members, neighborly disputes, and both criminal and civil cases.

**Moreover,** *the community tackles core issues like poverty, starvation, and water scarcity, ensuring that these challenges no longer plague its members.*

## TRANSFORMING CHALLENGES INTO OPPORTUNITIES: A CALL FOR SUPPORT

In our current challenging situation, there lies an opportunity for transformation. The growing demand for commercial products from various countries has led them to outsource from our nation. Rather than seeking purely financial assistance from the government, we anticipate their moral support.

The specific support we seek includes ensuring a stable supply of electricity and simplifying the formalities required to establish new units.

By facilitating the registration process as trusts, we can encourage more entrepreneurs to take the leap. Additionally, we propose that banks extend their support through mechanisms like overdrafts and key loans rather than rigid-term loans. Furthermore, local government authorities also streamline their processes without unnecessary red tape.

With this comprehensive support, numerous units can thrive not only within our nation but also globally, only in rural areas. These units play a crucial role in safeguarding the lives of their members. <u>Within the unit's boundaries, members enjoy freedom and safety while their dedication and skills determine their progress, future prospects, and financial stability</u>.

## ADDRESSING CHEATING: A CALL FOR GOVERNMENT ACTION

The government can only proactively combat cheating. Crafty individuals exploit unsuspecting victims, amassing wealth through dishonest means. Unfortunately, the common populace remains largely unaffected due to inadequate restrictions or bans that could safeguard their families.

Within our organization, we diligently monitor and curb any cheating tendencies among members. All legal activities pass through rigorous scrutiny by our management. The only vulnerability lies when members interact with external clients beyond our unit.

To address cheating in partnership businesses involving outsiders, the government has to take effective remedies. By tapping into the latent potential of our workforce, we can witness transformative changes within a few months. Fostering growth in rural areas will not only boost the economy but also enhance lifestyles.

Given our small membership, we meticulously collect and store detailed information on our computers. Any weaknesses in our system can be swiftly identified and rectified, thanks to our limited size.

Furthermore, our unit can collaborate with various government offices—Agriculture, Village, Block, Police Station, and post—alongside financial institutions. Their support can significantly aid our mission.

1. **Educational Focus**: The unit aims to educate all its members, encouraging them to interact with others in new and constructive ways. This shift from previous approaches fosters better communication and understanding.

2. **Non-Interference Policy**: The unit strictly avoids meddling in political party affairs or local government matters. Instead, it remains an independent body solely dedicated to the welfare of its members. Its collaborative approach resembles that of a corporate office.

3. **Government Collaboration**: While not directly involved in political beliefs, the unit's work results can benefit the government if desired. It operates as a business house, akin to a well-run corporation, with qualified staff selected exclusively from within the unit.

4. **Equal Rights and Property**: The unit functions like a family business, ensuring equal rights for all members. Differences in property investments are gradually equalized, and no one loses their excess holdings.

5. **Unit Members' Appeal for Support**: The members of the unit refrain from seeking any financial assistance from the state or central government. Instead, they earnestly pray for protection and moral backing as they navigate bureaucratic challenges within government offices. Their commitment to the unit's mission remains unwavering.

6. **Government Support and Delay**: Despite unexpected delays in obtaining robust legal protection, the unit persists in its efforts. The government's endorsement could transform the lives of its members in ways they never imagined. Their dedication

has already yielded significant benefits, including cost savings, efficient resource utilization, and economic growth across two-thirds of the global countryside.

## COLLECTIVE MANAGEMENT OF THE UNIT

Within our unit, there are thousands of members actively involved in its operation. The effectiveness of our management hinges on the unit's growth, and our self-motivated members contribute significantly. Rather than relying on the responsibilities of just a few individuals, our entire team aspires to collaboratively shoulder the unit's functioning based on their collective experience. A mere watchful eye is sufficient, given their wealth of life experiences. Let us empower them to do more than mere control—it's time for them to lead.

In this egalitarian environment, every member enjoys equal rights and responsibilities. Our vision is to operate like a corporation, where each of the 200 homes has its representative acting as the signing authority. Flexibility is key: any home can promptly change its representative or opt for a rotation every 12 months. This way, every member gets a chance to participate in the unit's governing body.

After each balance sheet, fresh teams can step up to lead, ensuring a fair and inclusive process. Only once the full cycle is complete can an individual be represented again.

*Together, we forge a path toward collective success and shared responsibility.*

## MEMBERS COLLABORATIVELY MANAGE THE UNIT

Within our organization, thousands of members actively participate in running the unit. The effectiveness of our management hinges on the unit's growth, and our self-motivated members contribute significantly. Rather than relying on a select few, the entire team aims to operate the unit collectively, leveraging their wealth of experience. A mere watchful eye suffices, as their life experiences empower them to do more than merely control.

In this setup, all members enjoy equal rights and responsibilities. Our plan is to function as a corporation, with each of the 200 homes represented by an authorized signatory. If any home wishes to change its representative, it can do so immediately or once every 12 months. This rotation ensures that every member has an opportunity to participate in the unit's governing body. After each balance sheet, newly formed teams take charge, ensuring a fair and inclusive approach. Only after a full cycle can an individual be represented again.

1. **Empowering the Unit with Fresh Ideas**: If you harbor innovative ideas to propel our unit to new heights, don't hesitate to share them during our initial meeting. Your proactive approach will position you as a leader among your peers. While seniority plays a role, every member deserves a chance to contribute.

2. **Navigating Unit Management**: As the unit operates under the guidance of the manager and their team (including yourself), newly elected members primarily handle policy matters. However, the manager will appoint skilled individuals to assist in suitable roles. Your relative unfamiliarity with day-to-day functions won't disrupt unit operations, so feel free to continue your work as usual.

3. **Recording Insights for Future Reference**: Although members may not derive special benefits from the unit, they represent their homes. During meetings, they can raise pertinent questions and valuable points, which should be meticulously recorded in the minutes. This practice ensures a repository of insights for future reference.

4. **Unlocking Potential in Rural Areas**: Our unit has the potential to transform dormant villagers into productive contributors.

While each villager possesses property, collaborative efforts are essential. Recognizing their limitations, they seek change in their rural surroundings. The bank, acknowledging the viability of project reports presented en masse by unit members, has played a pivotal role in rural progress. Implementing these projects rests not only with the unit manager and members but also with supportive bank officials, who can guide us toward familiarity and success.

## "A COMMUNITY'S COLLECTIVE ENDEAVOR FOR PROSPERITY"

In our close-knit community, **200 families**—comprising approximately **1,000 members**—have turned to local banks seeking financial assistance. These families, predominantly villagers, are determined to secure their livelihoods. To achieve this, they have collectively authorized our community unit to access financial resources.

Our democratic system is thoughtfully designed, emphasizing a systematic approach. We aim to shield our members from financial losses, sorrows, and hardships. The unit and the bank collaborate closely, ensuring that each decision aligns with our shared vision.

Despite past challenges, we remain resilient. Our unit boasts abundant resources scattered throughout our area. Now, we unite with a common purpose: to elevate our community and its residents. We envision ornamental landscapes, green and vibrant premises, and a clean environment. Above all, our agenda centers on the happiness and well-being of every individual within our unit.

# CHAPTER XIX

# THE UNIT AND ITS WEBSITE

In our endeavor to transform the countryside into functional units, we've created a cohesive entity. Now, it's time to unveil the unit's purpose to the public and market our products effectively. To achieve this, we must craft targeted advertisements.

In today's digital landscape, numerous technologies and websites serve as powerful channels to reach the masses. Our unit, nestled within the rural expanse, comprises 200 houses. All relevant information about every member is accessible through our unit's office. Recognizing the uniqueness of our venture, we've taken the step of establishing our own website.

1. **Website Outreach and Impact**: Our website aims to connect with a wide audience, reaching both our peers and the general public. By sharing comprehensive details and showcasing the successful execution of our services, we anticipate drawing significant interest. The functions we describe may serve as a guiding light for those facing adversity, helping them navigate challenging times and overcome obstacles.

2. **Unit System and Community Engagement**: Our unit system has the potential to resonate with unorganized rural populations. By disseminating knowledge and gathering additional insights, many individuals can discover meaningful solutions through our operational framework. Each unit functions as a corporate

office led by skilled managers and staff. To achieve our growth objectives, we seek substantial publicity and support from both the public and the government. This collaborative effort is essential for us to meet our targets effectively.

3. **Transparency and Government Interaction**: Transparency is our hallmark. We make our formalities and functions accessible to the general public. Government officials and departments can assess the progress and capabilities of each unit. This evaluation ensures that we receive diverse civil and other projects, aligning with our mission to serve the community effectively.

1. **Fostering Unity and Growth**: It's crucial to avoid unnecessary competition among sister units. Such rivalry can hinder our collective progress and unity. If a neighboring unit successfully markets a popular product with high yields, let's refrain from disrupting their efforts. Instead, we should explore alternative products to promote

2. **Transparency and Public Information**: While maintaining privacy policies, we'll ensure that general information about our unit is readily available to both members and the public. Our website will serve as a platform to showcase our offerings, including products and services. Visitors can learn about the detailed scope of our work and the value we provide.

3. **Product Details and Wholesale Opportunities**: Through our website, we'll highlight the products we produce and their availability. Whether wholesale or retail, buyers can access essential information, including minimum quantities and daily offer prices. Wholesale pricing will attract bulk buyers, and we'll also communicate our manpower needs openly.

1. **Strategic Website Integration**: Consider partnering your website with a marketing company that boasts a substantial network of sellers and buyers. By leveraging their portals, you can effortlessly showcase your products to a wide audience. Some of

these marketing platforms even act as mediators, ensuring fair transactions between buyers and sellers.

2. **Product Visibility and Pricing**: To attract potential buyers, publish categorized product listings along with their availability status. Whether you choose to display prices or not, this approach will facilitate sales, particularly for agricultural and allied products. Utilize this online medium as a second chance to market your offerings effectively.

3. **Embrace Uniqueness and Focus**: Encourage similar units to adopt the successful methods employed by your unit. Specialize in a select few products that other units do not produce. By concentrating your efforts, you'll create a high demand in the market, setting your offerings apart from the competition.

4. **Collaborate Instead of Compete**: Rather than engaging in cutthroat competition, prioritize collaboration. Seek out business opportunities and mutually beneficial partnerships. However, exercise discretion when sharing sensitive information about unit members—details like personal data, financial updates, and status should remain confidential. For promotional purposes, use your judgment to determine what information is essential to share.

1. **Product Listings and Inquiries**: The unit can post details about the products it wishes to sell or purchase, as well as the services it offers. Interested parties can inquire and respond through our agent portal. Regular monitoring by skilled staff ensures timely communication with concerned individuals.

2. **Guard Your Expertise**: Remember that your knowledge and skills are valuable assets. Avoid sharing them indiscriminately with the public. Instead, leverage them strategically to benefit the unit and its members.

3. **Empowering Rural Units**: Voluntary members play a crucial role in expanding the scope of such units. By collectively improving

the rural landscape, we can elevate the lifestyle of these areas from poverty to above-average standards.

4. **Maximizing Grants for Members**: If the government allocates grants to unit members, it is our responsibility to collect and utilize these funds effectively. Maintaining accurate records ensures transparency and prevents any loss to our members.

5. **Government Collaboration**: Establish strong ties with local government bodies to stay informed and claim relevant information promptly. This collaboration enhances our unit's effectiveness and impact.

1. **Comprehensive Fund Collection**: In addition to grants, we must diligently collect all funds earmarked for the development of our unit's area. These funds, whether directly related to the unit or its members, play a crucial role in our progress. We will meticulously document and submit all relevant details to the government authorities and our respective members within the stipulated timeframe.

2. **Project Execution and Accountability**: When undertaking project or developmental works, our unit strives for excellence. If government officials are involved in overseeing these endeavors, we should readily provide them with the necessary information upon request. Transparency and cooperation are key.

3. **Data Utilization for Future Works**: Furnishing detailed particulars of our projects to the government serves a dual purpose. Firstly, it aids in planning future works of a similar nature. Secondly, it allows us to forecast upcoming developments. The data we share becomes a valuable resource for informed decision-making.

4. **Cost Assessment and Reference**: By sharing project specifics with government authorities, we enable them to assess costs accurately. Furthermore, this information becomes a point of reference when calling tenders, estimating work, or seeking

quotations for similar projects in the future. Ultimately, it benefits both our unit and the government.

1. **Funds Collection and Reporting**: All grants and funds allocated to the unit or its members for the development of the unit's area must be diligently collected. The unit will be disbursed, and comprehensive details will be promptly submitted to government authorities and respective members.

2. **Project Execution and Accountability**: When undertaking projects or developmental works related to the unit, the government officials responsible for these tasks can provide necessary information to the government upon request. This ensures that all unit members are satisfied with the execution.

3. **Data Utilization and Cost Assessment**: Detailed information about such works can be furnished to the government, allowing them to utilize this data for future projects of a similar nature. Additionally, sharing particulars with government authorities enables cost assessment, serving as a valuable reference for future tenders, work estimates, and quotations. Ultimately, this benefits the government's planning and execution processes.

1. **Funding and Unit Development**:

All funds related to the unit or its members, including grants, must be collected. These funds are allocated for the development of the unit's area.

The unit's details will be distributed, and comprehensive information will be submitted to the government authorities and respective members in a timely manner.

2. **Project Execution and Accountability**:

When there are projects or developmental works related to the unit, the government officials responsible for these tasks can execute them to the satisfaction of all unit members.

If requested, they can provide the government with details about these works.

### 3. **Data Utilization and Cost Assessment**:

Detailed information about such works can be furnished to the government. This data can be used for future projects of a similar nature and to forecast upcoming developments.

The particulars shared with government authorities can help assess the cost of these works. Additionally, they serve as a valuable reference when calling tenders, estimating work, or obtaining quotations for similar projects in the future.

### 1. **Sustainable Work Through Units**:

Projects routed through these units will have a lasting impact, eliminating the need for recurring investments in the same work. Casual and skilled workers will find employment opportunities within their respective units. These projects encompass construction, infrastructure expansion, and other vital developments.

### 2. **Government Support and Unit Responsibility**:

The government can combat unemployment by allocating work to these units. Civil projects within the area can be entrusted to them. Since the work directly benefits the unit, its members will diligently oversee it, ensuring high-quality outcomes.

### 3. **Countryside Participation and Rural Development**:

For schemes to succeed, active participation from rural communities, especially at the grassroots-level, is essential. Without this engagement, many rural areas remain stagnant. Unit members must contribute actively to overall development.

1. **Gifts and Money Received:** It's common for some people to dismiss gifts or sums of money received effortlessly, especially if they don't seem sufficient to meet their immediate needs. Often, such funds end up being used for miscellaneous expenses. This trend is also observed when individuals receive government rural fund assistance.

2. **Inclusive Rural Growth:** When envisioning the progress of the entire countryside or rural area, it's crucial not to leave the grassroots-level population behind. Instead, we must actively engage with them and walk alongside them on the path of development.

3. **Collective Effort:** Regardless of age, everyone should contribute to overcoming present challenges and building a brighter future. Let's all participate wholeheartedly, leveraging our unique skills and abilities.

4. **Implementing the Scheme:** Adapt this scheme to your context for positive outcomes. As you identify your needs and collaborate with others, showcasing progress, the government will recognize your capabilities and allocate more developmental work accordingly.

1. **Engaging with Your Team and National-Level Projects**: When your team begins allocating funds for infrastructure within your unit, you become an integral part of their national-level schemes and projects. Your loyalty and dedication to the work play a crucial role. If you approach government authorities with confidence, you can actively contribute to successful government initiatives in your area or beyond. As these projects flow through your hands, you'll gain familiarity with their accounting procedures, estimate preparation, and quotations. Your ongoing assistance to the government ensures that you won't need to look back.

2. **Financial Accountability and Decision-Making**: By meticulously maintaining all accounts, you become a valuable resource.

Whenever the government requires details, you can promptly provide them via statements. Understanding the actual expenses incurred for specific projects empowers both you and the government to make informed decisions regarding financial matters.

1. **Effective Implementation of Public Works**: Public works should be executed by organized units. This approach offers several advantages for local growth. When managed by a unit, the work receives focused attention from its members, ensuring quality outcomes and minimizing recurring costs.

2. **Challenges in Our Developing Country**: In our developing nation, entrusting public works to individual contractors has proven costly. Substandard work often necessitates repeated efforts, draining public funds.

Interestingly, despite widespread malpractices, the public lacks the authority to intervene in construction matters. Third-party opinions from skilled experts often go unnoticed.

**3. A Solution: Entrusting Works to Units**: To mitigate substandard work, consider assigning projects to established units. The government can leverage their track records and assess their skills, abilities, and experience. This approach ensures better results and efficient resource utilization.

1. **Quality and Accountability**: The outcome of our work should endure for many years, satisfying not only the government officials but also our fellow unit members. We refrain from inflating costs beyond permissible limits during project execution, and we remain fully accountable for every task entrusted to us by the government.

2. **Ethical Conduct**: Within our unit, no individual engages in corrupt practices. Our adherence to established norms ensures

that personal gain is not prioritized over integrity. We do not seek private earnings or engage in unethical accounting practices. Corruption has no place in the work we undertake for government officials.

3. **Member Well-Being**: Our unit operates with the well-being of its members in mind. We eschew shortcuts and third-class approaches, focusing instead on ethical methods. Strict guidance and oversight prevent any deviation that could lead to career setbacks.

4. **Path to Growth**: As members, we have access not only to shortcuts but also to wide roads for growth. Embrace genuine and legal avenues; there's no need to accumulate funds illicitly for the unit. Let go of past habits and walk the path aligned with our unit's principles.

1. **Unit and National Contribution**: What you earn through hard work benefits not only yourself but also the entire nation. The government initiates numerous construction projects and other endeavors for public welfare. You can participate in these projects based on your goodwill and track record. Remember, the expectations you set for yourself often inspire greater achievements than those imposed by others.

2. **Daily Contributions**: As conscious citizens, we contribute significantly to the public fund through our everyday expenses—be it groceries, stationery, fuel, or other necessities. While income taxpayers play a crucial role in the economy, it's essential to recognize that the majority of the population contributes daily. Let's aim to strengthen our community, and in the future, we can also contribute directly through income taxes.

3. **Self-Reliance and Independence**: Rather than relying solely on government assistance, let's shift our mindset. The unit—comprising all families—should take responsibility for its well-being. Striving for self-sufficiency and independence is our shared agenda.

# CHAPTER XX

# CASTEISM CAN BE ABOLISHED

This is a suggestion that nobody else can bring its benefit to your hands – Its remedy is in your hands, say, purely within you. Long ago, individuals allocated tasks among their subjects to streamline work.

Over time, these divisions evolved into castes, such as carpenters, washermen, blacksmiths, barbers, fishermen, and countless others. Despite the passage of thousands of years, these caste distinctions persist, particularly in rural areas, even when individuals engage in different occupations. While the initial intention behind this classification might have been innocent, its impact is far-reaching.

Subsequently, religious leaders emerged, aiming to strengthen their faith by organizing these classified groups. Although the religion remained the same, they perpetuated differentiation through sub-castes, further entrenching the caste system.

However, it is essential to recognize that castes are not a relic of the past. Discriminatory practices rooted in caste continue to shape our society.

**FOR INSTANCE:**

1. **Discrimination in Daily Life**: Many youngsters are suffering the effects of this system. Matrimonial advertisements often seek partners from specific castes. In urban housing societies, separate elevators exist for residents and service workers, reinforcing

caste-based distinctions. Some households even deny basic courtesies like offering water to domestic workers.

2. **Normalization of Caste**: The discreet nature of caste-based discrimination doesn't indicate its decline; rather, it reflects its normalization. These practices persist, subtly perpetuating inequality.

3. **Reservations and Equality**: While some argue that reservations should only level the playing field initially, the heart of social inequality lies beyond economic deprivation. Caste-based reservations remain crucial to address historical discrimination and promote equal opportunity.

In conclusion, dismantling the caste system requires concerted efforts, education, and a commitment to equality. <u>Let us strive for a society where caste ceases to define our worth and opportunities</u>.

## BREAKING FREE FROM OUTDATED MINDSETS

In our society, certain individuals are still denied the right to sit alongside others or participate in communal gatherings due to restrictive norms. Despite technological advancements, the mindset remains entrenched and backward. It's time for change, and those who are suffering must take decisive action.

Waiting for others to initiate and correct your problems proves insufficient for your own lives and those of future generations. In this modern era, why wait for someone else? It's incumbent upon each of us to dismantle outdated systems within our communities. While these systems once served a purpose, times have changed.

Today, job opportunities are no longer dictated by caste categories. People engage in diverse professions—electricians, drivers, mechanics, clerks, officers, executives, and more. Across religions, caste divisions persist, perpetuating degradation and mental anguish.

Initiatives won't come from external sources. It's up to us. Going forward, government and other official documents should no longer label you based on caste, perpetuating backwardness. Removing these designations lies within our power—a step toward a more equitable present and future.

Before the classification system emerged, society recognized only two genders: men and women. However, over time, this binary framework evolved into a more complex structure, introducing the concept of higher and lower castes. This classification became particularly pronounced in rural areas.

Each caste carried significant social identification, and the system stratified people based on their birth. The high castes wielded authority over the low castes, often relegating the latter to subordinate roles. This hierarchical practice persisted, hindering unity and collective decision-making among rural communities.

Implementing this system was relatively straightforward because it aligned with the prevailing power dynamics. The ruling elite then, often referred to as the "Supremes," enforced this order. Despite efforts to eradicate classism, it endured.

The beneficiaries of this system perpetuated it, viewing it as a reward for their position.

As a result, genuine unity among people or collaborative efforts for their well-being remained elusive. Families struggled to secure their daily sustenance, and the specter of classism continued to impact subsequent generations. <u>In this context, some were even willing to make sacrifices, hoping for a better future</u>.

# SOCIAL CLASS AND CASTE SYSTEM: A COMPARATIVE VIEW

The division between social classes has historically conferred advantages upon the higher echelons of society. These privileged classes rarely intervened or corrected the disparities that existed. Interestingly, no socialists or other advocates stepped forward to guide or rectify the plight of the less fortunate.

Perhaps hidden agendas played a role, necessitating a discerning approach. Ultimately, this division boiled down to a binary distinction: men and women.

**The Lingering Influence of Religion, Castes, and Sub-Castes** Although this system took root long ago, its impact persists. Religion, castes, and sub-castes continue to wield significant influence over people's lives. Remarkably, the younger generation seems relatively unfazed by this deeply entrenched system.

<u>Perhaps they view it with a light-hearted perspective, allowing them to witness the relief it provides while acknowledging its historical roots</u>.

**Challenges Faced by Rural Communities** The plight of lower-level individuals in rural areas, who often prevent their children from accessing basic education, remains a global issue. These communities grapple with limited opportunities and face significant hardships.

**Interdependence and Caste Classifications** In these rural settings, people rely heavily on one another for their livelihoods. Meanwhile, caste divisions—established by certain individuals for their own convenience—persist. These classifications create disparities and perpetuate advantages for some while disadvantaging others.

**Historical Manipulation and Social Stratification** Throughout history, cunning manipulators deceived our ancestors, dividing them into various categories: high, medium, and low. These divisions were exploited to the detriment of the majority.

**Lack of Basic Education** Unfortunately, even fundamental education remains elusive for many in these communities. The absence of accessible learning opportunities perpetuates the cycle of poverty.

**Guidance** Despite the presence of practical advice on securing daily sustenance and achieving financial stability has been lacking. The financially disadvantaged continue to seek a path forward without clear guidance. The unit system will find a remedy for all the financial differences.

## EMPOWERING YOUR OWN PATH

**Uniting Rural Communities for Prosperity** The concept of this unit is to unite scattered rural communities, enabling them to collaborate and collectively transform their families and their rural areas into thriving paradises.

**Remember**, *your life is entirely yours. No one else will take the initiative to uplift you or your family. To achieve progress, hard work is essential, but it alone won't yield results without a well-thought-out plan.*

(THIS FORM SHOULD BE SUBMITTED BY ALL THE INMATES OF EACH MEMBER HOME)

**INSTRUCTION TO FILL UP THE APPLICATION**

## APPLICATION FOR FAMILY DETAILS

The unit seeks a transparent and candid report about you through this application. There's no need to embellish or conceal facts; the goal is to understand the reality of your family. As an applicant, you and your household members should provide truthful information.

Remember that once the unit is operational, all details will surface—so there's no room for secrecy. This applies not only to you but also to the unit and the government. If someone else fills out the application on your behalf, they must include their name, address, and mobile number below the application also s/he should be from the unit.

You can submit a duplicate of the form and receive an acknowledgment from the office. Keep the duplicate copy with you.

This form serves as the primary document for your household. It encompasses essential details such as members' ages, birth information, property specifics (including document number of property and right), encumbrance certificates, tax receipts, and related documents. Whenever possible, involve a fellow unit member to help explain the application's contents to you. The unit can input this format into a computer, fill it out, and provide a copy to you later.

About Me (100 Words or More)

I am a curious soul, perpetually seeking knowledge and adventure. My present life history is a patchwork of experiences—some mundane, others extraordinary. From the bustling streets of the city to the serene countryside, I've wandered, absorbing stories and unraveling mysteries. Life has taught me resilience, compassion, and the beauty of shared moments. As I pen these words, I am but a fleeting chapter in the grand saga of existence, eager to contribute my unique verse to the cosmic symphony.

About My Family (100 Words or More)

## ABOUT MY FAMILY

Our family is like a rich tapestry, intricately woven with threads of laughter, tears, and shared dreams. Each member contributes their unique color, creating a vibrant mosaic of love and togetherness. Let me introduce you to our cast of characters:

1. Mom: The heart of our home, her warm embrace, is a sanctuary for all our joys and sorrows.
2. Dad: The steady anchor, his wisdom and humor keep us grounded even during life's
3. storms.
4. Siblings: Partners in mischief, confidantes in secrets, and forever friends.
5. Grandparents: Their stories are the threads that bind generations together.
6. Pets: Furry companions who add their own brand of chaos and love.
7. Any special skill to any of them.

# HEAVENLY EARTH
## A VISION FOR RURAL PROSPERITY

**APPLICATION FORM FOR MEMBERSHIP**

**UNIT NME AND REGN No:**

**MEMBERSHIP NUMBER**

**Name and DOB...**

**D/o S/o: Sri / Late.**

**Address**

**House No: House Name:**

**Street No: Village:**

**Post: Pin Code:**

**Religion:**

**Mobile No: Tel.**

**E-mail Id:**

**Educational Qualification: Profession: Income M / Y**

**/ / Rs:**

**Total Members in your home:**

1) Name: DOB: S/o / D/o Sri. / Late

2)

3)

4)

5)

Ration Card No: issued on date: The office of issue. Status:

Names of members included in the card: All above, except the name if any: other than all above if any (with reason)

House electrified or not: Yes / No If No: reason:

Gas Connection: Yes / No If No: reason:

Water source: Well / Bore well / Water connection / fully depending on the neighbor / for drinking water only

Remarks, if any:

Source of income from Professional / Agriculture/ Casual Labor / Business / others (Strike which is not applicable / please give details)

Monthly / Annual:

Casual Labor: are you getting daily work?:

Any other earning member in your Home – If yes, name other than the details given above

Give details: Name: DOB Relation

Present monthly/annual income: Rs.

The total annual income of the family: Rs.

Words should not be less than 100 about you and your family based on the questions below, and if there is anything else that you wish to express about you and your family, it should also relate to the formation of this unit, what you are expecting, or your opinion.

1) Source of income to meet the two ends of every day's expenses out of income.

2) Is water an issue for your family? What do you think about solving it?

3) What about the Electricity connection to your home (Do you think you or your family cannot move forward without electricity?)

4) Gas connection to your house. Is it essential, like food?

5) Are you self-sufficient to meet family affairs? Are you a permanent employee / daily wager write all about you and your family in full?

The application form submitted should be with the following enclosure –

Whether you have your own house, if yes, details of the house say House No. rooms and accommodation details:-

Style and size of the house: Thatched shed / Mud wall with thatched roof, Stone wall with tiles roof, RCC (Strike which is not applicable / please give details) Years old:

Rooms: Rooms with attached: Study room: Yes/No Drawing / Hall: Yes / No. Kitchen: Yes / No Outside washroom: Yes / No Servant room Yes / No Others: Yes / No (Strike which is not applicable / please give details)

Do you have any loans? If yes, the loan amount was Rs. Dated: Present balance payable: as of date Rs. A certificate/ balance confirmation from the bank should be attached, besides an Encumbrance Certificate if applicable.

Whether the loan is regular: Yes / No

If No: any action proceedings against you?

Please give details and its present position: Sticky / Regular

Property details: The extension of land and ownership, other than the details given above to the family or its members.

1) Survey No. Extent other ID if any: in the name of:

2) Survey No. Extent – do-

3) Survey No. Extent – do-

Nature of Property Dry land / Wetland (Strike which is not applicable / please give details)

Is this property mortgaged for the housing loan? : Yes / No

Is this land used for agricultural purposes? : Yes / No

If this is agricultural land and it is not used for agricultural purposes, Please specify the reason


Any other loan or liability: Rs. Give details:

100 words at least:-

DECLARATION

I hereby agree that I accept the terms and conditions of the unit and obey the bylaws, rules, and regulations that are also amended from time to time. I will work for the unit without considering any personal interest but for the benefit of my family members and my neighbours; all the members are my family members. As a result of this, I confirm that I will work together with all other unit members to ensure the progress and prosperity of the unit. This unit is my family property. I will protect it.

I hereby solemnly affirm that the details given in this application are true to the best of my knowledge and belief. If any misleading or interpretation / wrong report, I am liable for any legal action against me.


Signature

Note:- While filling out the form, strike whichever does not apply to you

This format is in a Word file you can copy and fill up the details – the filled portion can be highlighted with a bold letter to enable you to trace it easily while checking and considering it. Read once again and confirm before submitting it for approval and confirm the related papers are attached. Individual applications should be submitted by not only the home but all their members separately. Do not copy others details and submit.

**(THIS FORM SHOULD BE SUBMITTED BY ALL THE INMATES)**

www.ingramcontent.com/pod-product-compliance
Lightning Source LLC
Chambersburg PA
CBHW031519150726
47990CB00001B/18